# PEARSON CUSTOM BUSINESS RESOURCES

Compiled by

## Intro to Macroeconomics

**Pearson Learning Solutions**

New York   Boston   San Francisco
London   Toronto   Sydney   Tokyo   Singapore   Madrid
Mexico City   Munich   Paris   Cape Town   Hong Kong   Montreal

*Senior Vice President, Editorial and Marketing:* Patrick F. Boles
*Associate Editor:* Ana Díaz-Caneja
*Development Editor:* Abbey Lee Briggs
*Marketing Manager:* Jack Cooney
*Operations Manager:* Eric M. Kenney
*Production Manager:* Jennifer Berry
*Rights Manager:* Jillian Santos
*Art Director:* Renée Sartell
*Cover Designer:* Renée Sartell

*Cover Art:* Courtesy of EyeWire/Getty Images and PhotoDisc/Getty Images. Photodisc, "Globe surrounded by business people on computer monitors," courtesy of Photodisc/Getty Images. Dave Cutler (Artist), "Man Dropping Coins Into Glass Jar,"courtesy of David Cutler/Images.com. Dave Cutler (Artist), "Three Coins in Glass Jar," courtesy of David Cutler/Images.com. Dean Turner, "Stock Vector: Global Finance" Courtesy of Dean Turner/iStockphoto. Hal Bergman, "Refinery Silhouette" Courtesy of Hal Bergman/iStockphoto. Dan Barnes, "Cargo Container Ship Aerial View" Courtesy of Dan Barnes/iStockphoto. Franc Podgorsek, "Stock Numbers" Courtesy of Franc Podgorsek/iStockphoto. "Customer in Line at Grocery Store" Courtesy of Digital Vision Photography/Veer Inc. Owaki-Kulla, "Pumping Gas" Courtesy of Flirt Photography/Veer Inc. Lynn Johnson, "Yunnan Province, People's Republic of China" Courtesy of Lynn Johnson/Getty Images, Inc. Thomas Bendy, "Student Typing" Courtesy of Thomas Bendy/iStockphoto.

This special edition published in cooperation with Pearson Learning Solutions.

Printed in the United States of America.

Please visit our web site at *www.pearsoncustom.com.*

Attention bookstores: For permission to return any unsold stock, contact us at *pearsonscustomreturns@pearson.com.*

Pearson Learning Solutions, 501 Boylston Street, Suite 900, Boston, MA 02116
A Pearson Education Company
www.pearsoned.com

ISBN 10: 0558935214
ISBN 13: 9780558935214

# Editorial Advisory Board

# Contents

# Preface

# Preface

## To the Student

### ECONOMICS: WHAT'S IN IT FOR YOU?

More than 230 years after the United States became an independent nation, it is one of the most technologically and economically advanced countries in the world. Its complex economic system produces and distributes goods and services daily and provides one of the world's highest standards of living. Yet we are not satisfied, because we, personally and collectively, have many economic problems. Can people find and keep jobs that provide them with the income to support themselves and their families? What are the prospects for improvements in people's economic well-being? Can you find a job that you like? What's more, the United States is not isolated from the rest of the world. Other peoples face similar, as well as different, problems. Unemployment, inflation, energy problems, downsizing, discrimination, deficits, debt, poverty, pollution, resource shortages, underdevelopment, and corruption in business and politics are problems that dominated global headlines in the last third of the twentieth century, and continue into the twenty-first century.

Economics, as one of the social sciences, helps us understand, think, and form opinions about and develop responses to these economic aspects of our social reality. Economics can be a tool that aids us in defining our successes and our failures, as well as in preserving success and correcting failure. It can contribute to our awareness. In an increasingly complex and confusing world, this tool can serve us personally and collectively as we strive to be responsible citizens of our communities, our nation, and our world. This book is dedicated to helping you to acquire that tool.

> We want to make economics as important as baseball and football scores. The minds are out there. It's a question of getting the attention.
>
> —Robert P. Keim, president of the Advertising Council, commenting on a public service campaign to "improve public understanding and awareness of the system," 1975

> Acting is a business—no more than that—a craft, like plumbing, or being an economist; it's been a good living.
>
> —Marlon Brando, actor, in a television interview with Dick Cavett, 1973

> An inhabitant of cloud-cuckoo land; one knowledgeable in an obsolete art; a harmless academic drudge whose theories and laws are but mere puffs of air in face of the anarchy of banditry, greed, and corruption which holds sway in the pecuniary affairs of the real world.
>
> —A definition of *economist* that won an award from the *New Statesman* in England, 1976

The questions in this book are not rhetorical. Each is intended to make you pause and think. Try to answer each question as you go along. Or use them to review each chapter after you have finished reading it.

1. Would you like to be an economist? Why or why not?
2. Why are you taking economics?
3. "Economics has [usually] been a countercyclical discipline; it flourishes when the economy flounders, and vice versa." Why do you suppose that is so?

## OBJECTIVES, OR WHAT WE HAVE DESIGNED THIS BOOK TO ACCOMPLISH

Before you begin your formal study, we would like to share the following list of what we consider the most important objectives of an introduction to modern economics:

❖ To produce some "cognitive dissonance." By this, we mean that we hope to present you with some ideas, facts, and ways of thinking that are new or different to you. Our hope is that these will challenge you to think, to work, and to learn. Is capitalism better than socialism? It might be, but then again, it might not be! We hope to open your mind to thinking about alternatives. What is "investment"? It is *not* simply buying a share of stock in a corporation or the stock market! Introductory economics may shake up some of your preconceived ideas and beliefs. And it may reorganize them into a *system* of thought.

❖ To give you perspective on the historical changes in the material conditions, economic institutions, and social relations of human society. The United States has not always been affluent, and capitalism has not always existed.

❖ To introduce you to a system of economic theories and ideas about the economic institutions of societies—and how those ideas and theories have changed over time. Even the conservative Republican Richard Nixon became a Keynesian in the 1970s. (We will learn more about Keynesian economics in Part 3, but basically it is an economic theory that suggests an important role for the government in guiding the overall economy.) But in the 1980s, Ronald Reagan's economic policies were based on a harsh critique of Keynesian economics; he emphasized the primary importance of business activity as opposed to the government. Bill Clinton's economic policies in the mid-1990s relied on an eclectic mixture of market-based, Keynesian theories and monetary policy that emphasized a positive role for government in influencing economic growth. The challenge of Newt Gingrich and the Republican Congress in the mid-1990s over the role of government and taxes and spending was based primarily on conservative thinking. George W. Bush in part continued this conservative tradition. The recent deep recession and financial crisis changed this debate as shortcomings of market freedoms were once again supplemented with additional government involvement in the economy.

3

❖ To convey to you *some* of the economic theories that economists, or groups of economists, regard as accurate descriptions and predictors of economic activity. For example, how do the two sides of a market, the buyers and sellers, interact to determine prices? We do not intend to give you a survey of all of economics, but to expose you to some of the most basic and useful economic concepts. There is too much of economics to try to do all of it in one semester or even a year; time is *scarce* (that's an economic concept).

❖ To focus on some contemporary economic issues—unemployment, inflation, growth, resource shortages, international trade, climate change, poverty and income distribution, multinational corporations, economic growth and development, and others.

❖ To expose you to the various, and contending, schools of economic thought. Not all economists agree on which theories or even on which problems are the most important. We hope that you will at least appreciate the variety of economic analysis—no matter which, if any, particular set of economic ideas appeals to you.

❖ To give you practice using economic concepts. We don't want you just to "input" the concepts in your head and "print them out" on tests. We hope that this text gives you opportunities to use economic concepts in solving real-world problems. Our intention is to provide you with real-world situations that allow you to apply economic concepts, ideas, and theories so that you may come to better understand the world you live in (and perhaps to change it!). We enthusiastically recommend that you read a daily newspaper. Regularly reading the newspaper will provide numerous real-world examples of economic problems (to integrate theory and reality). And applying economic concepts will help you understand them and figure out their implications. We may even be able to suggest solutions to some of these problems. How would you eliminate poverty?

❖ To give you a foundation in economic "literacy." You should be able to interpret some of the jargon of professional economists. You should also be able to identify the variables, ramifications, and possible explanations of and solutions to a variety of economic problems. We hope you develop a facility to evaluate economic ideas critically.

❖ To demystify economics so that you do not feel that the economy and its problems are too complex to understand and solve. Economics and economic policy ought not to be left only to the economists.

(CALVIN AND HOBBES © 1992 Watterson.Dist. by UNIVERSAL PRESS SYNDICATE. Reprinted with permission. All rights reserved.)

❖ To provide a foundation for future and continued learning. The world is complex. But economics will assist you in thinking critically and independently about our world. It can be one more tool that allows (and encourages) you to assume active citizenship in your community, your society, and your world.

Our hope is that we can excite you about economics, and that the insights you develop will make useful and creative contributions to your pursuit of a rich and meaningful life.

4. Are there any objectives we have missed? What are they? Do these objectives make sense to you? Why? Why not? In what ways are these objectives consistent with (different from) what you expected from introductory economics?

# Economics as a Social Science

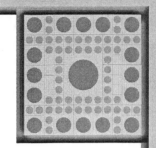

## ◆ Introduction

**W**hat is economics? And what can it do for us?

**Economics** is the study of how the productive and distributive aspects of human life are organized. The productive aspects include the activities that result in the goods and services that satisfy our day-to-day demands as human beings—for automobiles, cereal, clothes, movies, and so on. The distributive aspects are the ways a society makes these goods and services available to people in the society. Economics studies the history of production, distribution, and consumption of goods and services in different societies and countries, including the ways these aspects have changed over time. It seeks to help us understand the complexities of economic systems in the modern world.

Economics, as a social science, is thus an accumulation of human knowledge about one particular segment of social life: production, distribution, and consumption. Like the other social sciences, including geography, political science, psychology, and sociology, economics focuses on only one part of a rich and complex social life.

In this chapter, we examine economics as a social science. We will be concerned with its goals and methods, as well as its relevance to our lives. In addition, we will introduce briefly different fields in economics and the kinds of things that economists do. Finally, we will see that economists have some disagreements about what economics is and ought to be.

### Definitions

Key economic concepts are indicated by **bold type.**

# WHAT IS ECONOMICS?

Teachers of economics are concerned about how best to teach economics. Their concern stems from the importance of economic knowledge in the modern world and the difficulties of teaching that knowledge to students in a way that will prove useful to them. Out of this concern, many economists have attempted to define precisely what the key elements of economic understanding are and to concentrate on teaching these. A reasonable list of key elements of economic understanding would include the following:

❖ Practicing a reasoned approach to economic issues
❖ Mastering basic economic concepts
❖ Possessing an overview of the economy
❖ Identifying important economic issues
❖ Applying the concepts to particular issues
❖ Reaching reasoned decisions on economic issues

These elements provide some insights into the nature of economics as the study of the productive and distributive aspects of human life. Economic understanding encompasses both a body of knowledge and a way of thinking about the economic aspects of social life. It is concerned with practicing a reasoned approach; that is, economics presents an organized and logical way of thinking about economic life. It uses many basic concepts that focus our attention on key variables in economic activity. It provides us with an overall appreciation of the structure and complexity of the economic system in this country as well as those in other countries and in the global economy. It should help us identify the issues that will be important to us in our individual and social lives. In addition, economics helps us to reason and to draw conclusions about specific economic problems, their ramifications, and possible solutions.

In attempting to accomplish all of these tasks, one of the central concerns of economics is the development of **economic theory.** This task relates to the *method* of economics. While economics is concerned with social life and the vagaries of human beings, the development of theory requires that economics be as scientific as possible. An economic theory, for example, would try to explain why the prices of agricultural goods change from year to year as well as to predict how prices might change in the future.

Economists attempt to measure and collect facts about economic activity. In doing so, they try to discover certain patterns in the relationships between different components of economic life. When the facts suggest that these patterns express a constant relationship (in normal circumstances), economists may use them as the basis for economic theories. The theories of supply and demand are examples of such theories. These theories emerged out of observations of the behavior of prices of goods in markets and the ways prices changed over time. The theory developed from efforts to explain these changes. We can use these economic theories to gain insight into how goods and services are valued by society's members, how costly they are to produce, and what price they will sell for in the society, given different circumstances.

8

The function of economic theory, therefore, is to allow us to examine certain aspects of economic life, discover more or less constant relationships among different economic variables, and predict possible economic events. For example, the theories of supply and demand tells us that, most of the time, a desired article in short supply will command a relatively high price. From this we can conclude (theorize) that if the supply of that article is reduced, then its price is likely to go up even further.

Note that such statements are based on an **assumption**—an *if* statement—followed by a conditional conclusion. Economists love to make assumptions. Much of their theory is based on similar assumptions. In the final analysis, however, their theories must be judged by whether their conclusions and predictions conform with what actually happens in economic reality. In the case of supply-and-demand theory, frequent examples enable us to check the validity of the conclusions and predictions of this economic theory.

For example, in 1973, when the Middle Eastern oil-producing countries embargoed shipments of oil to the United States, Western Europe, and Japan, the supply of oil decreased, and the price *did* increase. Likewise, when there are good crops of wheat in the United States, the price of wheat is likely to go down; when crops are bad because of the weather, the price of wheat goes up. Whenever a freeze occurs in Florida, it sharply reduces the supply of Florida oranges, and this is followed by an increase in the price of oranges. In 2000, oil prices rose again as oil companies raised prices and the Middle Eastern oil-producing countries, now fearing lower returns, reduced supplies to Europe and the United States.

European motorists responding to fuel price increases in 2000.
(© Virginia Mayo/AP/Wide World Photos)

Higher gas prices prompted protests in Europe and complaints in the United States about the cost of filling cars, trucks, and fuel-guzzling sport utility vehicles. From 2004 through 2007, demand by Chinese and Indian industry, growing concerns about Middle East oil supplies, and increased speculation sent prices skyrocketing. In each of these cases, economic reality conforms with economic theory.

These examples highlight the *relevance* of economics. Economics and economic theories are concerned with problems and activities that are important to all of us as individuals and to our societies. The scope of economics can be international, national, regional, local, or personal. The problems and activities that are the subject matter of economics include such pressing concerns as recession, productivity, supplies of natural resources, efficiency, debt, unemployment, inflation, technological development, product distribution, advertising, poverty, alienation, the allocation of scarce resources, income redistribution, taxation, war, and a host of others. Economics identifies such economic problems, describes their ramifications, hypothesizes about their causes, predicts their future development, and prescribes solutions to them. In so doing, economics can build our understanding of the fundamental economic aspects of our social lives.

## One Method for Economic Theory

Milton Friedman, a Nobel Prize winner in economics, argued for a particular method in the construction of economic theory. This methodology, which he called "positive economics," has four basic components:

1. The process begins with a set of reasonable *assumptions* about some aspect of economic behavior. For example, one of the most important assumptions that we make is that the primary objective of firms is the maximization of profits.

2. Next, we try to identify some important economic *concepts* and construct some variables to measure them. For the firm, we will measure profit, cost, revenue, marginal cost, marginal revenue, and other variables. These are all functions of the economic activity of the firm.

3. Based on the assumptions we have made and the concepts we have identified, we develop some *hypotheses* and logical deductions about economic behavior. In the case of the firm, we theorize that the firm maximizes profit at a rate of output where its marginal cost equals its marginal revenue.

4. The final step is to *test the theory*. Does the hypothesis conform with observable events? When marginal costs do not equal marginal revenues, does the firm alter its decisions so that it can increase its profits?

Friedman emphasized that this method produces abstract economic theory; it simplifies and generalizes. The purpose, however, is to create a model of the economy that will help us evaluate and analyze the real-world economy. A model is an abstraction, or simplification, of the economy, not an exact replica of it.

*Source:* "Four Basic Components of Positive Economics" from Friedman, CAPITALISM AND FREEDOM. (1962) Copyright © University of Chicago Press. Used with permission.

## Economics and Economists

There are many fields within economics. Economic history focuses on how and why economic activity has changed over time. Urban economics focuses on analyzing the economic operation and problems of cities. Microeconomics is concerned primarily with the activities of smaller economic units, such as the household or the firm, and markets for goods and services. Macroeconomics has the much broader subject of the operation and health of an entire national economy. International economics deals with economic relationships and activities on a global scale. Economic thought treats the development of ideas by economists through the years. Economic development concentrates on theories and problems associated with the economic growth and maturation of national economies. Public policy economics is concerned with the analysis of proposals for dealing with public problems. Political economy highlights the relationships between economic and political institutions and how they affect each other. This by no means exhausts the list of the different fields in economics.

Given this wide variety of fields in economics, economists do many different things. Many people trained in economics as a discipline become teachers of economics in high schools, colleges, or universities. Many work in businesses, informing decision makers on current economic events and future economic forecasts. Since World War II, an increasing number of economists have found employment in government at the local, state, and federal levels. Economists also work for consulting firms, labor unions, public interest or lobbying groups, and international organizations.

With this diversity of employment experiences (and hence allegiances and perspectives), it should not be very surprising to find a healthy amount of "controversy" within the social science of economics. Economists, despite their efforts to build economic theory, often disagree with one another. They may differ about which problems are most important (or even, sometimes, that there are problems!), what the causes of a problem are, and which solutions to a problem are the best. Controversy in economics reflects controversy in life.

Nevertheless, most economists accept a large core of economic ideas. In addition, economists are unified by the goal of economics: building knowledge about the economic aspects of life.

Much of the debate among economists about what economics is and should be concerns its scope. The famous English economist Alfred Marshall (1842–1924) thought economics could be one of the most precise and scientific of the social sciences because it deals with observable and measurable data in the form of prices, quantities produced and sold, and incomes. In his *Principles of Economics*, he wrote:

> The advantage which economics has over other branches of social science appears then to arise from the fact that its special field of work gives rather larger opportunities for exact methods than any other branch. It concerns itself chiefly with those desires, aspirations and other affections of human nature, the outward manifestations of which appear as incentives to action in such a form that the force or

quantity of the incentives can be estimated and measured with some approach to accuracy; and which therefore are in some degree amenable to treatment by scientific machinery. An opening is made for the methods and the tests of science as soon as the force of a person's motives—not the motives themselves—can be approximately measured by the sum of money, which he will just give up in order to secure a desired satisfaction; or again by the sum which is just required to induce him to undergo a certain fatigue.

Other economists, however, have been less convinced by this argument. They point out that economics, as one of the social sciences, cannot divorce itself from the society in which it exists. The efforts of human beings to understand the world must necessarily be influenced by morality, ideology, and value judgments. In other words, economics cannot be totally scientific because the economist's understanding of the subject matter is affected by his or her evaluation of, opinions about, and conclusions concerning social issues. Economics as a body of thought functions to preserve, protect, and/or challenge existing social life—as well as help us to understand it. For some economists, then, economics should be a part of the effort to understand and *to improve* social existence. Joan Robinson (1903–1983), another English economist, wrote in *Freedom and Necessity:*

> The methods to which the natural sciences owe their success—controlled experiment and exact observation of continually recurring phenomena—cannot be applied to the study of human beings by human beings. So far, no equally successful method of establishing reliable natural laws has been suggested. Certainly, the social sciences should not be unscientific. Their practitioners should not jump to conclusions on inadequate evidence or propound circular statements that are true by definition as though they had some factual content; when they disagree they should not resort to abuse like theologians or literary critics, but should calmly set about to investigate the nature of the difference and to propose a plan of research to resolve it.... The function of social science is quite different from that of the natural sciences—it is to provide society with an organ of self-consciousness. Every interconnected group of human beings has to have an ideology—that is, a conception of what is the proper way to behave and the permissible pattern of relationships in family, economic, and political life.

For Robinson, then, economics must attempt to be scientific and rigorous, but since it is also concerned with the effort to create a better society, it must also devote itself to exploring areas that are more philosophical. It must recognize its ideological elements, and that, as one of the social sciences, it is also involved as a tool of analysis in the formation of public policy.

Along these lines, economists often divide their discipline between "economics" and what is called **political economy.** Economics in this sense is more concerned with explaining what can be measured and with developing theories about "purely" economic relationships. Political economy, on the other hand, is more concerned with the relationships of the economic system and its institutions to the rest of society and social development. It is sensitive to the influence of noneconomic factors such as political and social institutions, morality, and ideology in determining economic events. It thus has a broader focus than economics.

1. "The function of social science...is to provide society with an organ of self-consciousness." What does this mean? How does economics do this?

2. What, according to Robinson, is an ideology? What role do ideologies play in social development?

3. What does Robinson think is the task of economics as a social science? Do you agree with her or not? Would Alfred Marshall?

# PARADIGMS AND IDEOLOGIES

Not only do economists disagree about what economics is and should be, they often disagree about which economic problems are important, which theories are correct, and which economic policies are best. This is especially true over time, as the economic problems a society is likely to face change with changing conditions. Along with changes in economic problems and economic institutions, economic theories have also changed. The changes in economic theory and the differences among economists have two results that are useful to keep in mind while studying economics: First, there are different and sometimes contesting kinds of economic theory. Second, different economists begin their study with different assumptions.

## The Realm of Theory

Different periods of economic history (and different economic systems) have given rise to new economic theories. New or changed economic conditions and economic institutions have required different explanations and ways of thinking. Stated slightly differently, as crises have developed in economic matters when the old gave way to the new, economic institutions changed. The previous theories and notions became inadequate to explain the new conditions and problems, so economic thought also changed.

Thomas Kuhn, in *The Structure of Scientific Revolutions*, refers to such changes in scientific theory as changes in **paradigms.** A paradigm structures thought about a certain aspect of nature, life, or society. It delineates the scope of a discipline (the questions to be asked about a certain subject and the phenomena to be explained), as well as the method of the discipline (the criteria for accepting explanations).

Paradigms are usually widely accepted as providing a coherent and correct understanding of some aspect of life. However, as time passes, natural and social conditions may change, and new interpretations and new facts may become known. If so, the existing paradigm may be challenged or may be inadequate to explain these changes and a new and more widely accepted paradigm will eventually be developed. An example of this in the field of astronomy was the replacement of the Ptolemaic by the Copernican paradigm. The Copernican paradigm is now widely accepted, because it conforms with what we now know and observe—that the planets revolve around the sun.

**13**

Likewise, as economic crises occur and economic conditions change, one economic paradigm replaces another. Before the Great Depression of the 1930s, the dominant economic theory was classical economics, which argued that a laissez-faire, self-regulating market economic system would eliminate economic instability through the flexibility of markets. If overproduction of goods led to a decrease in production and an increase in unemployment, then the markets would respond to correct the situation. Prices would fall and stimulate consumption of those goods, thus eliminating the surplus. Wages would fall and stimulate the hiring of unemployed workers. To explain why overproduction or underconsumption would be unlikely in a laissez-faire market economic system, classical economics relied on Say's law, developed by the French economist J. B. Say (1767–1832), which held that supply creates its own demand. Say theorized that incomes paid out in the process of production of needed goods would always be sufficient to buy what was produced. The flexibility of prices and wages in self-regulating markets would ensure this result. However, when economists observed the severity and persistence of the Great Depression, they questioned Say's law. Consequently, they turned to a new paradigm, Keynesian economics, which offered an explanation for why depressions occur and what can be done about them.

Not only do paradigms change over time, two contending paradigms sometimes seek to explain the same aspect of economic life. Examining the same events and facts but differing in the use of key concepts and relationships, these contending paradigms offer conflicting (or at least differing) interpretations. At one time or another, or in different places, one or the other might be dominant.

An example of conflicting paradigms is the contrast between orthodox economics and Marxian economics. **Orthodox economics** accepts the assumptions of a competitive market economy and builds a theory around those assumptions. **Marxian economics** assumes a critical stance toward the existing market economic system and attempts to discover how it will and can be changed. Orthodox economics accepts capitalism, and Marxian economics criticizes capitalism and argues for socialism. A third paradigm, **institutional economics**, bridges Marxian and orthodox economics by focusing on the role of changing institutions and power in influencing economic affairs.

## The Realm of the Economist

Economists are human beings with differing ideas, theories, assumptions, and ideologies. As economic conditions and institutions have changed, so have economists' ideas, theories, assumptions, and ideologies. In different times and spaces, economists have differed. And in the *same* time and space, economists disagree. One way of clarifying this is to examine **ideology**. E. K. Hunt, in *Property and Prophets*, defines an ideology this way:

> [A set of] ideas and beliefs that tend to justify morally a society's social and economic relationships. Most members of a society internalize the ideology and thus believe that their functional roles, as well as those of others, are morally correct,

and that the method by which society divides its produce is fair. This common belief gives society its cohesiveness and vitality. Lack of it creates turmoil and strife—and ultimately revolution if the differences are deep enough.

At different times, different ideologies may dominate. At one time, Confucianism was the ideology of China. Later, the dominant ideology in China was that of Maoism and socialism. Catholicism and a concern with the next world was at the core of an ideology that dominated Western Europe; later, individualism and materialism held sway.

Ideologies influence the development of theory. For example, the ideology of individualism promoted the development of the economic theory of classical liberalism, and both accompanied the emergence of capitalism as an economic system. More recently, the combination of the ideologies of liberal democracy, the benevolent state, and individualism promoted the acceptance of Keynesian economics along with the emergence of the welfare state. From 1982 to 2007, with an increasing government presence in the economy, many economists (and politicians) with a conservative ideology argued for greater reliance on market forces.

Different ideologies concerning the goals of a society and an economic system may conflict. For example, differences in ideology underlie the division of Western economists today into three broad groups: liberal, conservative, and radical. Each group has its own ideas, theories, and ideologies. These are described in the next section.

4. What is your ideology?

5. Compare and contrast Hunt's definition of ideology with that of Joan Robinson.

## CONSERVATIVE, LIBERAL, AND RADICAL ECONOMICS

Milton Friedman (1912–2006) was a prominent conservative economist. John Maynard Keynes offered a liberal solution to the 1930s crisis of capitalism. Adam Smith, while recognized as a conservative today, was a radical in his day. Karl Marx offered a radical critique of capitalism.

What are some of the essential elements of conservative, liberal, and radical ideologies and theories? What are the differences among them? How do they interpret different economic issues, and what different solutions do they offer for economic problems?

**Conservative economists** focus on the operation of markets in a capitalist, free market economic system. They argue that private ownership of resources under capitalism assures economic and political freedom for individuals in that society. Individuals make their own decisions for their own private gains. Markets, where goods and services are exchanged, will then operate to produce economic well-being and growth for the society and the individuals within it. Markets, through the action of competition, enforce a result that is the best for everyone and uses resources efficiently. Consequently, conservatives see the profit motive as being one of the most important and positive aspects of capitalism. Firms, to meet their own interests in competitive markets, must produce exactly what consumers want at the lowest price. One further implication of conservative economics is that, since markets operate efficiently and produce economic growth, the government need not take an active role in the operation of the economy (beyond some important, fundamental obligations). In fact, most conservatives argue that excessive government intervention in the economy is the source of many of our economic problems.

The roots of conservative economics can be found in eighteenth-century classical liberalism. Modern examples of conservative economics include "free market" economics, supply-side economics, and monetarism. Conservative economists include Milton Friedman, author of *Capitalism and Freedom* and a Nobel Prize winner; Alan Greenspan, former chairman of the Federal Reserve System; and Robert Barro, *Business Week* columnist and Harvard economics professor. Ronald Reagan and John McCain are examples of politicians who believe in the ideas and the theories of conservative economics. Much of the advertising and educational efforts of corporate America utilize the logic and conclusions of conservative economics. *The Wall Street Journal* and *The Economist* newspapers take a consistently conservative position in their editorials.

**Liberal economists** accept the structure of the capitalist economic system and its basic institutions of private property and markets. They also agree with conservatives that, for the most part, this free-market system tends to produce efficiency and economic growth and that it protects individual freedom. However, they admit that the operation of the market system may produce problems. For example, it can't guarantee economic stability, it fosters an unequal distribution of income and economic power, often neglects some of the by-products of economic production and exchange such as pollution, and sometimes fails to provide necessary goods and services that can't be produced profitably. Liberals then usually point out that there is a solution to these problems that does not interfere with the basic structure of the economic system; they give the responsibility for addressing these problems to the government. The federal government can take responsibility for trying to achieve economic prosperity and price stability and to avoid economic depressions. It can attempt to redistribute income, and it can attempt to regulate the production of pollution in the economy. And, all levels of government can provide "public" goods such as parks, roads, schools, and police and fire protection. For liberals, the market works economic wonders, but they are qualified wonders; the active involvement of governments in some aspects of the market economy can improve its performance.

The theoretical underpinnings of most liberal economists can be found in Keynesian economics. Some liberals also find the ideas of Thorstein Veblen and other institutionalist economists to be helpful in framing their understanding of the economy. John Kenneth Galbraith of Harvard University wrote a number of important books about economics and the economy from Keynesian and institutionalist perspectives. Nobel laureate Paul Krugman, who teaches at Princeton University, is another liberal economist and an op-ed columnist for the *New York Times* and author of *The Conscience of a Liberal*. Jimmy Carter, Bill Clinton, and Barack Obama use the ideas and theories of liberal economics. *Business Week* magazine usually presents a relatively liberal editorial policy.

**Radical economists** tend to be very critical of the structures, institutions, operation, and results of capitalist economic systems. They do not deny that capitalism has been quite successful over the past several centuries in increasing the productive capacity of Western nations and the average standard of living for their inhabitants. However, radical economists suggest that the very operation of a market system based on private ownership creates different classes of people in capitalist societies. On the one hand are those who own productive resources, organize and control productive activity, and have the goal of earning profits for themselves. On the other hand are people who do not own any productive property and who rely on the sale of their mental and/or physical labor to earn a living. Radicals are quick to point out that there are inherent conflicts between these two groups over wages, working conditions, product safety, and economic power. It is this basic class structure of the society, radicals argue, that produces economic inequality, exploitation, and alienation. In addition, they conclude that capitalist production and growth are inherently unable to provide for public goods, ignore the social costs of productive activity, and lead to economic instability. Consequently, the efforts of the state (all levels of government) to deal with these problems

Lower East Side of Manhattan; New York
(© SuperStock.)

are merely Band-Aid solutions because they do not address the root causes—private ownership, production for profit, and a class society.

In the view of radical economists, solving modern economic problems such as poverty, income inequality, discrimination, and pollution requires alterations in the basic economic institutions of the society. Many radicals believe in nationalization, and many want to limit the existing power of corporations. Many would advocate much more significant redistribution of income in the United States (and the world). Some even call for social ownership and control of productive resources in pursuit of social goals of production.

Radical economics finds its roots in both institutional and Marxian economics. Although many radicals find the ideas of both Keynesian and conservative economics useful in understanding how capitalism and markets work, radicals depart in their evaluation of the operation and results of capitalism. For them, the negative aspects outweigh the positive. Samuel Bowles, David Gordon, and Thomas Weisskopf are radical economists who wrote *Beyond the Wasteland: A Democratic Alternative to Economic Decline*. This book contains their analysis of U.S. economic experience and presents a radical economic program for restructuring the economy and addressing many of its long-run problems. In his book *Contours of Descent: U.S. Economic Fractures and the Landscape of Global Austerity*, University of Massachusetts economist Robert Pollin argues that free-market policies have produced extensive poverty and increasing inequality. Along with Robert Pollin, writers for periodicals such as *Mother Jones*, *Z*, and *Dollars and Sense* express a radical point of view. Many of the ideas about economic priorities and policy articulated by Ralph Nader in his 2000, 2004, and 2008 presidential campaigns—for instance, increased income redistribution, significantly reduced military spending, and the promotion of environmentally responsible economic policies—are compatible with radical economics. The Green Party has a radical platform.

## Conservatives, Liberals, and Radicals on Poverty

From these brief descriptions of conservative, liberal, and radical economics, it should be possible to identify the basic approach that each would take to understanding a particular economic problem and suggesting solutions for it. But let's develop a single example: poverty. Conservatives tend to argue that poverty exists because of the particular attributes of individuals and their inability to earn high incomes in labor markets. Either they have the wrong skills or few skills, or they don't try or work hard enough. The solution, then, is either "It's appropriate that their economic rewards are low," or "They need to develop their marketable skills." If the society decides that it wants to facilitate the reduction of poverty, the most appropriate way might be through education. Individuals have to develop skills and work harder. Conservatives would not support anti-poverty programs because they represent government involvement with markets. Conservatives think that poverty can be reduced effectively only by the participation of responsible individuals in free markets.

Liberals maintain that, very often, the poverty of individuals is a result of circumstances beyond their control. Consequently, not only would liberals support a public role for education (and job training) to increase people's marketable skills, but, in addition, they would favor direct income redistribution to increase the purchasing power of poor people. This would reduce the burdens of poverty, but it also might create the chance for people to move out of poverty. Liberals would support food stamps and welfare for the poor.

Radicals generally would support governmental redistribution programs and certainly would oppose efforts to take economic benefits away from poor people. However, they would argue that redistribution programs have a very limited effect in eliminating poverty. Governmental programs have reduced poverty, but given the source of unequal incomes in private ownership of productive resources and the fundamental individualism of capitalism, the system cannot tolerate the amount of redistribution that would be necessary to eliminate poverty. Only massive redistribution of income to poor people or a radical restructuring of the institutions and goals of the economic system could significantly reduce the incidence of poverty in the United States.

The analyses of current economic problems are distinctive based on different ideologies and theories. And these differences are reflected in the variety of proposed solutions. Conservatives, liberals, and democratic socialists in the United States each proposed solutions to the financial crisis that began in mid-2007. Many conservatives argued that banks should simply be allowed to fail. These institutions took risks, and the cost is failure. Some liberals argued that these banks (Citi, BankAmerica, Wells Fargo) were "too big to fail," and support government bailout measures for these and other banks in order to protect the financial system and the economy. Democratic socialists proposed another option: Nationalize the banks that are too big to fail. Nationalization would shift the cost from the taxpayer to bank stock and bondholders—those who took risks by purchasing shares and lending to these now failing banks.

One of the fascinating aspects of modern economics is the controversy that surrounds our understanding of and efforts to deal with these problems. Conservative, liberal, and radical economics have all contributed to that analysis.

6. Which set of economic ideas do you think is dominant in the United States today?

7. Paul Sweezy, a U.S. Marxian economist, has written, "It seems to me that from a scientific point of view the question of choosing between approaches can be answered quite simply. Which more accurately reflects the fundamental characteristics of social reality which is under analysis?" Critically evaluate each of the different perspectives with respect to that statement. How are your answers affected by your own beliefs?

8. What is the difference between theory and ideology?

# ❖Conclusion

*There are many different fields within economics, the social science that focuses on building an understanding of how the economy—production, distribution, and consumption of goods and services—works. Economists do many different things, not the least of which is disagree with each other while at the same time working together to build economic theory.*

## Review Questions

1. What is economics? Is that what you thought economics is (or should be)?

2. What is the goal of economic theory? What is the test of an economic theory?

3. Why do economists disagree?

4. What is a paradigm? In your life have you ever replaced one paradigm with another?

5. What are the main differences among conservative, liberal, and radical economists?

6. Paradigms can offer contending explanations of the same reality. Sometimes the contention can reflect intense political, social, and economic struggles. Develop some examples of new paradigms for which the people suggesting them have been subjected to neglect, harassment, ridicule, or even punishment.

7. How might conservative, liberal, and radical economists respond to an issue like global climate change?

# Macroeconomics: Issues and Problems

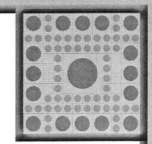

## ◆ Introduction

**T**his chapter begins our focus on macroeconomics, which examines the economy as a whole. Instead of studying individual parts of the economy, such as firms or labor unions, or concepts such as property and value, we turn our attention to entire sectors that make up our national and international economic system and to aggregate concepts and problems, such as recession, unemployment, inflation, interest rates, taxation, and budget deficits. These topics affect every one of us.

In this chapter, we will examine the goals of macroeconomics, review postwar U.S. macroeconomic trends, develop several tools that will aid our understanding of macroeconomic theory and macroeconomic policy, and define aggregate measures for economic activity in the National Income and Product Accounts. We will begin by considering the importance of macroeconomic theory and some of the ways macroeconomic policy might help to alleviate economic problems.

### MACROECONOMIC GOALS

In the early 1950s, the U.S. government accepted as its responsibility three basic macroeconomic goals: (1) economic growth, (2) full employment, and (3) price stability. Government policies should help the economy attain these goals. However, as we will see later, these goals are not necessarily compatible. Despite conflicts among these goals, many would agree that economic growth, full employment, and price stability are reasonable goals. We want people employed. Stable prices are good for most of us. And economic growth has become synonymous with a higher standard of living and economic progress.

From Chapter 13 of *Economics: A Tool for Critically Understanding Society*, 9/e. Tom Riddell. Jean Shackelford. Geoffrey Schneider. Steve Stamos. Copyright © 2011 by Pearson Education. Published by Addison-Wesley. All rights reserved.

## Economic Growth

Simply put, **economic growth** is the increased output of goods and services over time. Not only is growth assumed to be necessary and good, but more growth is assumed to be better than less. Economic growth, after all, creates employment and income.

To measure economic growth, economists have developed sophisticated tools that measure the performance of the economy and its annual rate of real growth. By using a method known as national income accounting (explained later in this chapter), they calculate the **gross domestic product (GDP)**—the total dollar value of all goods and services produced in a given year—and monitor its rate of growth. GDP has grown from $2 trillion in 1978 to $14.2 trillion in 2008. The United States continues to have the world's largest GDP. Once we have measured GDP, we can find the percentage change to calculate its growth rate from year to year. Table 1 shows recent and historic average growth rates.

During the 1960s and early 1970s, critics challenged the basic assumptions concerning economic growth, arguing that more growth does not necessarily mean an improved standard of living. Others now charge that the GDP merely quantifies the performance of the economy but does not reflect the qualitative dimension addressed by the question, What is the real societal value or cost of increased GDP growth?

Much of this critique stems from a consideration of the environmental aspects of increasing economic growth. Human health and well-being are endangered by toxic wastes and air and water pollution, while acid rain threatens the quality of our food supply. Issues including the demise of the rain forests, climate change, and population growth have reminded us that these are worldwide concerns. Growing ecological awareness in the context of energy and environmental crises has made us examine our values, attitudes, goals, and economic assumptions more intensely.

The economic growth controversy also focuses on issues of income distribution in the United States. Annual increases in economic growth do not lead to more equitable distribution of the increased output. Empirical data support the claim that despite the tremendous increases in GDP since World War II, the distribution of income in the United States did not change significantly until the 1980s, when it became *less* equal. Despite rapid economic growth in the 1990s and mid-2000s, income distribution continues to become even more unequal. Those who advocate economic growth often use the metaphor

**Table 1** Average Annual Rates of Growth, Unemployment, and Inflation

|  | 1950s | 1960s | 1970s | 1980s | 1990s | 2000–2008 |
|---|---|---|---|---|---|---|
| Real growth rate[a] | 4.0% | 4.1% | 2.8% | 2.7% | 5.4% | 4.1% |
| Unemployment | 4.4 | 4.8 | 6.2 | 7.3 | 5.8 | 5.1 |
| Inflation | 2.4 | 2.0 | 7.1 | 6.7 | 2.9 | 2.8 |

[a]In current dollars.
Source: *Economic Report of the President*, 1984, 1990, 2001, 2009.

"a rising tide lifts all boats." Indeed, "all boats" did rise during the period from 1993 to 2006, but the "boats" of the most wealthy in the United States rose the most.

Another concern is that economic growth may be too rapid, causing labor and input shortages, which in turn increase prices. In addition, economic growth has not evolved in a stable pattern. The United States has experienced ten major recessions since World War II. The instability characterized by fluctuations of the business cycle has been a primary feature of the postwar era.

## Full Employment

The attainment of high levels of employment has been a goal of the U.S. government since the passage of the Employment Act of 1946 following the Great Depression of the 1930s. Congress reaffirmed that goal in passing the Full Employment and Balanced Growth Act of 1978, which set targets of 3 percent inflation and 4 percent unemployment and directed the president to take steps consistent with these goals. These steps might include creating a more favorable business climate and establishing policies for direct federal expenditures, among others. The country has come closest to full employment mostly during times of war, and during the technology boom of the late 1990s.

**Unemployment** refers to people who would like to have jobs but don't. The Department of Labor defines people as unemployed when they are older than age sixteen, are actively seeking work, do not have a job, and have made some effort to find work during the past four weeks. The unemployment rate is the percent of people without jobs relative to the total number of people in the labor force (those with jobs or looking for jobs). About 63 percent of the U.S. population is in the labor force, and this base is used for the unemployment estimates. By 2008, almost 155 million of the 303 million people in the United States were in the civilian labor force. Table 2 shows unemployment rates for selected groups of workers from 1950 to 2008.

1. Does it surprise you that married men typically have lower unemployment rates than other groups of men (see Table 2)? Why or why not?

Economists have defined five basic types of unemployment:

1. **Frictional unemployment** is caused by the temporary mismatching of people with jobs because workers change jobs, employers seek new workers, and new people enter the labor market. All labor markets have frictional unemployment; even during the severe labor shortage of World War II, unemployment persisted at about 2 percent.

2. **Seasonal unemployment**, as the name implies, results from changing seasonal demand and supply for labor. Ski instructors seeking jobs in the summer and farmworkers laid off in the winter contribute to seasonal unemployment.

3. **Structural unemployment** presents a more serious problem. It results from permanent displacement of workers due to shifting product demand or technological changes that require new skills. The shift in demand from natural to synthetic fibers created problems of structural unemployment for places such as Fall River, Massachusetts. The mechanical picking of tomatoes caused many migrant farmworkers to become structurally unemployed. Such unemployment is a function of geography, as well as skill level, and mobility.

4. **Cyclical unemployment** is due to the decreased demand for labor during a downturn in the business cycle. The high unemployment of the 1930s was basically a problem of cyclical unemployment. The high unemployment rates of the early 1990s also were predominately cyclical.

5. **Hidden unemployment** is not included in the official unemployment rate and is probably the hardest concept to define and measure. Growing evidence suggests that many people would like a job if they thought one was available, but many have become so discouraged by their past failures to find employment that they have given up trying. Technically, such people are outside the labor force, but as a practical matter, they are unemployed and not offically counted as such. One sign that hidden unemployment exists is the rise in the labor force participation rate (the proportion of the total population seeking jobs) during the early stages of economic recovery. If more people seek jobs as the number of jobs increases, why weren't they part of the labor force when the unemployment rate was higher? In addition, many people work part-time but would prefer to work full-time. These people are counted as being employed.

**Table 2** Civilian Unemployment Rate by Demographic Characteristics, 1950–2008 (percent)

| Year | All Workers | By Sex and Age | | | Demographic Characteristic | | | By Selected Group | |
|---|---|---|---|---|---|---|---|---|---|
| | | Both Sexes, 16–19 | Males, 20 and Over | Females, 20 and Over | White | Black or African American | Hispanic or Latino Ethnicity | Married Men (Spouse Present) | Women Who Maintain Families |
| 1950 | 5.3 | 12.2 | 4.7 | 5.1 | 4.9 | — | — | 4.6 | — |
| 1960 | 5.5 | 14.7 | 4.7 | 5.1 | 4.9 | — | — | 3.7 | — |
| 1970 | 4.9 | 15.3 | 3.5 | 4.8 | 4.5 | — | — | 2.6 | 5.4 |
| 1975 | 8.5 | 19.9 | 6.7 | 8.0 | 7.8 | 14.8 | 12.2 | 5.1 | 10.0 |
| 1980 | 7.1 | 17.8 | 5.9 | 6.4 | 6.3 | 14.3 | 10.1 | 4.2 | 9.2 |
| 1985 | 7.2 | 18.6 | 6.2 | 6.6 | 6.2 | 15.1 | 10.5 | 4.3 | 10.4 |
| 1990 | 5.6 | 15.5 | 5.0 | 4.9 | 4.8 | 11.4 | 8.2 | 3.4 | 8.2 |
| 1995 | 5.6 | 17.3 | 4.8 | 4.9 | 4.9 | 10.4 | 9.3 | 3.3 | 8.0 |
| 2000 | 4.0 | 13.0 | 4.1 | 3.6 | 3.5 | 7.6 | 5.7 | 2.0 | 5.9 |
| 2005 | 5.1 | 16.6 | 4.4 | 4.6 | 4.4 | 10.0 | 6.0 | 2.8 | 7.8 |
| 2006 | 4.6 | 15.4 | 4.0 | 4.1 | 4.0 | 8.9 | 5.2 | 2.4 | 7.1 |
| 2007 | 4.6 | 15.7 | 4.1 | 4.0 | 4.1 | 8.3 | 5.6 | 2.5 | 6.5 |
| 2008 | 5.1 | 17.0 | 5.4 | 4.8 | 4.7 | 10.0 | 7.5 | 3.2 | 7.9 |

Source: *Economic Report of the President*, 1990, pp. 338–339; 2003, p. 326; 2008, pp. 334–335.

More than 10 million people (on the average) were unemployed during the recession of 1980 to 1982. (Princeton economist Alan Blinder called them "cannon fodder in the assault on inflation.") Although the number of unemployed fell to 6.5 million in 1989, it quickly rose to 9.4 million in 1992 as the result of the recession that began in 1990. Unemployment rates then trended downward to 4.0 percent in the recovery through 2000. By 2001, the economy was showing signs of recession as economic growth slowed and the unemployment rate increased to 4.7 percent in 2001 and peaked at 6.0 percent in 2003. In late 2003 and 2004, with increases in government spending and tax cuts kicking in to jumpstart the economy, growth had renewed, but joblessness remained stubbornly at 5.6 percent. By 2005, however, unemployment rates had dropped to 4.6 percent. The recession that began at the end of 2007 boosted civilian unemployment rates to 9.4 percent in June 2009. Unemployment has direct social consequences for unemployed individuals, their families, and communities facing closed factories, unemployment lines, and discouraged workers.

**Counting the Unemployed.**   Beyond the real costs to those unemployed and to lost output, there are also problems in simply counting and defining the unemployed in our economy. Critics claim that the national measures of unemployment actually understate the real rate of unemployment. They argue that a different definition and measurement technique would reveal a national "underemployment" rate of 9 to 16 percent.

David Gordon, who taught at the New School of Social Research, called attention to the problem of *underemployment* and suggested that it was a more appropriate measure than the traditional notion of unemployment. As a more meaningful statistic, it would give economists better information and be more instructive to policy makers. Gordon defined underemployment as the number of people who fall into any of the following four categories:

1. *Unemployed people*—those who are actively looking for work but unable to find a job

2. *Discouraged workers*—those who are unemployed and want work but have given up in frustration because they believe no jobs are available

3. *Involuntary part-time workers*—those employed part-time who want full-time work but are unable to find it

4. *Underemployed people*—those who are working full-time but earning less than the poverty level of income as specified by the Bureau of Labor Statistics (for an urban family of four, $21,200 per year in 2008, compared to approximately $13,624 per year paid to a person working full-time at the 2008 minimum wage).

We can use these categories to adjust the traditional measure of unemployment. In May 2009, the Bureau of Labor Statistics reported just over 9.1 million workers who were involuntary part-time employees. This compares to 4.5 million involuntary part-time workers in 2005. Discouraged workers were estimated at 792,000. An additional 1.4 million are marginally attached to the labor market but cite reasons other than being discouraged for not being employed. Such reasons might include transportation problems, family responsibilities, or ill health. When combined with the unemployed, these discouraged and involuntary part-time workers generated an "expanded unemployment rate" of over 12 percent in 2008.

2. Do you anticipate unemployment in your future? Why or why not? What are your "odds"?

3. Does it make any difference how we count the unemployed? Explain.

**Costs of Unemployment and Underemployment.** Unemployment is an economic (opportunity) cost. Every 1 percent of the labor force that is unemployed represents several billion dollars of potential GDP.

In addition, unemployment has social and psychological costs—crime, family disintegration, and increasing mental health problems, to name a few. An examination of the nature of unemployment in the United States also reveals an identifiable institutionalized process of discrimination according to race, gender, and age. This became increasingly evident as unprecedented numbers of minorities, women, and teenagers entered the labor force after January 1980. In January 2008, when the Bureau of Labor Statistics reported a national unemployment rate that averaged 5.1 percent, the unemployment rate for black or African Americans averaged 10 percent—and more than 30.0 percent for black teens.

A last consideration related to unemployment involves poverty and welfare. In 2007, the poverty rate for those who did not work was more than 8 times the rate for those who worked (21.5 percent versus 2.7 percent), and part-time workers were 6.0 times more likely than full-time workers to fall into poverty. For U.S. citizens who are neither employed nor receiving any form of income from unemployment compensation, Social Security, or disability, welfare is the only way to meet survival needs. In addition, there has been an increase in the percent of part-time jobs. While some workers opt for part-time schedules, some 4.7 million workers who hold part-time jobs prefer to work full-time. Part-time jobs are characterized by lower wages, lower skill levels, more limited promotion opportunities, and fewer benefits than full-time jobs.

## Price Stability

One thing that many people have in common is an aversion to **inflation**, which is an upward movement in the general price level. Deflation, in contrast, indicates a downward movement of the general price level. Price stability occurs when there is relatively little movement in the general price level.

The price level is measured by some sort of price index, such as the **Consumer Price Index (CPI)**. A typical price index measures the average level of prices in one year or period as a percentage of the average price level in some base period. The Consumer Price Index is computed by the Bureau of Labor Statistics (BLS). Each month the BLS surveys markets in some fifty urban areas for the prices of 400 "typical" consumer goods and services. The bureau then computes the CPI by measuring the present cost of this "basket" of items as a percentage of the cost in some base period:

$$\text{CPI} = \frac{\text{current cost of basket}}{\text{cost of basket in base year}} \times 100$$

The inflation or deflation rate then measures the percentage change in the price level:

$$\text{current inflation or deflation rate} = \frac{\text{current CPI} - \text{last year's CPI}}{\text{last year's CPI}} \times 100$$

In the 1970s, the U.S. economy experienced frequent periods of inflation. During the 1980s, 1990s, and through 2004, annual rates of price increase remained low overall but began increasing through 2007. Still, price increases have been greater than the overall inflation rate in some selected markets. For example, oil prices reached record levels in 2008 and college students have experienced rapid rises in the cost of tuition each year, as well as higher than average prices for textbooks. Between 2000 and 2006, potential home buyers were confronted by much higher than average housing prices. By 2008, however, the housing bubble had collapsed and home prices were decreasing.

Because rapidly increasing prices often affect our consumption and saving decisions, we tend to have a greater sense of well-being when prices are stable. We don't have to worry (as much) about whether our savings will suffice to send us to college or help maintain our standard of living after we retire. We do know, however, that inflation is not a problem for those who correctly anticipate it and take appropriate precautions. For example, if prices rise by 4 percent and workers are aware of these economic developments, they expect a 4 percent inflation rate. To keep real (inflation-adjusted) wages at the same level, workers will demand at least a 4 percent wage increase. They will also put their savings into assets that will yield at least 4 percent. With these adjustments, workers correctly anticipate inflation and insulate themselves from it. But, if wages rise by only 3 percent with a 5 percent increase in prices, workers' income will lose 2 percent in purchasing power.

Those hurt by inflation include people on fixed incomes, usually the elderly; those working under fixed-cost or fixed-wage contracts; and individuals or institutions who have lent money at an interest rate less than the current rate of inflation. Many contracts now allow for price fluctuations, and many pensions are adjusted for inflation. Financial institutions react to inflationary pressures by charging higher interest rates, or even variable interest rates pegged to bonds that reflect price or inflationary changes. Still, people prefer price stability as a way to avoid the necessity of forecasting correctly and adjusting behavior to that forecast.

During the 1970s, the United States experienced record levels of inflation caused by factors related to demand, supply, and expectations. Owing to the same factors, the 1980s brought an ebbing of inflationary pressures. Several unexpected forces entered into the scenario during the 1970s, all of which heightened the problem of inflation. In 1973, an embargo imposed by the powerful Organization of Petroleum Exporting Countries (OPEC) nations sent energy prices soaring. The reduced supply of oil caused the general price level to rise and output to fall. Shortages and price increases were also felt in the markets for food, metals, and other primary materials.

The 1970s also ushered in a period of increased government regulation. This time, instead of antitrust legislation, the government regulated various aspects of our living and working environments and promoted equal opportunity. While the social benefits of these regulations were widespread, they were also expensive, and these costs initially came on board during the 1970s. Accelerated government expenditures resulting from the Vietnam War added an estimated 3.25 percent to the underlying inflation rate, while the surge in oil prices, first in 1973 and again in 1979, added 4.75 percent. These factors alone explain an inflation rate of 8 percent during the 1970s.

At the beginning of the 1980s, events eased inflationary pressures. Oil prices began to drop as production increased and demand fell. The prices of other raw materials declined as well, due to overproduction in many of the developing nations. Deregulation, or the rollback of government regulations, in a number of industries increased competition and lowered prices. The value of the dollar restrained prices of imported goods, helping to lower inflation in the United States by providing a supply of cheaper imports and by keeping domestic prices in check as U.S. producers struggled to remain price-competitive. Labor made many concessions during the recession of 1980 to 1982, and these "givebacks" kept wages from rising. More importantly, the Federal Reserve cut the growth rate of the money supply to halt the inflationary trends, and lower inflation rates were gained at the cost of high rates of unemployment.

With the Federal Reserve policy continuing to target low inflation rates, the late 1980s through 2004 saw stable prices, averaging growth rates between 2 and 4 percent. This period was accompanied by relatively stable oil and resource prices, slow wage growth, and in the late 1990s, cheap imports. Oil prices began increasing rapidly in 2004 due to concern about Middle East oil supplies and increased oil demand by India and China. The effect of huricane Katrina's disruption of U.S. oil production in late 2005 and the Israel-Lebanon war in 2006 kept oil prices increasing at a robust rate. By the end of 2006, oil markets calmed and prices fell, just before rising to record level in 2008.

The goal of price stability is sometimes achieved due to good economic policy, good luck, or some combination of the two, particularly when factors outside the realm of domestic economic policy tools are operating.

4. Which of the three macroeconomic goals—growth, full employment, or price stability—is the most important to you? Why?

5. If you could add another goal to this list, what would it be? Explain.

## MACROECONOMIC TOOLS

To achieve the three macroeconomic goals of growth, full employment, and price stability, economists and government policy makers use economic theory to analyze the economy and to formulate macroeconomic policy. The primary macroeconomic tools are monetary and fiscal policy. Let's briefly define each of these and see how they are used.

The Federal Reserve System manages, coordinates, and controls the monetary system of the U.S. economy. Proper management of this system makes available the quantity of money necessary for desired economic growth at interest rates capable of inducing the desired levels of investment and spending. **Monetary policy** consists of tools that can change the amount of money and credit available in the economy. It is administered by the Federal Reserve System to achieve and promote economic growth, maximum employment, and price stability.

Through **fiscal policy**, the government manipulates its expenditures and taxation to attain the basic macroeconomic objectives. Fiscal policy is administered by the executive and legislative branches of the federal government and is coordinated with monetary policy.

Fiscal and monetary tools have both been part of contemporary macroeconomic policy as it has developed over the past sixty years. Several important issues and problems are associated with this policy. We shall examine a few of these in the context of the economic history of the post–World War II period, when monetary and fiscal policy became mainstays in a U.S. economy aiming to achieve the goals of growth, high employment, and price stability.

## The Rise of Pax Americana: 1946 to the 1960s

Just as the Victorian period in the late nineteenth century was dubbed "Pax Britannia," the period after World War II until the middle to late 1960s has been called "Pax Americana." The world seemed ripe for economic quests and successes by the United States. The three decades that followed, however, saw a reduction in U.S. power in the international economic arena. The U.S. position continued to worsen until conditions taking advantage of economic growth, improvements in levels of employment, stable prices, and deficit reductions arose in the mid-1990s.

By the end of World War II, many important institutions characteristic of the U.S. economy were already in place. Monopolies and large corporations had been present since the turn of the century, and the 1930s brought increasing levels of government intervention in the economy. After the prolonged recession and depression of the 1930s and the wartime economy of the 1940s, the setting was ripe for the United States to push ahead and prosper. The 1950s arrived with abundant potential and opportunity; Europe and Japan lay in ruin, and the United States possessed the only productive industrial capacity not debilitated by the war. These industries were immediately called on in the effort to rebuild Europe and Japan, as well as to meet the increased demands for consumer goods and services that had developed in the United States during the war. In the decade following the war, U.S. economic growth skyrocketed. Real weekly earnings increased at an average of 2.3 percent per year. Productivity increases held steady at 3.2 percent, and real GDP growth was about 4 percent. Unemployment averaged 4 percent. When unemployment rose to 5.5 percent in the recessions of 1949, 1954, 1958, and 1960, inflation slowed to 2 percent.

As the prosperity of the 1950s passed into the 1960s, the government began to actively participate in the growth that had earlier been dominated by the private sector. The new federal interstate highway system was the highlight of federal expenditures of the 1950s. These expenditures continued into the 1960s and were joined by a federal Model Cities program that contributed to the U.S. urban infrastructure. In 1964, Congress passed a tax cut specifically designed to increase income—the first planned policy action of its type. Later in the 1960s, the Great Society program was put into place to reduce poverty. Only now are we realizing the successes of these programs—as well as some of their shortcomings. The 1960s also brought the war in Vietnam and a demand for more federal expenditures to finance it.

Also by the 1960s, Japan and the industrial nations of Western Europe had rebuilt their factories, and their economies were strengthened. Increased foreign production challenged U.S. goods in world markets, and U.S. economic growth slowed. In the international sphere, the dollar, which serves as the "key currency" in all international transactions, was coming under economic attack as other nations regained their prewar economic positions. This pressure eventually led to a devaluation of the dollar and a new system for determining international exchange rates.

## The Decline of Pax Americana: The 1970s to Mid-1980s

During the 1970s, U.S. economic growth and strength were challenged from several sides. The oil embargo of 1973, coupled with agricultural shortages, showed the vulnerability of the U.S. economy (and others as well) to supply shocks on a world level. A severe recession in the mid-1970s sent unemployment to 9 percent. As the economy began to recover in 1977 and 1978, inflation sky-rocketed to 13.3 percent. In the last half of 1979, the Federal Reserve put in motion a series of credit restraints that sent the economy plummeting into yet another recession. Economic growth slowed, and throughout the decade, growth was due almost entirely to rising employment and not greater productivity. The service sector dominated the employment growth of the seventies, with many dead-end, low-paying jobs providing entry for an expanding labor force.

While the 1970s were marked by record levels of inflation in the United States, the early 1980s witnessed both the highest levels of unemployment since the 1930s and the lowest levels of inflation since the 1960s. In 1981, the economy experienced a recession and modest recovery, then plunged into the deepest recession since the Great Depression. This recession can largely be explained by actions of the Federal Reserve, which was using monetary policy to actively restrict growth in the supply of money between late 1979 and 1982.

Monetary ease and historically high government expenditures and tax cuts combined to generate the recovery of 1983 to 1984, which, despite very slow economic growth, persisted until 1989. Unemployment fell as some workers headed back to the factories and many others moved into the service sector. Inflation remained stable at 3 percent, but increases in real weekly earnings averaged only 0.3 percent. The economy, however, had been left with very high real rates of interest, resulting at least partially from large government expenditures and tax cuts creating deficits. Throughout the 1980s, the federal government incurred large and persistent budget deficits. High interest rates hurt the economy by hindering job creation and investment in new plants, equipment, and housing. These high rates of return also attracted foreign money to the United States and kept the value of the dollar high through 1985. This promoted the importation of relatively cheap foreign goods, helping consumers but hurting U.S. producers, who lost out in two ways: Not only were more foreign goods purchased in the United States, but fewer U.S. products were exported to the rest of the world. In the early 1980s, high interest rates also affected debt-plagued developing nations, whose debt payments mounted with each rise in the U.S. interest rate.

6. Why do you think inflation might rise when unemployment is low? Explain.

7. What is debt? How does it arise? Do you worry about going into debt? Why?

## The U.S. Economy: The Late 1980s and Early 1990s

During the 1980s, the Federal Reserve continued to increase the money supply, resulting in lower interest rates. During this period of sustained growth and low inflation, a stock market crash in the United States wiped out some $500 billion of wealth, signaling that not all was well with the U.S. economy. By the end of the week of October 19, 1987, nearly $1 trillion of wealth had vanished.*

The repercussions of the crash were felt throughout the world. Quick intervention by the Federal Reserve assured both confidence and sufficient liquidity to underwrite any instability that might spread to the banking and credit industries. Indicators showed the economy to be in reasonable health; the 6 percent unemployment level was the lowest in a decade, prices were stable, and economic growth had been led by a massive consumer spending boom. There were, however, economic as well as structural and institutional problems that prompted the dramatic decline in the New York Stock Exchange on that day, referred to as Black Monday.

After the 1987 crash, the underlying U.S. debt, low saving rate, and institutional problems persisted. The economic recovery of the early 1980s continued, with economic growth averaging just over 3.7 percent between 1987 and 1989. In 1989, unemployment reached its lowest point since 1973, when it fell to 5.3 percent. After this, growth stagnated and an economic slowdown continued through 1992.

## A Rebirth of Pax Americana: 1992 and Beyond

A buoyant recovery followed the 1989 to 1992 recession and was characterized by increased investment, strong productivity growth, lower levels of unemployment,

---

*Some people call this wealth "paper wealth." It accumulates from the changing value of stock prices.

and steady economic expansion without any signs of inflation. Indeed, the economic growth experienced in the United States between the trough of the recession in 1991 and peak of the upturn in 2000 was the longest economic expansion on record.

Growth between 1992 and 1997 was accompanied by changes in corporate organization including downsizing. While the rate of growth was initially slow, it increased steadily. The president and Congress paid increasing attention to budget and trade deficits and were successful in reducing budget deficits. The income gap between the haves and have-nots continued to widen, with women and children bearing the brunt of the effects of income redistribution. Although an impressive number of jobs were created between 1982 and 1988 and 1992 and 2000, the number of less-educated workers vying for those jobs reduced the real earnings of high school graduates and dropouts alike. Rank-and-file workers experienced an 18 percent decrease in real (inflation-adjusted) wages between 1973 and 1997, while corporate chief executive officers watched their pay increase by an average of 19 percent (66 percent after taxes). Homelessness became a national problem.

Financial crises in Asia, Latin America, and Russia in 1997 and 1998 failed to stem the economic expansion in the United States. Rather, as countries in these areas experienced a deep economic downturn, their falling currencies and lower wages signaled cheaper exports to the United States. The relatively low prices of imports from these areas kept U.S. prices low.

With inflation well under control, investment continued to increase, and economic growth became even more rapid, reaching an extraordinary level of 6 percent in 1999 before falling to more normal and sustainable rate of 4 percent in 2000. Employment remained strong as growth kept unemployment hovering around 4 percent between 1997 and 2001. With rising income, productivity increases, and moderation in public policy, budget deficits turned into surpluses in 1999 and 2000 for the first time since World War II. Internationally, U.S. growth rates were much stronger than those in Europe and Japan. Despite this remarkable period of economic expansion, the U.S. infrastructure—the stock of highways, bridges, and water and sewer lines that had contributed to growth in the 1950s and 1960s—continued to deteriorate. Fewer U.S. workers were covered by health insurance and the number of uninsured children grew.

By early 2001, a recession was underway. After a decade of uninterrupted and often accelerating growth, postwar unemployment record lows, and vigorous productivity increases, growth did finally slow and a number of economic "shocks" prolonged the slowdown into 2003. In March 2001, the high-flying stock market, largely propelled by technology and .com stocks, began a quick descent, with most stock measures dropping more than 20 percent, wiping out an estimated $4.7 trillion in "paper" wealth from the change in value of stock prices. The Federal Reserve pumped money into the economy and targeted much lower interest rates designed to stimulate investment and consumer spending. Congress passed a series of tax cuts with the hope of increasing the economic stimulus.

In the fall, more economic shocks left the economy reeling. The terror attacks of September 11, 2001, had profound impacts on all aspects of American lives, including the economy. Uncertainty and confusion surrounding the attacks led investors and consumers to be more wary about expenditures. And, while Americans were still trying to deal with the after-effects of September 11 and plan for the future, a series of corporate scandals led to the failure of several large firms, including Enron (the seventh largest firm in the United States in 2000), and Arthur Andersen, one of the (then) "big five" accounting firms. War in Iraq, declared in March 2003, also had economic consequences.

The lowest mortgage rates in four decades, low interest rates, increases in government spending and tax cuts, resilient consumers, and a buoyant housing market stimulated economic activity. By late 2006, economic growth and productivity returned. Initially, lethargic job creation and discouraged workers, accompanied by growing budget deficits and trade deficits (despite a weaker U.S. dollar), continued to cause concern, but by the end of the year and throughout 2007 the unemployment rate remained at a low 4.6 percent. Inflation began to rise in 2007 and 2008 due to high commodity prices, including record oil prices; however, prices stabilized in late 2008. The financial crisis that began in 2007 spread to the rest of the economy in 2008 as consumers cut spending and businesses decreased investment expenditures. Unemployment began to rise, reaching 9.4 percent in mid-2009. Between 2007 and the second quarter of 2009, some $14 trillion in wealth was lost due to decreases in the stock market and the drop in house prices as the housing bubble burst. Because of the global spread of the financial crisis, the U.S. dollar initially rose against most major currencies and the strong dollar dampened an already lethargic export sector. The failure and near failure of several large financial institutions, along with a growing number of U.S. corporations entering bankruptcy, resulted in continuing and increasing job losses. Firms entering bankruptcy included Linens 'n Things, Eddie Bauer, Circuit City, Chrysler, and General Motors. The government injected funds into the economy through the Troubled Asset Relief Program (TARP) and stimulus package, and the Federal Reserve created a number of funding and lending facilities to help supply liquidity to a financial system that had ceased lending and creating credit. Health care and health insurance coverage remained a topic of public discussion as health care costs continued to rise, as did the numbers of uninsured.

As we continue our discussion of macroeconomic goals, we see that while full employment, low inflation, and economic growth are important, other goals also might be beneficial, but little agreement exists as to what these additional goals might be, or which economic problems should have priority.

8. What has happened to the recession since 2009? What has stimulated the rapid or slow or no growth? Has unemployment increased? Inflation? Why or why not?

9. List five macroeconomic goals you think are important for this millennium. Briefly explain your choices.

# NATIONAL ACCOUNTING MEASURES

As we chart macroeconomic goals through the next few years, it is important to understand what these concepts mean and how we measure them. The scheme of National Income and Product Accounting was developed to put economic growth measures into perspective. These measures give quantifiable definitions to the activities of the major macroeconomic actors (consumers, businesses, governments, and the international sector) and show how they interact to generate production, consumption, and investment.

To help understand the ways in which the economy continues to change over time, economists collect and analyze data that measure economic variables. Economic measurement is usually designed to aid forecasting and explanation of economic events, or it may be used to compare the size or the value of things. When economists speak of the value of the annual output of a nation, they refer to gross domestic product (GDP), published in quarterly reports issued by the Department of Commerce. The media, politicians, and others who regularly comment on economic affairs await the Commerce Department reports in order to assess whether GDP and its accompanying growth rate are up or down. Economists then assess these results and often qualify them—for example, GDP was up 2.5 percent over last quarter, but prices have been increasing by 3 percent at the same time.

In December 1991, the Bureau of Economic Analysis began to emphasize GDP in place of gross national product (GNP). The distinction between the two accounting measures is that GDP includes the income earned by foreign residents and companies in the United States, but not the income earned by U.S. citizens and corporations abroad. The change from GNP to GDP occurred because GDP more closely follows the short-term economic performance of the economy and because most other countries use GDP as their primary accounting measure.

In fact, for the United States, the difference between GNP and GDP has usually been very small. In a typical year, the income earned by foreign-owned businesses and noncitizens in the United States is very close to the income earned by U.S. citizens and companies abroad. Therefore, the differences between GNP and GDP nearly cancel each other out in the United States. However, in small countries with much business activity by foreign companies, the two measures may be significantly different.

Economists and policy makers use GDP and the rest of the National Income and Product Accounts as the basis for many decisions. We therefore will spend some time looking at the components of these accounts.

There are two basic ways of arriving at final figures for the various accounting measures:

1. The *goods- or expenditures-flow approach* focuses on the prices and quantities of goods and services sold.

**FIGURE 1**  The Income and Spending Flows

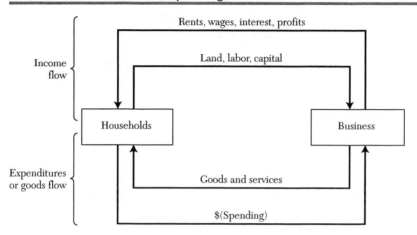

2. The *income-flow approach* focuses on income paid to those producing goods and services.

These approaches appear in the circular flow diagram in Figure 1. We can measure either the top part of the circular flow (the income flow) or the bottom part of the circular flow (the goods or expenditures flow) to arrive at equal measures of national income.

The definitions, relations, and data in Tables 3 and 4 show the derivation of GDP with the goods-flow approach. GDP consists of the total expenditures of the four sectors that purchase goods and services:

$$GDP = C + I + G + (X - M),$$

where $C$ represents the expenditures made by consumers, $I$ is investment expenditures made by the business community, $G$ is expenditures on goods and services by government, and $(X - M)$ represents net exports, or exports $(X)$ minus imports $(M)$. GDP grows or declines due to changes in consumption $(C)$, investment $(I)$, government expenditures $(G)$, and/or net exports $(X - M)$. Figure 2 illustrates the percentage change of each of these measures between quarters from 2007 through the second quarter of 2009. Note how the percentage change in consumption spending fell until the first quarter of 2009 as consumers responded to the recession by decreasing their spending. This had the effect of decreasing GDP. Note as well that gross private domestic investment only began to decline in the fourth quarter of 2008. When investment spending falls, it too produces a negative effect on GDP—so GDP will fall, unless decreases are offset by an increase in other measures. The income-flow approach entails summing the various forms of income received from the production process, so when the percentage change in an income stream like wages and salaries falls, GDP will fall unless another income stream, like profits, offsets the decline.

**Table 3** Relation of Gross Domestic Product, Net National Product, National Income, and Personal Income

| The sum of | Billions of Dollars | | |
| --- | --- | --- | --- |
| | 1996 | 2000 | 2008 |
| Personal consumption expenditures (C) | 5,151.40 | 6,757.30 | 10,057.90 |
| Gross private domestic investment (I) | 1,117.00 | 1,832.70 | 1,993.50 |
| Government consumption expenditures and gross investment (G) | 1,406.40 | 1,743.70 | 2,882.40 |
| Net exports of goods and services (X – M) | −98.70 | −370.70 | −669.20 |
| EQUALS: Gross domestic product (GDP) | 7,576.10 | 9,963.10 | 14,264.60 |
| PLUS: Receipts of factor income from the rest of the world | 228.40 | 370.60 | 789.30 |
| LESS: Payments of factor income to the rest of the world | 237.30 | 374.90 | 665.10 |
| EQUALS: Gross national product (GNP) | 7,567.20 | 9,958.70 | 14,397.80 |
| LESS: Consumption of fixed capital | 858.30 | 1,257.10 | 1,832.30 |
| EQUALS: Net national product (NNP) | 6,708.90 | 8,701.60 | 12,565.50 |
| LESS: Indirect business tax and nontax liability | 617.90 | 769.60 | – |
| Business transfer payments | 32.20 | 41.70 | – |
| Statistical discrepancy | −74.60 | −87.70 | 138.10 |
| PLUS: Subsidies less current surplus of government enterprises | 17.50 | 27.90 | – |
| EQUALS: National income (NI) | 6,150.90 | 8,002.00 | 12,427.40 |
| LESS: Corporate profits with inventory valuation and capital consumption adjustments | 654.70 | 946.20 | 1,476.50 |
| Net interest | 403.30 | 567.20 | 682.70 |
| Contributions for social insurance | 689.70 | 705.60 | 995.70 |
| LESS: Taxes on production (–) M subsides | – | – | 983.10 |
| Net Business Transfer Payments | – | – | 103.60 |
| PLUS: Personal interest income | 1,056.70 | 1,034.30 | – |
| Personal dividend income | 738.20 | 396.60 | – |
| Personal income receipts on assets | – | – | 2,037.70 |
| Government transfer payments to persons | 230.60 | 1,037.10 | – |
| Business transfer payments to persons | 23.00 | 30.70 | – |
| Personal current transfer receipts | – | – | 1,869.10 |
| EQUALS: Personal income (PI) | 6,451.70 | 8,281.70 | 12,100.60 |
| LESS: Personal tax payments | 863.80 | 1,291.90 | 1,457.30 |
| EQUALS: Disposable personal income (DPI) | 5,587.90 | 6,989.80 | 10,643.30 |
| LESS: Personal outlays | | 6,998.30 | 10,450.70 |
| Personal consumption expenditures (C) | 5,151.40 | 6,757.30 | 10,057.90 |
| Interest paid by consumers | 146.30 | 212.20 | 248.90 |
| Personal transfer payments | 16.30 | 28.80 | 144.50 |
| EQUALS: Personal savings (S) | 273.90 | −8.50 | 192.70 |

Note: Dollars are not constant dollars.

Note: Numbers do not add up to the totals shown because of adjustments or inclusion of minor categories. In 2006, revisions changed the accounting for items shown as dashes (–).

Source: *Survey of Current Business*, April 1997; April 2001, 2004, 2009.

**Table 4**   Definitions of Primary Account in Table 3

---

*The sum of*

1. ***Personal consumption expenditures (C)*** consist of the market value of purchases of goods and services by individuals and nonprofit institutions and the value of food, clothing, housing, and financial services received by them as income in kind.

2. ***Gross private domestic investment (I)*** consists of acquisitions of newly produced capital goods by private business and nonprofit institutions and of the value of the change in the volume of inventories held by business. It covers all private new dwellings.

3. ***Government consumption expenditures and gross investment (G)*** consist of government expenditures for compensation of employees, purchases from business, net foreign purchases and contributions, and the gross investment of government enterprises. This measure excludes transfer payments, government interest, and subsidies.

4. ***Net exports of goods and services (X − M)*** measures the excess of (1) domestic output sold abroad over purchases of foreign output, (2) production abroad credited to U.S-owned resources over production at home credited to foreign-owned resources, and (3) cash gifts and contributions received from abroad over cash gifts and contributions to foreigners.

EQUALS

5. ***Gross domestic product (GDP)*** is the market value of the newly produced goods and services that are not resold in any form during the accounting period (usually one year).

PLUS

6. ***Receipts of factor income*** from the rest of the world are the moneys received from foreign affiliates of U.S. corporations. The moneys take the form of interest, dividends, and reinvested earnings.

LESS

7. ***Payments of factor income*** to the rest of the world are the payments to foreign residents of interest, dividends, and reinvested earnings of U.S. affiliates of foreign companies.

EQUALS

8. ***Gross national product (GNP)*** is the market value of the newly produced goods and services that are not resold in any form during the accounting period (usually one year).

LESS

9. ***Capital consumption allowance*** is an allowance for capital goods that have been consumed in the process of producing this year's GDP. It consists of depreciation, capital outlays charged to current expense, and accidental damage.

10. ***Net national product (NNP)*** is the net creation of new wealth resulting from the productive activity of the economy during the accounting period.

---

# POTENTIAL PROBLEMS WITH THE NATIONAL INCOME ACCOUNTS

The measures in the National Income Accounts are corrected for inflation with the use of a price index. Also, use of a value-added approach in the measurement process avoids possible double-counting. There are, however, criticisms of the accounts that have not been addressed. Particularly troublesome are issues of what is and what is not included in the National Income and Product Accounts. Let us see how some potential problems have been avoided and discuss some that remain.

**Table 4**  Continued

LESS

**11.** *Indirect business tax* consists primarily of sales and excise taxes, customs duties on imported goods, and business property taxes. These taxes are collected from businesses and are chargeable to their current costs.

EQUALS

**12.** *National income (NI)* is the total income of factors from participation in the current productive process.

LESS

**13.** *After-tax corporate profits* with inventory and capital consumption adjustments subtracts federal and state taxes levied on corporate earnings and depreciation allowances from orporate profits.

**14.** *Net interest* is interest earnings minus interest liabilities and part of national income.

**15.** Contributions for *social insurance* consist of payments by employees and the self-employed.

PLUS

**16.** *Personal interest income* includes all interest payments made to persons.

**17.** *Personal dividend income* includes that part of corporate profits returned to stockholders.

**18.** *Transfer payments* (government and business) consist of monetary income received by individuals from government and business (other than government interest) for which no services are currently rendered.

EQUALS

**19.** *Personal income (PI)* is income received by households, as opposed to income earned by households.

LESS

**20.** *Personal taxes* consist of the taxes levied against individuals, their income, and their property that are not deductible as expenses of business operations.

EQUALS

**21.** *Disposable personal income (DPI)* is the income remaining to persons after deduction of personal tax and nontax payments to general government.

LESS

**22.** *Personal consumption expenditures (C)*—this is the same as item 1.

EQUALS

**23.** *Personal savings (S)* may be in such forms as changes in cash and deposits, security holdings, and private pension, health, welfare, and trust funds.

## Real versus Nominal GDP

These definitional relationships ignore many difficult and rather perplexing problems. First, there is the problem of the yardstick, money. This is a very flexible yardstick, since dollars are most often worth more or less as time passes (usually less). To solve the flexibility dilemma, economists use index numbers, meaning they compare a "market basket" of selected goods and services from one accounting period with a similar "basket" from some previous accounting period, or base year.*

---

*In January 1996, the Bureau of Economic Analysis (BEA) released new estimates for the national income and product accounts, moving to a system that uses chain weights instead of fixed weights in the adjustment of real GDP, to remove biases caused by the fixed-weight price system of the past. The formula for this adjustment is no longer as simple as the common market basket example using fixed weights. By adopting the chain-weighting system, the BEA hopes to provide more accurate measures of real GDP. For additional information on these changes, see the 1996 *Economic Report of the President*, pp. 48, 50, and 59.

**FIGURE 2**  Contribution to U.S. GDP Growth, % change on previous quarter (annualized)

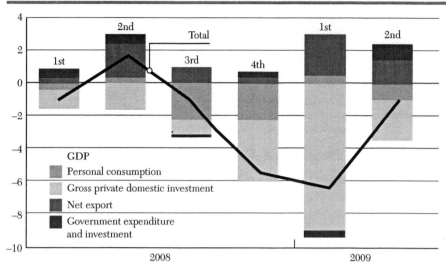

Source: *Thomson Reuters Datastream.*

Thus, they can avoid the perils of price instability by inflating or deflating the dollar value accordingly. For example, if prices increase at a rate of 5 percent during a year, a good that cost $100 at the beginning of the first year would be priced at $105 at the beginning of the next. Using a price index, this item would be valued at $100 in constant dollars. This device allows us to remove the effects of price changes from GDP, so that we can measure the changes in *real* output and better assess the actual physical volume of production in the two periods.

The GDP deflator is a systematized equation that has been shown to be a reasonable indicator of how much the national product has gained or lost due to recession or inflation. For example, in 1979 GDP went up by 12 percent, but prices went up by 11.3 percent, so real GDP increased by only 0.7 percent. Figure 3 shows the variation between real and nominal GDP since 1999.

## Value-Added Accounting

A second problem encountered in the national income accounting framework is the actual counting process. We can either count the final products produced or sum the amount of value added by each stage of the production process. For example, to enter a loaf of bread into the accounting scheme, we could use the final sale price of the loaf of bread, or we could sum the value added to the loaf of bread by the wheat farmer, miller, baker, grocer, and so on. Both methods should yield the same result, but in the final-product method, there is often a chance of double-counting the components of production. Therefore, the value-added approach is preferred.

## What Is Counted in GDP?

The significance of the accounts also has been called into question. These accounts are primarily derived from market transactions with known prices and quantities, but some market transactions are excluded. Excluded transactions include capital gains and losses as well as all illegal transactions. (What would the illegal drug market add to the GDP?) Also excluded is the economic activity of the underground economy—individuals who earn but do not report income on services they render or goods they produce, for example, cash paid for baby-sitting. Barter exchange also is part of the underground economy. The size of the underground economy has been estimated at 5 to 30 percent of GDP. Other industrial nations are estimated to have underground economies comparable to that of the United States.

**FIGURE 3** GDP in Current and Constant Dollars 1999–2009

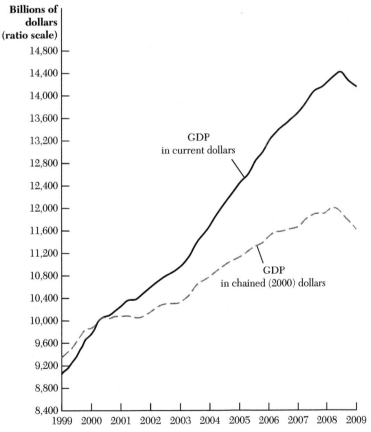

Source: U.S. Department of Commerce, *Economic Indicators*, May 2009.

The accounts also include some imputed values for nonmarket transactions. For example, imputed values are added for owner-occupied homes (room and board services exchanged for). But imagine what would happen to the accounts if we made yet another nonmarket inclusion, the value of unpaid child care provided by parents. If families simply exchanged child care with their neighbors each day and paid one another $50 or more a day (the estimated market worth of child care services), their production would be included in the accounts. These activities are productive; they are services. Currently, however, they are neither measured nor included in the National Income Accounts.

Marilyn Waring, a political economist and former member of the New Zealand Parliament, has suggested in her book *If Women Counted: A New Feminist Economics*, that throughout the world, accounting systems that define productive activity, as well as the economic analysis and teaching that sustain them, automatically exclude the nonmarket activities of women. To this point she quotes retired Harvard economist John Kenneth Galbraith:

> That many women are coming to sense that they are instruments in the economic system is not in doubt. But their feeling finds no support in economic writing and teaching. On the contrary, it is concealed and on the whole with great success, by modern neo-classical economics—the everyday economics of the textbook and classroom. This concealment is neither conspiratorial nor deliberate. It reflects the natural and very strong instincts of economics for what is convenient to influence economic interest—for what I have called the conventional social virtue. It is sufficiently successful that it allows many hundreds of thousands of women to study economics each year without their developing any serious suspicion as to how they will be used.

> —Marilyn J. Waring, *If Women Counted*, HarperCollins Publishers, 1989.

10. How will you be used by the economic system? Does it matter? Why?

11. What are "natural" instincts? Do you trust them?

The National Income Accounts are often misrepresented as an indicator of social well-being. In 1995, Clifford Cobb, Ted Halstead, and Jonathan Rowe published an article in *The Atlantic Monthly* entitled "If the GDP Is Up, Why Is America Down?" The article noted that the U.S. economy was performing in textbook fashion, with productivity and employment increasing and inflation remaining at low levels, but people didn't "feel" better. Indeed, President Clinton later called it a malaise. These authors argued for new measures for economic progress that would "change the social and political landscape":

> The GDP is simply a gross measure of market activity, of money changing hands. It makes no distinction whatsoever between the desirable and the undesirable, or costs and gain. On top of that, it looks only at the portion of reality that economists

choose to acknowledge—the part involved in monetary transactions. The crucial economic functions performed in the household and volunteer sectors go entirely unrecognized. As a result the GDP not only masks the breakdown of the social structure and the natural habitat upon which the economy—and life itself—ultimately depend; worse, it actually portrays such breakdown as economic gain.

Economic "bads," such as pollution and deaths due to lung cancer attributed to smoking cigarettes, actually increase the GDP. These social costs are not subtracted from, but added to the GDP. As we spend more and more to clean up the environment, the spending *adds* to our national product. As cigarette sales increase, GDP increases. As hospital costs for increased numbers of cases of lung cancer and emphysema occur, GDP increases. GDP, in other words, is not a measure of overall welfare.

The environment think tank, Redefining Progress, has constructed what it calls a genuine progress indicator (GPI). The GPI tries to monitor "sustainability"—or the conflict between sustaining human life and the integrity of nature... or living satisfactorily without destroying our environment. Thus the GPI monitors human consumption of resources *and* our contentment with our social, personal, and civic life. In other words, the GPI takes some economic "bads" such as environmental degradation into account. Figure 4 compares trends in per capita GPI with trends in per capita GDP in the United States since 1950. Although GDP has risen over that period, the level of GPI has barely changed.

12. Can you give other examples in which individual or societal welfare is diminished but GDP is increased?

Social scientists are attempting to construct a qualitative index that measures social welfare. Thus far, the index is quite crude, but it shows that nations with the highest GDP do not necessarily have the highest social welfare ratings, while a few countries with extremely low GDP have *relatively* high standings on the social welfare index.

The United Nations has constructed a Human Development Index (HDI) that measures a set of average human achievements in a single index. These achievements include life expectancy at birth, adult literacy rate, and per capita income. Table 5 lists the top twenty countries according to a recent HDI.

13. Why is it important to collect data on all of these different macroeconomic variables?

**FIGURE 4**  Genuine Progress Indicator and GDP for the United States, 1950–2004

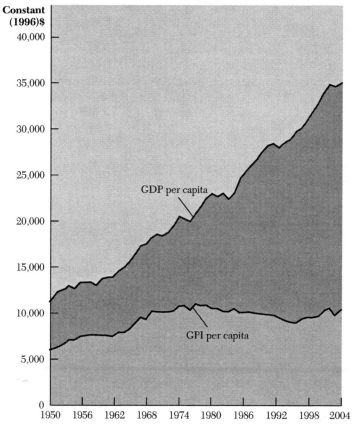

Source: Data from Redefining Progress, *Genuine Progress Report,* 2006. p.4

**Table 5**  Top Countries Rated with the UN's Human Development Index

| Rank | Country |
|------|---------|
| 1. | Iceland |
| 2. | Norway |
| 3. | Canada |
| 4. | Australia |
| 5. | Ireland |
| 6. | Netherlands |
| 7. | Sweden |
| 8. | Japan |
| 9. | Luxembourg |
| 10. | Switzerland |

(continued)

**Table 5** Top Countries Rated with the UN's Human Development Index (continued)

| Rank | Country |
| --- | --- |
| 11. | France |
| 12. | Finland |
| 13. | Denmark |
| 14. | Austria |
| 15. | United States |
| 16. | Spain |
| 17. | Belgium |
| 18. | Greece |
| 19. | Italy |
| 20. | New Zeland |

Source: Data from United Nations, *Human Development Report.* Copyright © 2008 The United Nations. Used with permission.

# Conclusion

*This brief overview of macroeconomic problems and issues and summary of aggregate economic measurements provides a conceptual framework for describing relationships among important economic variables. While it is clear that recent trends in the U.S. economy have left us with many questions concerning future directions, we need to ask ourselves, To what extent does contemporary macroeconomic theory adequately explain our current economic reality?*

## Review Questions

1. Why do you think full employment, economic growth, and price stability were selected as the basic macroeconomic goals in the United States? Can you think of other possible goals? Explain.

2. The three goals are often at odds with one another. Has the relative emphasis of these different goals changed over time? Why?

3. What do you see as some of the costs associated with unemployment? Inflation?

4. Do events elsewhere in the world affect the U.S. economy? Give some examples.

5. Is it possible to establish an effective body of macroeconomic policy using only fiscal tools or only monetary tools? Why or why not?

6. Do policy measures aimed at alleviating one set of economic problems sometimes make others worse? Should a policy action be undertaken to aid one aspect of the macroeconomy to the detriment of another? Explain.

7. Examine a daily newspaper (e.g., *The New York Times*) for a few days, and see how many articles address macroeconomic issues and problems. Make a list of the macroeconomic terms, concepts, and issues that you find.

8. Why should reports of current levels of GDP be received with care?

9. What do the National Income and Product Accounts measure?

10. Increasing numbers of women have entered the paid labor market during the past three decades. What impact would you expect this to have on GDP? Explain.

# Macroeconomic Theory: Classical and Keynesian Models

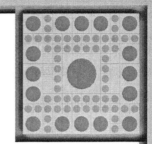

## ❖ Introduction

**T**he tenets of classical macroeconomic theory formed by Adam Smith, David Ricardo, John Stuart Mill, and others, which focused on growth, were carried pretty much intact through the nineteenth century. Economists in the latter part of that era concentrated more on the microeconomic concepts of utility and production than on the total economy. This chapter will provide a guide to our current understanding of the macroeconomy, discuss four major parts of the classical doctrine, illustrate their use, and then examine the Keynesian critique of classical macroeconomic theory and its inability to deal with high unemployment in the depression-plagued world of the 1930s.

In this chapter, we also will start to construct an economic model that is used for analyzing economic activity and forecasting the outcome of policy measures and/or economic shocks. This aggregate demand–aggregate supply model builds on macroeconomic models of income and output, and adds to that the effect of including money (through monetary policy). We formulate the Keynesian model, which combines with monetary theory to form the underlying foundation for macroeconomic analysis.

The completed aggregate demand–aggregate supply graphs resemble market supply and demand graphs, but this resemblance is where the similarity ends. Information about financial markets, goods and service markets, and economic policy are reflected in an aggregate demand–aggregate supply analysis, which tells us how those markets respond to economic events, including policy decisions. We will be able to assess aggregate output and price levels for the economy when the model is completed.

From Chapter 14 of *Economics: A Tool for Critically Understanding Society*, 9/e. Tom Riddell. Jean Shackelford. Geoffrey Schneider. Steve Stamos. Copyright © 2011 by Pearson Education. Published by Addison-Wesley. All rights reserved.

*We begin with Keynes's theory which challenged long-standing economic traditions. Some view the Keynesian contribution as a new paradigm, while others view it as simply a major revision of classical theory. The classical model we discuss in this chapter was never formally set up as such by any of the classical economists. Rather, Keynes drew together the foundations from the writings of the classical economists and constructed the model primarily as a foil against which he could contrast his model in* The General Theory of Employment, Interest, and Money.

# THE **BIG** PICTURE

## An Introduction to the Classical Model

If we were to summarize the contributions of various classical and neoclassical economists prior to the Great Depression of the 1930s, they would share the view that a capitalist economy (using an analogy of Cambridge economic historian Mark Blaug) generated its own automatic pilot. If there were disturbances in various markets creating disequilibrium prices, then wages or interest rates would adjust so that equilibrium in markets would once again be attained. For example, if there was not enough saving among the public to generate required levels of investment, the interest rate would be bid up—attracting more saving and lowering investment—and equilibrium would be restored, as we see in Figure BP.1

If there was unemployment, wages would be bid down until employers would be willing to hire those unemployed, thus restoring labor market equilibrium (Figure BP.2).

**FIGURE BP.1**  Saving and Investment in the Classical Model

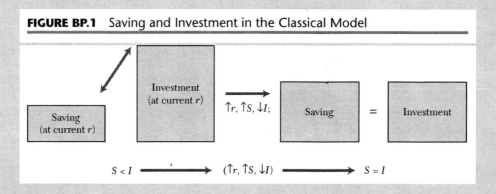

**FIGURE BP.2** Labor Market Adjustment in the Classical Model

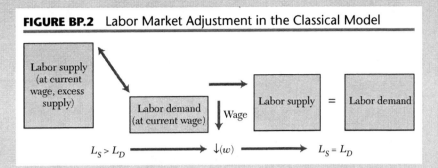

$$L_S > L_D \longrightarrow \downarrow(w) \longrightarrow L_S = L_D$$

All one needed to do was wait. The automatic pilot takes over, markets adjust, and equilibrium is restored. But the Great Depression, which was felt throughout the world, found capitalism's markets slow to restore equilibrium. Prices fell and gluts occurred. Wages fell and unemployment increased. The economy crashed before the automatic pilot restored order.

# THE CLASSICAL MODEL

We will now discuss four specific elements of the classical model that show how economists analyzed unemployment, inflation, and growth, particularly when the economy suffered during the Great Depression. We will begin by examining the quantity theory of money and the equation of exchange, which was used to show the relationship between money and prices. Next we will briefly examine the goods and labor market, Say's law, and the credit market in the classical model.

## The Quantity Theory of Money

A major tenet of classical economic theory is the **quantity theory of money**. Most often this is expressed by the **equation of exchange**:

$$MV = PQ,$$

where $M$ is the money stock in the economy, $V$ is the income velocity of money (the rate of turnover of money), $P$ is the price level, and $Q$ is the level of real national income (real GDP). This equation appears simple enough—perhaps too simple, for when it is examined carefully, it becomes an identity. It is true because it is by definition true. This is because of the definition of velocity—the rate at which money moves through the economy during a given period, or the number of times a piece of money gets spent:

$$V = \frac{PQ}{M}$$

Since national income is a measure of all output ($Q$) in a country for a year multiplied by the price ($P$) of each good or service, $V$ is equal, in effect, to national income in a given year divided by the total amount of money available (on the average) during that year.

The classical economists elaborated further on each of the variables in the equation of exchange. They proposed that each of the variables in the equation is affected by both external and internal forces. $Q$, or national output, is determined primarily by real factors that change slowly over time, such as capital, technology, resource availability, and labor. The quantity of money ($M$) would not influence these variables in any significant way. The classical economists argued that the income velocity of money ($V$), on the other hand, is determined by institutional factors that are also independent of any change in the money stock ($M$). Some of these institutional factors are population density, custom, transportation factors, the state of the art of banking, and wage payments and practices. With $Q$ and $V$ unaffected by changes in the supply of money, the level of prices ($P$) is directly related to changes in the quantity of money ($M$).

Since $Q$ and $V$ were defined as relatively constant, this means changes in the quantity of money produce nearly proportional changes in the price level. Thus, if the quantity of money in the economy doubles, the price level is likely to double as well. In terms of output and employment in the economy, money, therefore, does not matter very much; in terms of wages and prices, however, it matters a great deal. The following equations show this:

$$M\overline{V} = P\overline{Q} \qquad \Delta M = \Delta P$$

Assuming that $\overline{V}$ and $\overline{Q}$ are constant at a point in time, any changes in the quantity of money ($\Delta M$) must lead to changes in prices ($\Delta P$).

The classical economists viewed money as neutral in that it satisfies no direct utility or want. It merely reflects real activity in the economy. It serves as a veil behind which the *real* action of economic forces, such as the growth of the national product and employment, are concealed. Yet money was viewed as a lubricant for the economy, keeping it well oiled and enabling it to run smoothly and effectively. In the classical model, money does not affect the level of output. The labor market plays a role in determining output.

## The Goods and Labor Markets in Classical Economics

A second part of the classical model centers on the production of goods, or real output. Equilibrium output is determined by the demand for and supply of labor. Increases in the demand for labor increase output ($Q$), and decreases in the supply of labor decrease output. In the classical system, the level of output is determined by full employment. The equilibrium real wage defines the level of full employment in the labor force. Anyone willing to work at the prevailing equilibrium wage will be employed—the quantity supplied of labor equals the quantity demanded of labor. Anyone unwilling to work at that wage is regarded as not desiring to work, and therefore not classified as unemployed. As long as wages are flexible (both upward and downward) in the classical world, no conflict will arise. Full employment, as they defined it, is the norm. This fully employed labor force will produce an equilibrium level of goods and services ($Q$) for the economy.

## Say's Law

A third part of classical macroeconomic theory is Say's law, named for the French economist Jean Baptiste Say (1767–1832). In its oversimplified form, the "law" is often expressed as supply creating its own demand. Businesses in the process of producing or supplying goods and services for the market will pay wages or rents to employees, landlords, and others engaged in producing the product. That income may be used to purchase goods supplied by the firm or goods supplied by other firms. The act of production, which supplies goods to the market, at the same time generates income to workers and others, who in turn demand goods and services in the market and spend the dollars they earn on those products. For every dollar of product produced, a dollar of income is created and spent.

Say's law, which is important to both the Keynesian and classical models, explains the flow of goods and the flow of income. The supply, or output, that "creates its own demand" consists of the goods and services produced by the firms or businesses. The factors of production (land, labor, and capital) receive returns of rents, wages and salaries, and interest and profits for their part in the production process. Over time, with expanding population, higher income levels in the household sector create more demand for goods and services. The household sector then spends this income on the goods and services that have been produced, thereby creating an income stream for the business sector. As a result, the aggregate expenditures on goods and services by the household sector will equal the aggregate supply of those goods and services produced by the business sector. Equilibrium occurs when aggregate income or output equals aggregate expenditures.

## The Classical Credit Market

Thus far we have assumed that Say's law means all income received during the production process will be spent on goods supplied by producers. But what if some of that income is saved? The classical model accounts for both saving and investment in its analysis of the credit or loanable funds market. Any income saved by consumers will flow into the business sector as investment, through the credit or loanable funds market. In this market, a flexible interest rate adjusts to yield an equilibrium between saving and investment.

The classical model assumes that both saving ($S$) and investment ($I$) are functions of the rate of interest ($r$): $S = f(r)$, and $I = f(r)$. The supply of credit comes from people who save. Income not spent is saved in the credit market. The classical economists assumed that higher interest rates cause people to save more because of the higher return on any money they save. Therefore, interest rates are directly related to saving. As Figure 1 shows,

**FIGURE 1** The Classical Credit Market

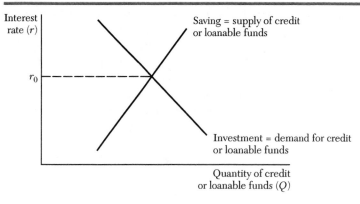

this gives us an upward-sloping curve that represents saving or the supply of credit or loanable funds.

Investment is inversely related to the interest rate. If businesses must borrow funds at high interest rates to finance investments, they will be less willing to borrow and invest. So, at higher interest rates, investment will be low; at lower interest rates, investment will be higher. Investors, like savers, make decisions based on the interest rate. In Figure 1 the downward-sloping curve represents investment or the demand for credit or loanable funds. At $r_0$ the amount saved is motivated by the amount invested; what isn't spent by some is borrowed and spent by others.

## FLAWS IN THE CLASSICAL MODEL

Between 1860 and 1929, the U.S. economy generally displayed rapid economic growth. The phases of growth tended to be cyclical, with upswings in economic activity accompanied by downswings, but with an overall upward trend in economic activity averaging about 2 percent per year. We call these recurrent swings in business activity **business cycles**. Figure 2 shows a hypothetical series of business cycles. Note that periods of growth and peaks are followed by periods of slump and troughs.

**FIGURE 2** Business Cycles

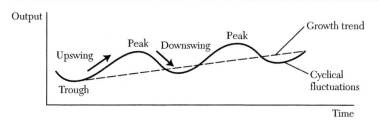

Economists have offered many explanations to account for business cycles. While few classical economists fully explained these fluctuations, economists who followed them offered explanations ranging from increases in sunspot activity to theories suggesting problems in overconsumption and underinvestment, monetary expansion and contraction, and innovation trends. Indeed, compelling arguments have been made for most of these in explaining cycles of growth.

1. If you were to extend Figure 2 to include this year, where would the economy be? In an upswing? A downswing? A peak or a trough? Why?

When economic conditions were in the downswing or trough of the cycle, as in the 1930s, classical economic theory explained the resulting levels of unemployment by insisting that those out of work were voluntarily or temporarily unemployed. They believed that businesses could make more employment opportunities by reducing the prevailing wage rate. As wages fell, the amount of labor demanded by businesses would increase. According to classical theory, these unemployed workers would be more than happy to work as long as their wages were above zero. However, during the Great Depression, as wages dropped lower, the number of people out of work actually rose. The classical system failed to explain this.

## THE GREAT DEPRESSION

The Great Depression lasted for ten years, from 1929 to 1939, and left enduring imprints on millions of Americans. It resulted from many different phenomena that seemed to culminate all at once. Some people who are interested in business cycles believe that short-, medium-, and long-run cycles all reached bottom at the same time. Certainly, more than just the 1929 stock market crash sustained the Great Depression for such a long period. Despite the robustness of the stock market before its fall, several industries in the economy were essentially weak.

Agriculture and manufacturing were perhaps the most important sectors contributing to the duration of the Great Depression. As the United States grew in the first few decades of that century, the number of agricultural workers fell. Hurt by the exploitation of the rail and storage bosses, and burned by their own speculative activities in land, more and more farmers were leaving or selling out to join the urban migration or to become tenants. The number of independent farms dropped by 40 percent during the 1920s. Output, however, was increasing, and the inelastic demand for farm production did little to help farmers. Unlike the other industries, in which greater supplies meant lower prices and increased demand, demand did not increase for the lower-priced agricultural products. In addition, the European export market declined, as European agricultural production was restored following World War I.

In manufacturing, conditions were mixed. Many people in business foresaw a time of weakness, and although sales, prices, and output were at all-time highs, employers cut back their workforces substantially, especially in the mines and mills. Only in the service and construction industries did employment levels hold their own, for these were areas in which men and women could not yet be displaced by technology. Growth increased throughout the 1920s, but workers were no better off than before. Wages and employment levels simply did not increase. Profits, on the other hand, swelled rapidly, as did the concentration of economic power in the hands of a few wealthy individuals. Profits in 1929 were three times those of 1920. But firms were not reinvesting. This was partially because firms had no incentive to invest; supply was already greater than demand.

The weaknesses in these two industries are directly linked to other causes of the depression: the lopsided distribution of income, with 5 percent of the population receiving about 30 percent of all income, and the lack of new investment by the business sector. In addition, the existing banking system was troubled. A series of unexpected and urgent demands by customers on some poorly managed banks created fear among all bank depositors, so that even economically sound banks were subjected to "runs" (when large numbers of depositors withdrew their money) and potential failure. Some 5,000 of the nation's banks failed during the Great Depression. Other factors added to the instability: Several European governments defaulted on U.S. loans, and in the United States, Congress adopted a balanced-budget philosophy that, by increasing taxes and reducing government expenditures, helped to worsen an already bad situation.

From this description, you can see that the U.S. economy had fundamental problems at the time of the stock market crash. From the widespread prosperity of the early 1920s, the late 1920s saw a lack of capital formation, overproduction of goods and services, and an agricultural glut, in addition to international disequilibrium and deep-seated psychological effects of the crash. All these led to prolonged instability, which caused many businesses, organizations, and institutions to collapse and brought havoc to the lives of unemployed workers, the heads of failed businesses, and their families and friends. The depression of the 1930s was a time of severe unemployment and poverty for the men, women, and children who endured it. More than one-third of the nation was unemployed or living in poverty. Conditions were abysmal for all but a few of the well-to-do.

As conditions worsened worldwide, the U.S. Congress passed the Smoot-Hawley Act imposing a 45 percent tariff on a third of U.S. imports. Other nations retaliated with high tariff barriers to protect their domestic industries from U.S. imports. Retaliation led to even higher tariffs and very high prices on all imported goods. World trade slowed dramatically. During this same period there was a severe contraction in the supply of money, which worsened financial conditions. Between 1929 and 1932, in the United States, 85,000 businesses failed, and stock values decreased from $87 billion to $19 billion. Manufacturing and farm income decreased by 50 percent. By 1933, the GDP had declined from $104 billion in 1929 to $56 billion, and unemployment stood firmly at 25 percent, with 12 million people unemployed. Despite the human misery that swept the nation, Secretary of the Treasury Andrew Mellon advised, "Liquidate labor, liquidate stocks, liquidate the farmers, liquidate real estate."

# ENTER JOHN MAYNARD KEYNES

The most important work of John Maynard Keynes (1883–1946) came at a time when the classical model was most under fire because of its inability to account for continued and worldwide depression with the masses of unemployed in the 1930s. Keynes watched the economic importance of his native Britain continue to wane after World War I, as the rapid growth of the United States and continental Western Europe accelerated. He developed his ideas and critique of the classical model slowly over a long period of time. Much of his writing was highly critical of the British authorities. Keynes was one of the first to recognize the implausibility of the British attachment to the gold standard for international payments and to object to the Versailles Peace Treaty after World War I. (He believed correctly that it would be impossible for Germany to meet the reparations called for by the treaty.)

During the 1930s, the major question being asked in each world capital was what to do about the depression. According to the classical doctrine, the simple remedy was to reduce wages to eliminate the excess supply of workers. But wages were falling, and more unemployment resulted, not less, violating Say's law. Supply was not creating its own demand. The circular flow was not working as it should. Markets were not adjusting to an equilibrium position as laissez-faire predicted. Classical theory and economists who were following these classical tenets were in a quandary.

Keynes focused on unemployment and argued, "The postulates of the classical theory are applicable only to a special case and not the general case ... and not ... those [conditions] of the economic society in which we actually live." In so doing, he illustrated the futility of the classical scheme, particularly Say's law and the limited circular flow.

## Capitalism's Savior

John Maynard Keynes is endlessly fascinating. A product of Eton, Cambridge, and the British Treasury, he was also a member of the Bloomsbury group, that influential collection of writers, artists, and intellectuals in London that included Virginia Woolf and E. M. Forster. A top academic and public policy polemicist, he also ran an insurance company and made a fortune in the markets. The philosopher Bertrand Russell considered Keynes's mind the "sharpest and clearest" he had ever encountered. "When I argued with him," Russell said, "I felt that I took my life in my hands, and I seldom emerged without feeling something of a fool."

But it is as an economic innovator that Keynes is best remembered. Keynes changed how economists study business cycles, price levels, labor markets, and economic growth. His insights have largely kept downturns in the business cycle over the past half century from turning into depressions. "Keynes's lasting achievement is the invention of macroeconomics," says Deidre McCloskey, an economic historian at the University of Illinois at Chicago.

Indeed, Keynes can lay claim to playing a crucial role in saving capitalism and, perhaps, civilization during the Great Depression. Despite millions of unemployed workers in the industrial nations, economic orthodoxy demanded that government do nothing or, worse yet, tighten the purse strings. Little wonder that the totalitarian solutions of fascism and communism exerted such pull. U.S. Treasury Secretary Andrew W. Mellon expressed a widespread sentiment among elites when he said in 1930 that the depression would "purge the rottenness out of the system. High costs of living and high living will come down. People will work harder, live a more moral life. Values will be adjusted, and enterprising people will pick up the wrecks from less competent people."

Keynes battled against such harsh counsel. With his landmark 1936 book, *The General Theory of Employment, Interest, and Money*, he persuaded a generation of thinkers and leaders to abandon a near-theological belief in balanced budgets. He showed how economies could get trapped in recession or depression—and argued that government could break the spiral by borrowing to finance public spending that stimulated consumer activity and restored business confidence. His ideas helped create

the golden era of postwar growth, and two institutions he championed in the 1940s still operate on a global scale, the International Monetary Fund and the World Bank.

Keynes is the philosopher-king of the modern mixed economy. It's a sign of his influence that there are no true believers in laissez-faire left. We are all Keynesians now. Governments routinely run deficits during downturns to increase the overall level of demand and, hence, employment. And many economists believe Japan's long stagnation in the 1990s largely reflected timid policy makers unwilling to boldly use the levers of fiscal and monetary policy.

Like Adam Smith and Karl Marx before him, Keynes believed economics wasn't merely about studying the efficient allocation of resources. For him, the good life meant beauty, art, love, morality—the passions that define civilization—and the value of economics lay in its pursuit of the stability and wealth that would allow our passions to flower.

Source: "Capitalism's Savior" by Christopher Farrell, *Business Week*, April 12, 2004, p. 20.

Today in the United States there is a resurgence of support for Keynesian economics. As the recession that began in the fourth quarter of 2007 deepened, many economists looked to lessons learned from the past to find solutions for that crisis.

# THE **BIG** PICTURE

## The Keynesian Model

### Part 1: Consumption, Saving, Investment, and Income

During the 1930s, nations mired in the Great Depression suffered massive levels of unemployment; little if any investment; falling prices (deflation); and reduced production. John Maynard Keynes's *The General Theory of Employment, Interest, and Money*, published in 1936, offered a macroeconomic analysis that challenged the time frame for market adjustment and the argument that the economy was best left unregulated. One message of the Keynesian theory is that market forces won't reliably generate full employment in a society. Market forces take too long—and are perhaps too weak—to return an economy to full employment in a timely way. In addition, the economic and social costs are too high to wait for market adjustment in the national and international markets for goods and services.

Several Keynesian assumptions about economic behavior differed from some assumptions of the classical model. For example, Keynes viewed full employment as *one possible equilibrium*; the classical model viewed full employment as *the only equilibrium* possible. Keynes noted that the economy could be in equilibrium when labor was fully employed, when it was underemployed, or even when it was over fully employed.

Equilibrium in Keynes's theory occurred when aggregate expenditures equaled aggregate output or national income—and that could be at full employment or not. Keynes noted that unemployment was part of the normal process of economic expansion and contraction in capitalist economies. Economies based on capitalism to this point displayed a history of expansion when employment increased, followed by economic contraction that left large numbers of people unemployed for substantial periods of time, without any sign of an automatic pilot reversing the trend. But, for Keynes, there was hope that an economy enduring

recession and unemployment could be restored to full employment quickly with government borrowing and government spending. Since the economy could be in equilibrium below full employment, there was no reason to think the economy would reach full employment—or adjust on its own. Thus, a *decisive actor* replaced the automatic pilot.

Two building blocks of the Keynesian model are the consumption function; viewing savings and investment adjustment through income, not interest rate changes; and the Keynesian multiplier.

***Consumption*** Income can either be consumed or saved and Keynes viewed both consumption and saving as functions of income, so that as income increased, consumption would increase—but not by as much as the increase in income—with the remaining income saved (Figure BP.3). By examining the relationship between income and consumption expenditures in a country over time, we find that as income rises, consumption also rises, and that there is a fairly stable relation between consumption and income.

**FIGURE BP.3**  Saving, Consumption, and Income

| Consumption | | |
|---|---|---|
| | = | Income |
| Saving | | |

***Savings Equals Investment*** In Keynes's explanation of macroeconomic relationships, just as in the classical system, in equilibrium, saving must equal investment. Keynes argued that consumers most often make spending decisions based on changes in their income, not changes in interest rates in the economy. If we think about what drives our decision, say to purchase a new pair of jeans, it is our income that we consider, not the current interest rate. So, since in the Keynesian model consumption and thus saving are functions of income, it is changes in income that equate savings and investment. For example, if investment is greater than saving, increased investment will generate higher levels of income that will raise both consumption and saving, and the economy reaches equilibrium (Figure BP.4).

***The Multiplier (k)*** In the circular flow we can observe that business payments to the factors of production (income in the form of wages, rents, and profits) will be used by households to purchase goods and services produced by businesses (Figure BP.5).

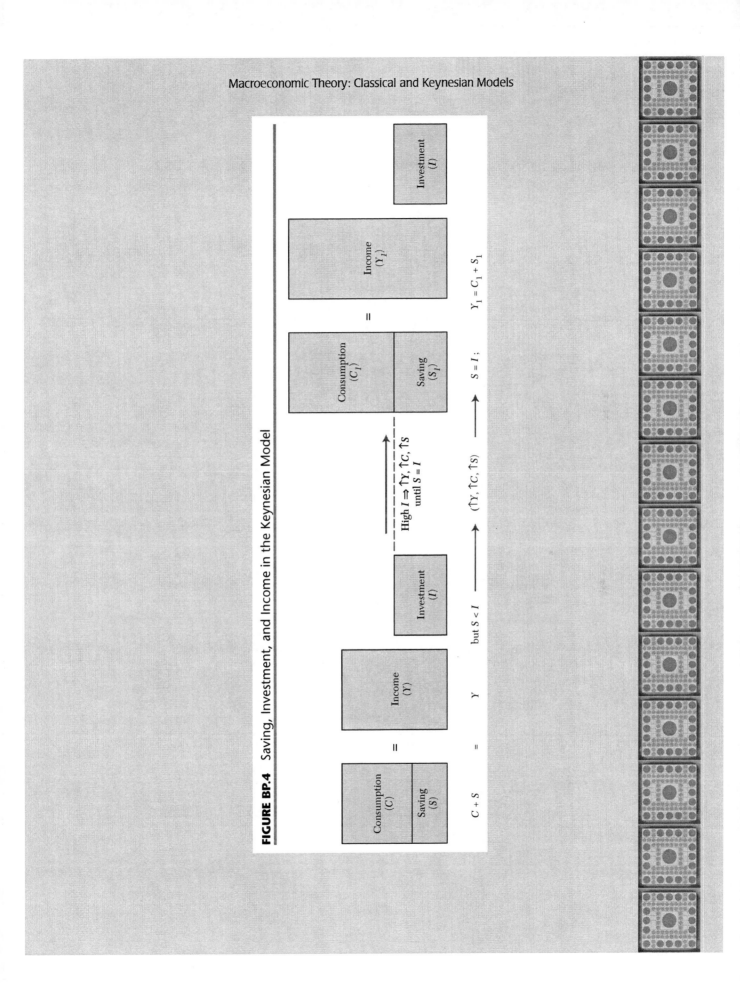

**FIGURE BP.4**  Saving, Investment, and Income in the Keynesian Model

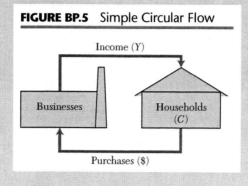

**FIGURE BP.5** Simple Circular Flow

But Keynes pointed out that not all of income households earn will be spent on business-produced goods and services. Some will be saved—a leakage from the circular flow (Figure BP.6).

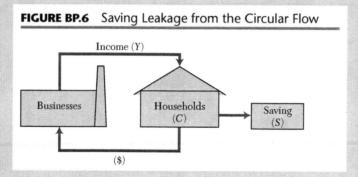

**FIGURE BP.6** Saving Leakage from the Circular Flow

To restore equilibrium to the system, business must *inject* investment expenditures that add new facilities, technology, and tools, as we see in Figure BP.7.

But Keynes saw these investment expenditures as a source of higher income since investment has a multiplier effect on income. In other words, an increase in investment will increase income by much more than the initial investment expenditure.

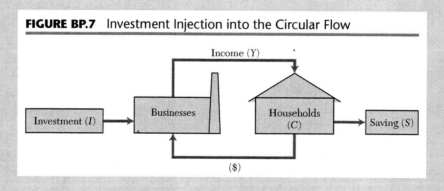

**FIGURE BP.7** Investment Injection into the Circular Flow

Let's see how that works. First, the initial investment expenditure becomes income in the economy. The expenditure on that investment is received by the seller as income (Figure BP.8).

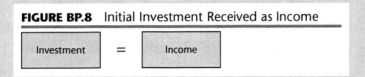

**FIGURE BP.8**  Initial Investment Received as Income

Investment  =  Income

When income is received, some will be spent or used for consumption—perhaps on groceries and shoes, and the rest on replacement materials (glass, concrete). The amount spent on consumption adds to the income stream. If consumption ($C$) averages three-fourths of income, 75 cents of each dollar of income ($Y$) is spent as consumption and 25 cents is saved. So here $C_1$ is added to $I$ as part of income. Now the grocer and shoe dealer and concrete supplier have additional income—three-fourths of which will be consumed; one-fourth saved. The three-fourths adds income. The multiplier continues through this responding effect to finally increase income by the multiplier times the change in investment. The multiplier depends on the percent of income that is consumed and saved. For our example, when consumers spend three-fourths of their income, the multiplier is 4. An increase in investment spending of $1,000 would result in an increase in income of $4,000. The higher the percentage of expenditure out of each dollar, the higher the multiplier. (If a nation's public spends four-fifths of each dollar of income, the multiplier is 5.) We can see each of these additions to income from the initial $1,000 investment in Figure BP.9.

To see how this works in a possible real-life example, consider a business that invests $100,000 in new computer equipment. This generates $100,000 in income for the computer manufacturer. Using a multiplier of 4 (above), the computer manufacturer will spend three-fourths of the $100,000, or $75,000, on purchases from suppliers, workers, and other goods or services. The suppliers and workers will continue the spending cycle, with three-fourths of $75,000, or $56,250, worth of purchases—perhaps on CDs, groceries, gasoline, amusement parks, and so forth. The spending cycle continues until the total increase in income generated by the $100,000 investment in computer equipment increases income by $400,000, which equals the multiplier (4) times the initial investment ($100,000). We can see the result of the initial investment expenditure leading to the continuing responding effect in Figure BP.10.

**FIGURE BP.9**  The Keynesian Multiplier Effect

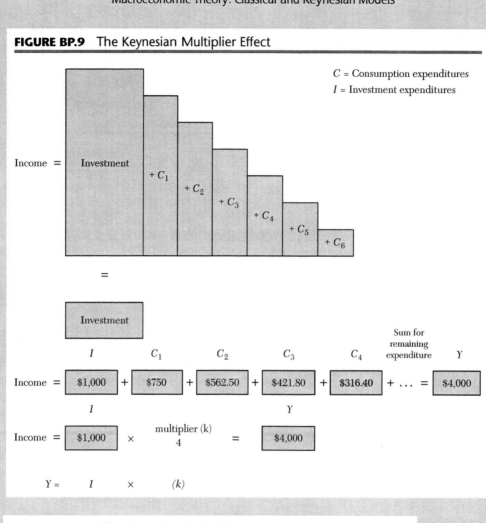

$C$ = Consumption expenditures
$I$ = Investment expenditures

Income = Investment $+ C_1$ $+ C_2$ $+ C_3$ $+ C_4$ $+ C_5$ $+ C_6$

=

Investment

|  | $I$ | $C_1$ | $C_2$ | $C_3$ | $C_4$ | Sum for remaining expenditure | $Y$ |
|---|---|---|---|---|---|---|---|
| Income = | $1,000 | + $750 | + $562.50 | + $421.80 | + $316.40 | + ... = | $4,000 |

| | $I$ | | multiplier (k)<br>4 | | $Y$ |
|---|---|---|---|---|---|
| Income = | $1,000 | × | | = | $4,000 |

$$Y = I \times (k)$$

**FIGURE BP.10**  The Keynesian Multiplier

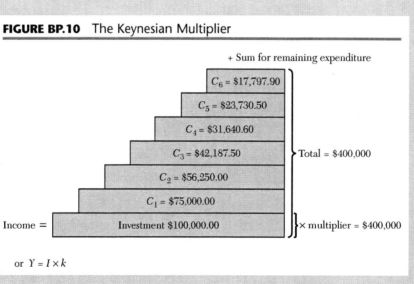

+ Sum for remaining expenditure

$C_6$ = $17,797.90
$C_5$ = $23,730.50
$C_4$ = $31,640.60
$C_3$ = $42,187.50     Total = $400,000
$C_2$ = $56,250.00
$C_1$ = $75,000.00

Income =     Investment $100,000.00     × multiplier = $400,000

or $Y = I \times k$

## The Keynesian Model: The Details

Keynes defined aggregate expenditures as the sum of consumption expenditures, investment expenditures, government expenditures, and net exports. He and some contemporary economists recognized that there are leakages (transfers of funds out of the income and spending flows) and injections (additions of funds to these flows). Leakages include saving, taxes, and purchases of goods and services in international markets (imports). With each of these leakages, income flows out of domestic economic activity and thus out of the circle in the circular flow diagram of the classical economists. Saving and hoarding remove money from the spending stream·and occur when households, deciding that future consumption is better than present consumption, put their money into savings accounts at banks, into the stock market, or under their mattresses. Taxes leave the spending stream of the household and business sectors and are turned over to the government. Imported goods and services from other nations increase the goods and services received by households but reduce the total domestic spending, since these dollars go abroad to pay for the goods and services received.

In contrast to leakages, funds can enter into or be added to domestic economic activity. These injections into the income and spending stream may take the form of government spending, investment, and the sale of goods in international markets (exports). Government spending, like consumer spending, increases the income received by the business sector, since government and consumer purchases are made of business products. Government spending may also go directly to the household sector in the form of wages, transfer payments, or income supplements, which in turn will increase.spending as well. **Investment** occurs when the business sector creates new capital in the form of new plants,

**FIGURE 3**  The Circular Flow with Leakages (L) and Injections (IN)

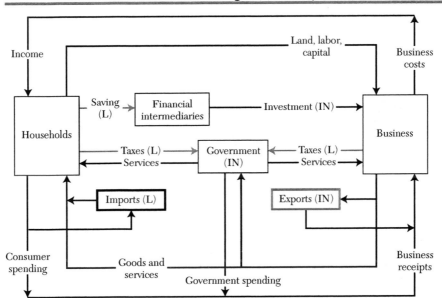

additions to equipment, and the buildup of inventories, or existing stocks of goods and services. Investment is, in effect, business spending. Exports create an injection into the income stream, since businesses have a new market for their products and receive income. Figure 3 illustrates the dynamics of these flows, with leakages indicated as (L) and injections as (IN).

For the economy to be in equilibrium, the injections must equal the leakages. As a result, aggregate expenditures for goods and services in the economy will equal the aggregate output or income. This establishes an equilibrium level of income and output that may or may not be at full employment. According to Keynes, an economy can have an infinite number of equilibrium positions, one of which is at full employment. The equilibrium depends on the level of spending in the economy. The classical economists, however, saw one and only one equilibrium—the one that exists at full employment.

Keynes recommended that governments use spending policies to counter cyclical upswings and downswings. These policies could cure a full range of economic maladies. In a depression, increased government spending would increase the levels of income, employment, and output. To ward off inflation, government spending could be cut and/or taxes increased.

The Keynesian model has remained a prevailing economic paradigm for the past half century. It has not always been successful, and economists have continued to add to and revise its core. Despite the challenges of the 1980s, however, it still solidly forms the basis for much of New Keynesian macroeconomic theory and is the basis for current economic policy. The late Nobel Prize recipient and monetarist Milton Friedman perhaps stated it best when he said, "We are all Keynesians now."

# THE KEYNESIAN ECONOMIC MODEL

In the discussion that follows, we will describe the assumptions, methods, and implications of the full Keynesian model, exploring the sources of spending and how they affect aggregate output or GDP in any period.

## Consumption

To begin our construction of a simple Keynesian model, we will first examine the assumptions and hypotheses for the consumption function. The importance of consumption on economic activity is fairly straightforward. In 2007, the U.S. population spent 83 percent of personal income on goods and services. Consumption is simply purchasing of goods and services, spending of income for necessities and luxuries. The level of consumption depends on many things, including income, interest rates, price levels, and expectations, along with the other financial assets the consumer might possess. But as one might well expect, consumption is primarily a function of income. In our simplified version of the Keynesian model, we will express consumption as

$$C = f(\text{DPI}),$$

**FIGURE 4**   The Consumption Fuction

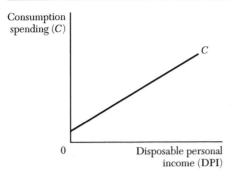

where $C$ is the consumption of individuals over some period of time, DPI is disposable personal income, and $f$ is a functional notation.* In what Keynes called a "fundamental psychological law," he states, "As a rule and on the average, [people] are disposed to increase their consumption as their income increases." In other words, as your income increases (perhaps after graduation and upon securing a better job), your consumption spending will rise as well—but, says Keynes, not by as much. This relationship can be expressed graphically with consumption ($C$) measured on the vertical axis and disposable personal income (DPI) on the horizontal axis. Since consumption is an increasing function of disposable income, as DPI increases, $C$ will also increase (see Figure 4).

What happens to the income *not* spent on consumption? People save it. *Saving* is any part of income that is not spent on consumption. There is nothing left to do with it. (Burning it isn't rational, and Keynes assumes that we are all rational.) We can express the relationship between income, consumption, and saving as follows:

$$DPI = C + S,$$

where DPI is disposable personal income, $C$ is personal consumption expenditures, and $S$ is personal saving. Saving is a residual of consumption.

Saving occurs when individuals defer present consumption and keep the funds for future use. People save for many different reasons: precaution or fear of what might lie ahead, financial independence, or pride or avarice. In contrast to the classical model, which assumes that saving is a function of the rate of interest, Keynes assumed that consumption expenditures are a priority, and we save whatever funds are left after we make these consumption expenditures. No matter how much a high interest rate

---

*Studies have shown consumption to be a linear function of income, or $C = a + b$ DPI where $C$ is the consumption of individuals over time, $a$ is the intercept of the consumption function (or $C$ where DPI = 0), $b$ is the slope of the function, and DPI is disposable income (that is, GDP − depreciation − taxes − undistributed corporate profits + transfer payments). DPI, then, is income that a household has available for consumption spending. Since $a$ is positive, individuals must consume some amount of food, clothing, and shelter even if they have no income.

might make us want to increase our saving, we pay for food, housing, and other necessary consumption expenditures first. Whatever is left can be saved. So in the Keynesian model, saving, like consumption, also is a function of income:

$$S = f(\text{DPI})$$

2. Do you or your family behave as though $S = f(\text{DPI})$ or $S = f(r)$? Which comes first, the mortgage or rent payment, grocery and clothing expenditures—or saving?

Before we proceed further in the analysis of consumption and saving, it is important to establish a reference position (or helping line) to make it easier to discuss the relation of the level of consumption spending to the level of income. This helping line is a 45° line from the origin of the consumption-income axis (see Figure 5). The 45° line represents the locus of equilibrium points where total spending equals total output or disposable personal income (DPI). If firms produce $3.0 trillion worth of goods and services, and spending in the economy equals $3.0 trillion, we will be at point $A$ on the 45° line. Each of these points is on the 45° line, which bisects the origin and represents a level of spending just equal to a corresponding level of disposable personal income (DPI). Here and throughout the Keynesian analysis, we assume that *prices are constant.*

We can now use the relationship between expenditures and income in examining consumption. Since the 45° line bisects the 90° angle, at any point on the 45° line, income (DPI) will equal consumption. For example, at point $A$, DPI = $C$ = $3.0 trillion; at point $B$, DPI = $C$ = $4.0 trillion. If we superimpose the consumption curve on this 45° line, we can compare the relationship of consumption spending to the actual level of disposable personal income in the economy.

**FIGURE 5**   The 45° Line

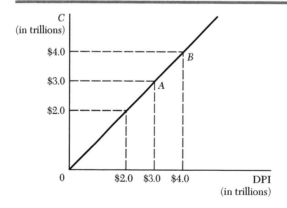

**FIGURE 6**    The Consumption Function and the 45° Line

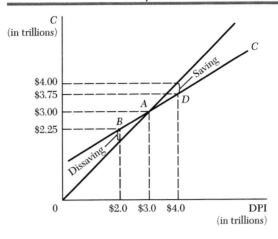

In Figure 6, at point *A*, consumption and disposable personal income are equal, since the consumption curve passes through the 45° line at that point. Saving equals 0 (since $S = \text{DPI} - C$, and $3.0 trillion − $3.0 trillion = 0). At point *D*, however, consumption (*C*) is less than disposable personal income, indicating that saving occurs. Since disposable personal income is $4.0 trillion and consumption is only $3.75 trillion, $0.25 trillion must be saved. At point *B*, consumption is greater than disposable personal income; income is $2.0 trillion, but consumption spending is $2.25 trillion. Dissaving is taking place to allow the desired level of consumption. Dissaving consists of borrowing or drawing down other financial assets in order to purchase products for current consumption. Individuals on low fixed incomes frequently dissave, as do young people starting families or households. (Note that even when income is 0, there is some amount of consumption spending.)

 3. Do you dissave now? Do you expect to dissave in the next year or two? Draw a curve on the graph in Figure 7 indicating what you expect your consumption pattern to look like for the rest of your life. At what periods do you think you might be dissaving?

**FIGURE 7**    Your Consumption Function

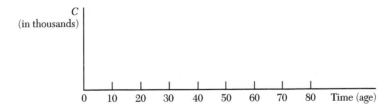

**Table 1**  Data for Hypothetical Consumption Function

| DPI (in Trillions) | C (in Trillions) | MPC = ΔC/ΔDPI |
|---|---|---|
| $2.0 | $2.25 | 0 |
| | | 0.75 |
| 3.0 | 3.00 | |
| | | 0.75 |
| 4.0 | 3.75 | |

## Marginal Propensity to Consume

From the information given thus far, we can determine two ratios: the average propensity to consume (APC) and the **marginal propensity to consume (MPC)**. APC is simply $C$/DPI. MPC is the ratio between the *change* that occurs in consumption with some given change in disposable personal income:

$$MPC = \Delta C / \Delta DPI,$$

where $\Delta$ is a symbol for change, $C$ is consumption, and DPI is disposable personal income. In the previous example, if disposable personal income increases from $3.0 trillion to $4.0 trillion, consumption increases from $3.00 trillion to $3.75 trillion. The change in disposable personal income is $4.0 trillion – $3.0 trillion, or $1.0 trillion; the change in consumption is $3.75 trillion – $3.00 trillion, or .75 trillion. The MPC, then, is $\Delta C/\Delta DPI = $0.75 trillion / $1.0 trillion, or 0.75 (see Table 1). For every additional dollar of disposable personal income, consumers use $0.75 for consumption and save the remaining $0.25 (see Table 1 and Figure 8).

The relationship MPC = $\Delta C / \Delta DPI$ is also the slope of the consumption function* (see Figure 8). Note that the consumption function is a straight line only when MPC is constant at all levels of disposable personal income.

**FIGURE 8**  Marginal Propensity to Consume

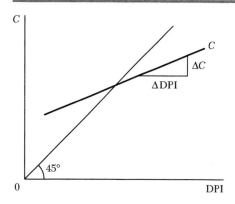

---

*MPC is the slope of the consumption function, or $b$ in $C = a + b$ (DPI).

This will seldom occur in practice, since each individual as well as each income-earning group reacts differently to changes in income. However, to simplify the analysis, in most cases we will assume a constant MPC (and thus a straight-line consumption function).

4. How might your reaction to a change in income be different from that of Warren Buffett, Tiger Woods, J. K. Rowling, or Oprah Winfrey? From that of a poor person?

## Saving

Given that saving is a residual of consumption (DPI = $C + S$, so $S = $ DPI $- C$), we can analyze the saving function as we did the consumption function. Data for a saving function are derived in Table 2 and graphed in Figure 9.

## Marginal Propensity to Save

We can also express the average propensity to save (APS) and the **marginal propensity to save (MPS)**. APS is the ratio of saving to disposable personal income, $S$/DPI. MPS is the ratio of the change in saving to any change in disposable personal income:

$$\text{MPS} = \Delta S / \Delta \text{DPI}$$

In Table 3, we find MPS using the data for $S$ we derived earlier.

**Table 2** Derivation of Saving Function from Consumption Data

| DPI (in Trillions) | C (in Trillions) | S = DPI − C (in Trillions) |
| --- | --- | --- |
| $2.0 | $2.25 | −$0.25 |
| 3.0 | 3.00 | 0.00 |
| 4.0 | 3.75 | 0.25 |

**FIGURE 9** The Saving Function

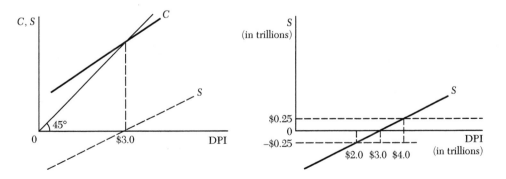

**Table 3** Data for Hypothetical Saving Example

| DPI | S (in Trillions) | MPS = $\Delta S / \Delta DPI$ |
|---|---|---|
| $2.0 | –$0.25 | |
| | | 0.25 |
| 3.0 | 0.00 | |
| | | 0.25 |
| 4.0 | 0.25 | |

Note that MPS + MPC = 1. This must be true, since the change in $C$ and the change in $S$ must add to the whole of every new dollar of disposable personal income.*

## Consumption and Real GDP

We have just seen how consumption ($C$) changes when disposable personal income (DPI) changes. What causes changes in disposable personal income? Disposable personal income changes whenever real GDP ($Y$) changes or when there is a change in tax rates. As long as tax rates are constant (which we will assume they are for this analysis), real GDP ($Y$) is the only influence on disposable personal income. In equations we can write this as follows:

$$DPI = Y - Tx$$

because we are assuming that

$$Tx = 0, DPI = Y$$

Consumption therefore depends not only on disposable personal income, but also on real GDP. In the sections that follow, we will add other variables that determine real GDP ($Y$), including investment expenditures, government expenditures, and net exports.

## Investment and the Two-Sector Model

The simplest Keynesian model describes the behavior of two sectors in the economy: the household and business sectors. This simple model ignores the government and foreign sectors. We represent total spending by individuals and businesses as follows:

$$AE = C + I,$$

where AE is income or real GDP, $C$ is consumption, and $I$ is investment. In equilibrium, $Y = AE$; all aggregate expenditures (AE) become someone's income ($Y$). Consumption represents spending by households, and investment

---

*$DPI = C + S$
$\Delta DPI = \Delta C + \Delta S$
$\Delta DPI/\Delta DPI = \Delta C/\Delta DPI + \Delta S/\Delta DPI$
$1 = MPC + MPS$

consists of business spending on additions to plants, equipment, inventories, and newly constructed housing. Inventories may be goods of any type, from raw material inputs to intermediate and finished products. Together, consumption and investment make up the aggregate expenditures for goods and services produced. In the preceding sections, we learned about consumption, but we know little about investment.

In this simple two-sector model, we assume that investment is determined outside the model itself.* For example, if Microsoft decides to invest $1,000, it makes the decision without considering the variables included in this model. Expected profits, interest costs, or business confidence might be more important to investment decisions than income and consumption levels. Graphically, then, investment would be constant at all levels of GDP, as shown in Figure 10.

In the two-sector model, we know that aggregate expenditures (AE) equal consumption plus investment (AE = $C + I$) and that the resulting GDP ($Y$) can be spent or saved ($Y = C + S$). For equilibrium in the macroeconomy, income ($Y$) and expenditures (AE) must be equal ($Y =$ AE). A level of spending produces a level of income, which, in turn, generates the same level of spending, and so on (as in the circular flow of activity). Putting these two equations together tells us that in the two-sector Keynesian model, the only leakage, saving, must equal the only injection, investment. This describes the equilibrium condition for the model: when aggregate income ($Y = C + S$) equals aggregate expenditures (AE = $C + I$), then $S = I$.

$$Y = AE$$
$$C + S = C + I$$
$$S = I$$

**FIGURE 10**   The Investment Function

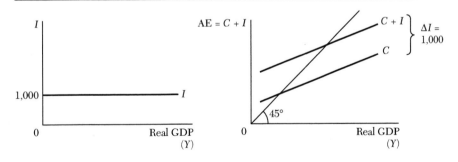

*Investment in a more sophisticated model is a function of changes in income, since as GDP increases, businesses will likely increase their level of investment. Investment decisions also depend on interest rates, expected inflation, expected profits, depreciation, and other factors. Investment fluctuates over time and plays a major role in accounting for business cycles. With a more sophisticated model, our analysis can include investment decisions more typical of businesses. For simplicity, however, we use the less complex model and assume that investment decisions are given and constant.

**Table 4**  Data for Hypothetical Investment Function

| Y | C | S | $I_p$ | $I_a$ |
|---|---|---|---|---|
| $6.0 T | $5.75 T | $0.25 T | $0.25 T | $0.25 T |
| 6.5 | 5.50 | 0.50 | 0.25 | 0.50 |

Several factors are important in the $S = I$ relationship. First, saving and investment are done by two different groups of people for totally different reasons. Second, realized (or actual) saving must equal realized (or actual) investment. There is no guarantee that the dollar amount of investment *planned* by the business sector will be the same as the saving planned in the household sector.

Using the data in Table 4, which assumes planned investment spending of $0.25 trillion, we can illustrate this with an example. $I_p$ equals planned investment, and $I_a$ equals actual investment. Figure 11 shows that the equilibrium income level in this simple model is at point $A$, where the $C + I$ line intersects the 45° reference line. This graph is sometimes referred to as the *Keynesian cross*. Here, AE = $C + I$ = $6.0 trillion, $C$ = $5.75 trillion, and $I$ = $0.25 trillion. All higher and lower levels of income are not at equilibrium; planned $S$ does not equal planned $I$, and planned aggregate expenditures do not equal planned aggregate income. At $Y$ = AE = $6.0 trillion, $C + I = C + S$ and aggregate expenditures equal real GDP. Only at the $6.0 trillion equilibrium point does planned investment equal actual investment ($I_p = I_a$).

**FIGURE 11**  Equilibrium Level of Income

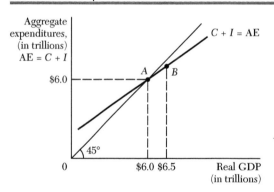

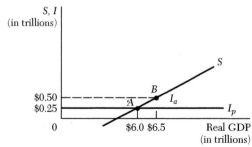

At disequilibrium position $B$, $C = \$6.0$ trillion, $S = \$0.50$ trillion, and $Y = \$6.5$ trillion. Here, intended saving is greater than intended investment, since saving is $\$0.50$ trillion and investment is only $\$0.25$ trillion. With $I_p$ at $\$0.25$ trillion, there will be an unplanned increase in inventories; some of the goods produced will not be sold, because consumers desire to increase their saving balances. At $Y = \$6.50$ trillion (GDP), $C + I = $ (only) $\$6.25$ trillion (and $C + S = \$6.50$ trillion). Aggregate output is greater than aggregate expenditures. Total output is $\$6.50$ trillion, but total spending is only $\$6.25$ trillion. Therefore, inventories increase by $\$0.25$ trillion. Since the increase in inventories is counted as investment, $I_a$ will increase to $\$0.50$ trillion. Actual saving equals actual investment.

5. In the next time period with an accumulation of inventories, what do you expect the $I_p$ response of business would be? What does this do to the equilibrium level of income where aggregate expenditures equal real GDP and $S = I$?

Since planned $S$ is greater than planned $I$, however, this is not an equilibrium position. With increased inventories, which were unplanned, producers will cut back production and lay off workers. As output is cut, income will also be reduced. This movement will continue until an equilibrium is reached where aggregate expenditures equal aggregate output or income. This new equilibrium occurs at point $A$, where $C + S = C + I$, and where planned $S$ of $\$0.25$ trillion equals planned $I$ of $\$0.25$ trillion. This equilibrium may be or may not be at full employment. Unlike the classical model, the Keynesian model may have equilibrium conditions at greater than full, less than full, or full employment.

## Changes in Investment and the Keynesian Multiplier

Once the economy is in equilibrium, it tends to remain unchanged until some disturbance occurs, such as a change in the level of investment. Suppose investment increases from $\$0.25$ trillion to $\$0.45$ trillion, a change of $\$0.20$ trillion. This change is graphed in Figure 12.

How much does income increase as a result of this $\$0.20$ trillion increase in investment? What is the new equilibrium level of income? Here, the **Keynesian multiplier (k)** has its effect. When additional investment enters the model, the equilibrium level of income ($Y$) increases by some multiple of the change in investment. This multiple (called the Keynesian multiplier) equals $1/(1 - MPC)$ or the ratio between the change in income and the change in investment ($\Delta Y / \Delta I$).

To demonstrate how the multiplier works, consider a nursery that decides to expand by adding a greenhouse costing $\$200,000$. The first round of spending is $\$200,000$, which is added to the income stream. The contractor and workers who built the greenhouse now have the $\$200,000$ (as income)

**FIGURE 12** An Increase in Investment Spending

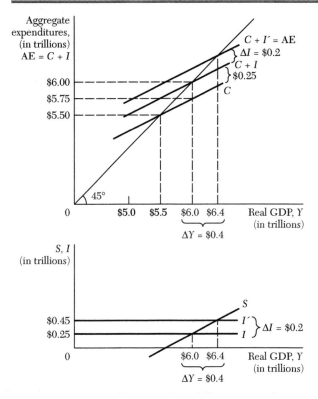

and will respend it according to the MPC. If the MPC is 0.5, the contractor and her workers will spend $100,000 and save the remaining $100,000. The $100,000 then enters the income stream (as other people's income); half of that will be spent and half saved in the third round. Table 5 illustrates this process.

**Table 5** Keynesian Respending Effect

| Expenditure for Greenhouse | | | |
|---|---|---|---|
| ΔI = $200,000 | ΔY | ΔC = 0.5 ΔY | ΔS = 0.5 ΔY |
| Round 1 | $200,000 | $100,000 | $100,000 |
| Round 2 | 100,000 | 50,000 | 50,000 |
| Round 3 | 50,000 | 25,000 | 25,000 |
| Round 4 | 25,000 | 12,500 | 12,500 |
| Round 5 | 12,500 | 6,250 | 6,250 |
| Round 6 | 6,250 | 3,125 | 3,125 |
| Etc. | | | |
| Total* | $400,000 | $200,000 | $200,000 |

*The rounds continue until they have generated $200,000[1/(1 − 0.5)] = $200,000 × 2 = $400,000 in new income. The initial increase in spending is multiplied through the economy.

In the example of a nursery adding a greenhouse, the MPS of 0.5 yields a multiplier of 2. Thus, the $200,000 increase in investment will generate $400,000 of new income. In Figure 12, an increase in $I$ of $0.2 trillion will produce a new equilibrium level of Y = $6.4 trillion? (representing a "multiplied" increase in $Y$ of $0.4 trillion).

6. What is the new level of consumption in Figure 12 at $Y$ = $6.4 trillion? What is the level of saving? `

## A Simple Derivation of the Multiplier

The Keynesian multiplier gives us the amount of income (GDP) generated by an increase in spending. We know that at equilibrium in the Keynesian model, $\Delta I = \Delta S$ If both sides of this identity are divided by $\Delta Y$ the right side of the equation becomes MPS:

$$\frac{\Delta I}{\Delta Y} = \frac{\Delta S}{\Delta Y} = MPS = \frac{1}{\text{the multiplier}}.$$

To get the multiplier ($k$), we invert the equation:

$$k = \frac{\Delta S}{\Delta Y} = \frac{\Delta Y}{\Delta S} = \frac{1}{MPS}.$$

Since MPC + MPS = 1, we can restate this in terms of MPC:

$$\frac{\Delta Y}{\Delta I} = \frac{1}{1 - MPC} = k.$$

Example: Given MPC = 0.75

$$k = \frac{\Delta Y}{\Delta I} = \frac{1}{1 - 0.75} = \frac{1}{0.25} = 4.$$

In this example, for each $\Delta I$, real GDP ($Y$) will increase by 4 times $\Delta I$.

## The Three-Sector Model

To add a bit more realism, we can add the government sector to the simple two-sector Keynesian model. *Government expenditures* (G) are purchases of goods and services by the government during a given period. Like investment, we will assume in this extension of our simple model that government spending is determined outside of the Keynesian model. For example, Congress decides to spend $G = G_0$. This means there is a given level of government spending for goods and services at all levels of income, as shown in Figure 13.

Once we add government spending to the model, aggregate expenditures become AE = $C + I + G$, as shown in Figure 14. Now, in our three-sector model, we have

$$AE = C + I + G,$$

where aggregate expenditures (AE) equal the sum of consumption ($C$), investment ($I$), and government expenditures ($G$). In our three-sector model, real GDP ($Y$)

**FIGURE 13** The Government Spending Function

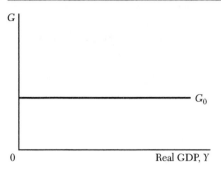

will equal the sum of consumption ($C$), saving ($S$), and—now that we have introduced the government—taxes ($Tx$):·

$$Y = C + S + Tx$$

Given our definition of disposable personal income (DPI), we can also state this as:

$$Y = \text{DPI} + Tx$$

In equilibrium, $Y = \text{AE}$, so the two sides of our three-sector model are equal:

$$C + S + Tx = C + I + G$$

To simplify, we subtract $C$ from both sides of the equation, in equilibrium (when $Y = \text{AE}$):

$$S + Tx = I + G$$

The 45° line again represents equilibrium points where aggregate spending equals aggregate output or income. Expenditures for goods and services are now made by consumers, investors, *and* the government, creating the aggregate expenditures graph for the three-sector economy. The equilibrium level of income is $Y_a$ where $\text{AE} = Y = C + I + G$. At any other level, $Y \neq C + I + G$.

**FIGURE 14** The Keynesian Model with $C$, $I$, and $G$ Spending

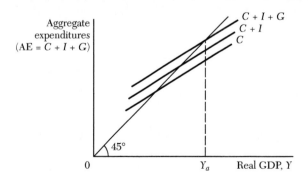

**76**

Government expenditures include expenditures by state and local governments as well as by the federal government. Currently, about 17.5 percent of the GDP is made up of purchases by the government. The government buys a wide range of goods and services, from paper to computers to military equipment. The government makes such purchases to support its normal operations or as part of programs designed to stimulate the economy when the business cycle is declining, as Keynes suggested in his *General Theory*. Transfer payments from the government are not included as part of these government purchases.

The size of $G$ may change. Indeed, the government may make decisions that will affect the level of income in the economy. These expenditures are often aimed at *directly* changing the level of income—perhaps from a level not at full employment to a new equilibrium level at full employment. Government expenditures for goods and services are subject to the Keynesian multiplier just as investments are. Government spending becomes income that enters the spending flow as recipients consume and save at increased levels by their MPC and MPS. Any increase in $G$ will increase $Y$ by an amount equal to $\Delta G / (1 - \text{MPC})$.

We can analyze the results of government spending by looking at a purchase of a new defense system at a total cost of $0.5 trillion. Figure 15 shows that aggregate expenditures have increased from the equilibrium position at $8 trillion (where $\text{AE} = C + I + G$). If the marginal propensity to consume remains at 0.5, the multiplier is 2. The increase in income that results from the purchase of the defense system is $k \times \Delta G = 2 \times \$0.5$ trillion = $1.0 trillion. The new equilibrium level of income is therefore $9 trillion ($8 trillion + $1 trillion).

**FIGURE 15**   Effects of Increased Government Spending on the Equilibrium Level of Income

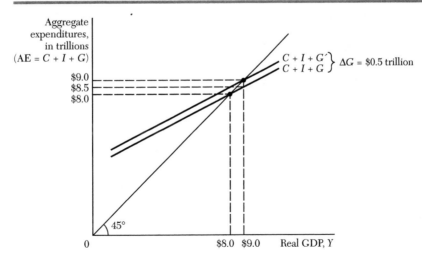

An increase in government allocations for research for the space program and NASA will boost the economies of Huntsville, Alabama; Houston, Texas; and Cape Canaveral, Florida, as well as increasing the enrollments in aerospace engineering courses. Cuts in government expenditures reverse the Keynesian multiplier effect. A decrease in defense spending, such as military base closures, will have the effect of contracting the economies of Alameda, California, and Charleston, South Carolina. Entire communities will be affected by the decreasing income and increasing unemployment levels.

7. What kinds of government spending programs would stimulate growth in your area? What are a few government spending programs that would help us all?

## The Four-Sector Model

Thus far, we have extended our economic model by adding *injections* of investment expenditures and government purchases of goods and services into the spending flow and observing how the Keynesian multiplier affects each of them. There is, of course, one more injection into the spending stream, and that comes from the foreign sector through foreign trade. Whenever U.S. goods and services are exported to other nations, dollars flow into the U.S. economy in payment for these exported goods. These dollars then enter the spending stream as injections. On the other hand, imports take money out of the income flow, since goods and services come into the country in return for dollars that flow out of the U.S. income stream and into the income stream of the exporting nation.

In dealing with both of these flows, we will use the quantity *net exports*, which is simply $X - M$, where $X$ represents exports and $M$ accounts for goods and services imported into the nation. If $X - M$ is positive, then money is flowing into the U.S. income stream. If $X - M$ is negative, then money is flowing out of the U.S. income stream as imported goods and services flow in. A positive net export figure ($X - M > 0$) will mean additional income, as $Y$ expands. If net exports are negative ($X - M < 0$), $Y$ will fall.

We can express this four-sector model as an equation:

$$AE = C + I + G + (X - M)$$

Now aggregate expenditures (AE) equals the sum of consumption ($C$), investment ($I$), government expenditures ($G$), and net exports ($X - M$). Real GDP ($Y$) is still equal to the sum of consumption ($C$), saving ($S$), and taxes ($Tx$):

$$Y = C + S + Tx$$

As noted previously, we can also say that real GDP equals disposable personal income (DPI) plus taxes: $Y = \text{DPI} + Tx$. In equilibrium, $Y = \text{AE}$, so the sum of their components is equal:

$$C + S + Tx = C + I + G + (X - M)$$

We can simplify by subtracting $C$ (consumption) and $M$ (imports) from both sides of the equation. Thus, in equilibrium (when $Y = \text{AE}$),

$$S + Tx + M = I + G + X$$

The equilibrium level of income is at the point where the total for expanded aggregate expenditures intersects the 45° line. When imports to the United States exceed exports, more goods and services are coming into the country and more income (money) is going out of the country. Net exports are negative. The equilibrium level of income will be lower.

Domestic and foreign economic policies may directly affect import or export expenditures or both.

# THE BIG PICTURE

## Wrap-Up

Thus far The Big Picture has looked only at two sectors in the economy: consumers, through their consumption expenditures (*C*), and businesses through investment expenditures (*I*). And we discovered how investment expenditures work through the Keynesian multiplier (*k*) to increase income (real GDP) by more than the initial investment expenditure.

We must now complete our examination of aggregate expenditures (AE)—which to this point includes only investment (*I*) and consumption (*C*) expenditures. To complete the model we must also add government expenditures (*G*) and the expenditures of the international sector, which we define as net exports (*X* − *M*).

Thus, if we put the features of the Keynesian model together using the building blocks we've explained above, we see that equilibrium in this model is where aggregate expenditures (AE) is equal to aggregate output or real GDP (*Y*) (see Figure BP.11).

**FIGURE BP.11** The Keynesian Model—Four Sectors

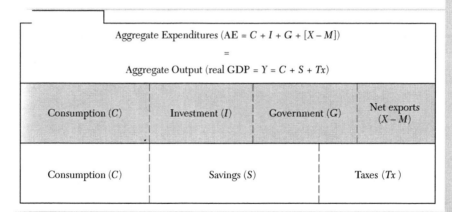

| Aggregate Expenditures (AE = $C + I + G + [X - M]$) | | | |
|---|---|---|---|
| = | | | |
| Aggregate Output (real GDP = $Y = C + S + Tx$) | | | |
| Consumption (*C*) | Investment (*I*) | Government (*G*) | Net exports (*X* − *M*) |
| Consumption (*C*) | Savings (*S*) | | Taxes (*Tx*) |

# Conclusion

*We have examined the impact of the Keynesian multiplier on several sectors of the economy and noted that income (output) expands by the value of the multiplier times the value of the injection. Prices do not change in the Keynesian model as a result of changes in aggregate expenditures. In this chapter we have examined only how changes in injections affect income. We have made many assumptions about investment and spending decisions; the economy is somewhat more complex than our model. Nevertheless, the model helps us begin to understand how the macroeconomy functions.*

*The Keynesian model gives us a theoretical framework within which to analyze how the aggregate economy operates and to examine the sorts of macroeconomic problems one might expect to encounter and how we might develop stabilization policies to try to correct them. If real GDP exceeds aggregate expenditures, we can expect a lower level of national income. Conversely, if aggregate expenditures exceed real GDP, we would expect an expansion of economic activity and a higher equilibrium level of national income. An equilibrium level is where real GDP (Y) equals aggregate expenditures (AE = C + I + G + [X − M]).*

## Review Questions

1. What phenomena caused the Great Depression? Why did it continue for so long? Why did it affect so many sectors of the economy?

2. What did your grandparents or your great-grandparents and their families do during the Great Depression? How were they affected by the economic conditions of the time?

3. Why would the classical economists distinguish between real factors and monetary ones as influences of the variables in the equation of exchange? What is the implication of prices increasing as the quantity of money increases?

4. Why might Keynes's theory be called a "depression theory"? Can you make a few arguments as to why it might command a more general use?

5. What were Keynes's major criticisms of the classical theory?

6. What are leakages? Why are they called leakages? How do leakages differ from injections?

7. Why must leakages equal injections in the Keynesian world for an equilibrium level of income to exist?

8. In the Keynesian circular flow diagram (Figure 3), do leakages and injections ever leave the economy permanently? How are they fed back into the economy?

9. If depressions become self-fulfilling prophecy, can inflationary periods also be self-fulfilling? What would you expect the Keynesian prescription to be in such a case?

Use the information in Figure 16 to answer Questions 10–17.

10. Explain in words why the equilibrium would be $4 trillion if there were no saving, investment, or government spending. What would be the level of output at this income level?

**FIGURE 16** A Problem on the Keynesian Model

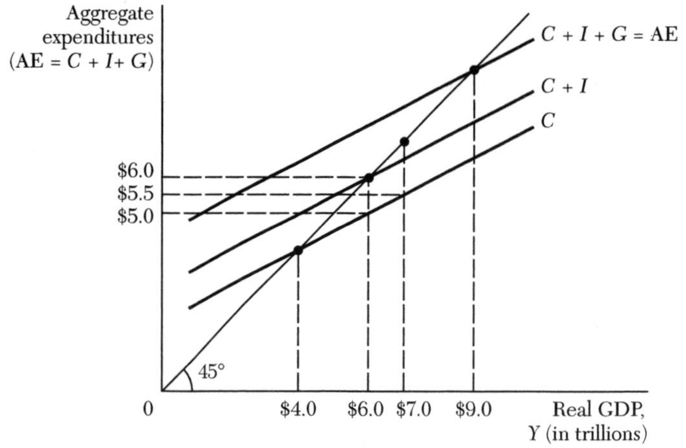

The intersection of income or output (AE) and aggregate expenditures (Y) = $9.0 trillion.

11. Why would the consumption function (if extended) intersect the spending axis at a positive value? What does this mean? Is it realistic?

12. The slope of the consumption function tells us that as real GDP increases, consumption (increases/decreases) but at a (slower/faster) rate. Is this realistic?

13. What assumptions are required to draw an investment function parallel to the consumption function? How realistic are these assumptions? What is the amount of desired investment in Figure 16?

14. Assuming no government expenditures, what is the level of saving at $Y = \$6$ trillion? What is the level of desired investment at $Y = \$6$ trillion? Why is $Y = \$6$ trillion an equilibrium level (with $C = I$)?

15. What would be the level of saving if the real GDP ($Y$) were at $7 trillion? What is the level of desired investment at this level? What forces are at work at a real GDP of $7 trillion? What will be the equilibrium level of real GDP?

16. What is the MPC in Figure 16?

17. Assume that real GDP is $6 trillion but real GDP of $9 trillion is needed to generate enough jobs for full employment. What level of government spending will be necessary to achieve full employment?

18. Why is there a multiplier effect for injections into the U.S. economy? What determines the multiplier?

19. How do net exports affect real GDP? Can real GDP be reduced by net exports? How?

# Fiscal Policy: Government Spending and Taxation

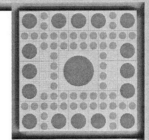

## ❖ Introduction

For the past fifty years, the federal government has been officially committed to maintaining employment, price stability, and output. The **Employment Act of 1946** states,

*The Congress hereby declares that it is the continuing policy and responsibility of the Federal Government to use all practicable means consistent with its needs and obligations and other essential considerations of national policy, with assistance and cooperation of industry, agriculture, labor, and state and local governments, to coordinate and utilize all its plans, functions, and resources for the purpose of creating and maintaining, in a manner calculated to foster and promote free competitive enterprise and the general welfare, conditions under which there will be afforded useful employment opportunities, including self-employment, for those able, willing, and seeking to work and to promote maximum employment, production, and purchasing power.*

*Within the framework of these economic objectives, the government establishes and implements its* **fiscal policy**—*actions of taxation or government spending that are designed to change the level of income.*

*According to Keynesian theory, when poverty, unemployment, or inflation rises, the government has tools to try to fix each problem. The existence of unemployment and poverty suggests a need for government spending and/or transfers. These may take the form of unemployment and welfare benefits, food stamps, Medicaid, or a variety of other payments, or they may be purchases of goods and services. Other possible remedies are increases in employment opportunities and decreased tax levels. The government may try to stimulate employment by directly adding programs that put people back to work—for example, through a series of tax credits or advantages for those*

From Chapter 15 of *Economics: A Tool for Critically Understanding Society*, 9/e. Tom Riddell. Jean Shackelford. Geoffrey Schneider. Steve Stamos. Copyright © 2011 by Pearson Education. Published by Addison-Wesley. All rights reserved.

*firms increasing employment and investment. Recently we have seen several of these policies implemented as part of the government stimulus package aimed at alleviating the recession that began in late 2007. To combat inflation, fiscal policy requires spending reductions and/or tax increases. Cutbacks of all types and tax increases restrict household and business spending. Fiscal policy can also be used to affect aggregate supply; for example, a tax cut might be designed to lower business costs, increasing supply.*

*While normally we think of the federal government as the major purchasing, borrowing, and taxing authority, state and local governments are very active in the process as well. In some cases, however, state and local governments exacerbate economic problems (pursuing* procyclical *rather than* countercyclical *measures—for example, spending during times of economic expansion rather than during times of contraction and cutting spending during recessions.).*

*Fiscal policy is also subject to the constraints of the political process. At the federal level, the president receives advice on fiscal policy from the Council of Economic Advisors (CEA) and the National Economic Council created in the 1990s to coordinate policy making. Some of the advice is accepted and successfully makes its way through the bureaucratic channels, but other advice does not. In addition, the president receives advice from the Office of Management and Budget. Meanwhile, in addition to its own committees, Congress has the Joint Economic Committee and Congressional Budget Office to assist in legislative decisions on government spending and taxation. Policy studies in all these bodies are constantly ongoing. Often the dynamics of these public offices, plus the host of private organizations engaged in economic research, lead to a profusion of mixed analysis and advice. Since each advisory body has its own priorities and operates under its own assumptions about economic growth, policy recommendations vary widely.*

*This chapter will explore how each type of fiscal action works. Some fiscal policies may directly affect the level of imports and/or exports as well as the domestic economy. We will explore these implications and deal with the shortcomings and advantages of using fiscal policy to address economic problems. We will also explore the budget process of fiscal policy's major player, the federal government. The discussion of the federal budget includes the impact of federal debt on the economy, balanced budgets, and the difference between structural and cyclical budget deficits.*

## FISCAL POLICY

The tools of fiscal policy may be selected to resolve a particular problem, or they may occur automatically with a given change in economic conditions. The former uses constitute **discretionary fiscal policy**. The automatic, nondiscretionary forms of fiscal policy are called **built-in stabilizers**. Examples of built-in stabilizers include the progressive income tax system, unemployment insurance, and all other compensatory programs that come into effect when income levels are low and that are shut off when income levels are high. As economic activity decreases during a recession, income is lost. This threatens additional decreases in economic activity. However, as unemployment increases, unemployment compensation *automatically* increases income and spending to slow a cumulative decrease in economic activity. Additionally, during a recession, people find themselves in lower tax brackets, which reduces the tax bite on individuals as their incomes fall.

1. If income is increasing at a highly inflationary rate, how do progressive income taxes help to stabilize the economy automatically?

# THE BIG PICTURE

## Fiscal Policy

When government officials pass a bill to increase public spending on the interstate highway system or to repair the nation's infrastructure, once undertaken, these projects work like expenditures on investment. An increase in investment spending worked through the multiplier through respending. Fiscal policy also works through the multiplier to increase income in the economy by more than the initial policy expenditure. In our example, if Congress approved a $10 billion expenditure on the highway system, we would find that the initial $10 billion spent would increase national income through the multiplier. This first $10 billion could be spent to employ designers, engineers, and asphalt firms and to purchase concrete and orange safety barrels. After this first round of spending, the designers, engineers, firm owners, concrete makers, and so forth would spend three-fourths of the $10 billion (or $7.5 billion) on supplies, labor, and other goods and services. Next, laborers, suppliers, and others will spend three-fourths of this new $7.5 billion (or $5.63 billion) of income on groceries, clothing, entertainment, and other goods and services. And the process continues until the initial $10 billion expenditure on highways results in $40 billion in income in the economy.

Instead of authorizing expenditure increases or cuts (which work in reverse), policy makers might consider a tax policy. This would involve tax cuts (to increase income) or tax increases (to decrease income). Tax policies also have a multiplier

**FIGURE BP.1**   The Effect of Expenditure and Tax Policies on Income.

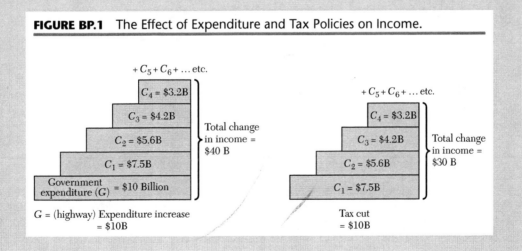

effect, but the tax multiplier is not as large as the investment and government expenditures multiplier since some portion of the income received from a change in tax policy is saved. Because there is no initial one-time expenditure, the effect is to reduce the multiplier by 1. In our earlier example, the expenditure multiplier was 4, and this tax multiplier would be 3 (or 4 − 1). The effect on the economy of reducing taxes by $10 billion to increase income would cause total income to increase by $30 billion, or by $10 billion less than by increasing highway expenditures by $10 billion. Figure BP.1 illustrates the difference in the two outcomes.

## Government Spending

The government often adopts a fiscal policy position when politicians and public opinion consider employment levels to be inadequate—for example, if the full-employment level of income is thought to be at $5.7 trillion and income is currently $5.1 trillion. In this situation, a substantial amount of unemployment is likely, and the government can opt for fiscal action that will increase employment and boost the level of income by $0.6 trillion ($5.7 trillion − $5.1 trillion).* In its arsenal of policies are spending, taxing authority, and the ability to issue transfer payments (income supplements such as Social Security and welfare paid to individuals). Since transfer payments are not for current productive services, they are not included in the yearly national product accounts but enter the income-spending flow as part of the personal income tally.

Government spending on goods and services such as military operations, the space program, and public buildings will have the largest expansionary impact on income in the economy, since the full amount of spending enters the economy in the first round. In the case of transfer payments and tax reductions, some of the impact in the first round is "leaked" into savings. Table 1 provides an example of the difference.

In the example, the equations show the amount of government spending or tax reductions necessary to increase the level of income by $0.6 trillion (or $600 billion), assuming MPC in the economy is 2/3. The first set of equations addresses government spending. With an MPC of 2/3, we can use the formula $k = 1/(1 - \text{MPC})$ to determine that the multiplier is 3.† Knowing the multiplier ($k = 3$) and the desired level of income ($\Delta Y = \$600$ billion), we have enough information to determine the necessary amount of government spending ($\Delta G$):

$$\Delta Y = k \times \Delta G$$

$$\Delta G = \Delta Y/k = \$600 \text{ billion}/3 = \$200 \text{ billion}$$

---

*Conversely, we could establish an example in which inflation was the primary problem, with income being above the full employment level. For example, income could be at $5.7 trillion, with the full employment level at $5.1 trillion. In that case, the policy measures would be the opposite of those we discuss in the following sections.

† $k = \dfrac{1}{1 - \text{MPC}} = \dfrac{1}{1 - \frac{2}{3}} = \dfrac{1}{\frac{1}{3}} = 3$

**Table 1**  Multiplier Effect of Government Expenditures and Tax Cuts

| Spending Sequence | ΔG = $200 billion | ΔTx = $300 billion |
|---|---|---|
| Round 1 | | |
| (direct expenditure) | | (indirect expenditure $\Delta Tx \times MPC = \Delta Y$) |
| | $\Delta G = \Delta Y = \$200B$ | $\Delta Y = \$300 B \times 2/3 = \$200B$ |
| Round 2 | | |
| ($\Delta Y \times MPC$) | $\$200 B \times 2/3 = \$133 B$ | $\$200 B \times 2/3 = \$133 B$ |
| Round 3 | $133 B \times 2/3 = \$90 B$ | $\$133 B \times 2/3 = \$90 B$ |
| Round 4 | $90 B \times 2/3 = \$60 B$ | $90 B \times 2/3 = \$60 B$ |
| Round 5 | $60 B \times 2/3 = \$40 B$ | $60 B \times 2/3 = \$40 B$ |
| Round 6 | $40 B \times 2/3 = \$27 B$ | $40 B \times 2/3 = \$27 B$ |
| Round 7 | $27 B \times 2/3 = \$18 B$ | $27 B \times 2/3 = \$18 B$ |
| Round 8 | $18 B \times 2/3 = \$12 B$ | $18 B \times 2/3 = \$12 B$ |
| Round 9 | $12 B \times 2/3 = \$8 B$ | $12 B \times 2/3 = \$8 B$ |
| etc. | Total          $600 B | Total          $600 B |

Our policy recommendation, then, is that the government build a (big) dam at a price of $200 billion to increase income by $600 billion to the full employment income level of $5.7 trillion. This is illustrated in Figure 1.

Although the example shows that the needed increase in income is $600 billion, policy decisions certainly are not made by such quick calculations. Partisan politics and economic philosophies play a crucial role in these decisions. We might recommend the construction of a dam, but each of the 435 representatives and 100 senators has his or her own plan, which often involves a particular congressional district or state. This and the following examples describe technical economic "solutions" to extremely complex economic, political, and social problems—what theoretically needs to happen to achieve economic goals. This is one reason "shovel ready" highway projects that are spread across the country have bipartisan support.

2. Clip a recent newspaper article on some federal, state, or local economic issue. What, besides the economics of the problem or policy, does the article address?
3. In the example you found, are the various positions based on ideology, economic theory, or rhetoric?

## Tax Policy and Income Effects

If the government decides it wants to accomplish the desired income increase of $600 billion through a cut in taxes, it must decide how much of a tax reduction is needed to generate new increases in income equal to the $600 billion. Since tax cuts are initiated through a different channel for their progression

**FIGURE 1**  Effect of Increased Government Spending

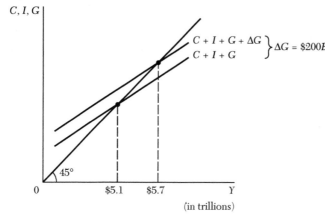

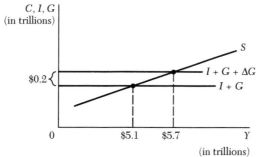

within the economy, we must address the behavior of leakages, rather than the effects of injections on spending flows. The crucial difference between the effect of leakages and that of injections occurs during the first round of spending.

Instead of $200 billion being directly spent on a dam, the $200 billion in tax cuts goes into the pockets and bank accounts of the taxpayers. According to the marginal propensities given, taxpayers will save part of the $200 billion and spend the remainder. With an MPC of 2/3, the first action is to consume 2/3 of $200 billion, or $133 billion, and save $67 billion. Thus, only $133 billion *initially* enters the total income stream, instead of the $200 billion that would enter in the case of government spending.

The *tax multiplier* is therefore less than the spending multiplier—in fact, 1 less*:

$$k - 1 = k_{tx}$$

$$k_{tx} = -\text{MPC}/(1 - \text{MPC})$$

---

*This can be derived as follows:

$-k_{tx} = [1/(1 - MPC)] - 1$

$$= \frac{1}{(1 - \text{MPC})} - \frac{(1 - \text{MPC})}{(1 - \text{MPC})} = \frac{\text{MPC}}{(1 - \text{MPC})}$$

$k_{tx} = -\text{MPC}/(1 - \text{MPC}).$

(Note the negative sign for the tax multiplier, since a tax *cut* will increase income.) Using our previous example, to get a $600 billion increase in income with a tax multiplier of 2 (because $3 - 1 = 2$ ), the following decrease in taxes must occur:

$$\Delta Y = -k_{tx} \times \Delta Tx$$

$$\$600 \text{ billion} = -2 \times \Delta Tx$$

$$\Delta Tx = -\$300 \text{ billion}$$

In other words, as detailed in Table 1, taxes must be reduced by $300 billion to increase income by $600 billion. (The impact of a tax cut on equilibrium income is outlined at the end of the chapter.)

## Transfer Payments

The logic behind the macroeconomic effects of changes in transfer payments is essentially the same as those of tax cuts. Transfer payments, however, redistribute income, while tax cuts may not. Looking at the impact of transfer payments on the economy, we find that the income of households will increase. In our example, the change in spending during the first round will be two-thirds of $300 billion, since part of the transfer will be consumed and the remainder will be saved. The **transfer multiplier**, like the tax multiplier, is $k - 1 = k_{tr}$ (note that the transfer multiplier is positive, since an increase in transfers will increase income). Transfer expenditures worth $300 billion would be necessary to raise income by $600 billion.

4. If Social Security transfers were to increase by $4 billion and if MPC were 0.9, how much of an impact would this transfer package have on the economy?

The government, of course, might choose one or any combination of tax, spending, or transfer alternatives. It also might decide to pass legislation to encourage new consumer or investment spending. Tax credits and incentives have been used in recent years to stimulate certain industries that might be suffering more than others. During a housing slump in 1974, Congress gave a 5 percent income tax credit to purchasers of newly constructed homes. In 2009 an $8,000 tax credit was offered to first-time home buyers. These measures were designed to pick up a depressed housing industry, as well as to stimulate economic activity in general. Unemployment benefits were extended during the 1990–1993, 2001, 2007–2009 recessions so that those who were unable to find jobs during the normal benefit period could receive an additional six weeks of benefits.

# PROBLEMS WITH FISCAL POLICY

With these "mechanical" fiscal fixes firmly in mind, it is well to remember that problems are likely to arise in the determination of fiscal policy. The political machinery involved in fiscal decisions is often slow, the product of many lags. Additionally, policies of state and local governments offer their own brand of fiscal effects, which more often than not are ill-timed for national objectives because of interest costs, spending capacity, and political considerations.

## Lags and Lumps in Fiscal Measures

From the discussion thus far, it seems that full employment in the economy requires only a mighty snap of the government purse strings. Several rather sticky problems emerge in the deployment of these strings, however. One problem encountered early on is the time it takes simply to recognize that a problem exists—in other words, a *recognition lag*. Another is trying to estimate MPC and thus the multiplier effect that each expenditure might have on the economy. Additionally, government spending tends to be lumpy. Projects are normally large and are generally confined to a reasonably small geographical area. Constructing a flood wall in Lewisburg, Pennsylvania, will probably not help alleviate unemployment in Dubuque or Detroit.

Legislation also tends to move slowly through Congress. By the time funds are allocated, new and different problems might emerge. During this time, higher resource prices might increase the inflation rate, and the expenditure of government funds would only add to the problem of rising prices. The enactment of tax policies takes time. For example, the 1964 tax cut was proposed in 1963 and approved after more than a year of hearings. This particular tax cut was an example of Keynesian economics well thought out and proposed, but legislative reluctance delayed the cut for over twelve months. Oftentimes a conflict between the president and the Congress leads to bitter policy debates. We refer to the undue passage of time before a proposed policy measure is signed into law as the *legislative lag*.

Execution presents another delay in transferring the legislation into action. Tax policies tend to be faster and more efficient after passage, but spending packages may be hung up in a bidding and allocation process for months. This has been called the *implementation lag*.

Finally, once the legislation for government spending or tax cuts is enacted and executed, time passes before the policy becomes effective. Results from empirical econometric models show that this *reaction lag* can be as long as a year or more before even part of the policy has affected GDP.

## Procyclical Tax and Spending Policy

In the introduction to this chapter, we mentioned that policies of state and local governments have their own fiscal effects. These governments are active in spending and taxing as well as in issuing transfers. Often, however, they use their tools at the "wrong" time in the business cycle. Federal fiscal policy is usually designed to counter inflationary and recessionary trends in economic activity. Yet local government spending often occurs when fiscal "good times" prevail. Voters more readily approve bond issues for schools, libraries, or parks during boom periods, so these construction projects add to the boom. In the same vein, when times are hard, state and local governments often have difficulty financing new spending projects that might stimulate the economy, thus reinforcing a recession. The recession that began in 2007 caused state and local governments to lay off workers, reduce work hours, and cancel projects as growing unemployment rates and lower income and corporate tax revenue diminished state treasuries.

5. What does Keynesian theory tell you about this kind of spending? What would be the economic effects?

6. Is there any salvation to the procyclical spending of state and local governments? (What happens when bond issues to finance libraries and schools are passed?)

# FISCAL POLICY IN ACTION: THE AMERICAN RECOVERY AND REINVESTMENT ACT (ARRA) OF 2009

The American Recovery and Reinvestment Act (ARRA) is the name of the $787 billion stimulus package created to counter the recession that began in late 2007. The act was signed into law on February 17, 2009, and is the largest single stimulus package in U.S. history. The act includes funds for tax cuts, infrastructure investment, expansion of unemployment benefits, education and training, health care, and energy. Table 2 lists the overarching categories within ARRA and the funds that are allocated to each of these areas. Tax cuts account for 37 percent of the allocation and relief to state and local governments accounts for 18 percent.

According to Recovery.gov, the website developed for ARRA to provide up to date information and transparency for the general public, the act is designed to:

❖ Save and create more than 3.5 million jobs over the next two years.

❖ Take a big step toward computerizing Americans' health records, reducing medical errors, and saving billions in health care costs.

**Table 2** American Recovery and Reinvestment Act Funding

| Category | Amount ($Billions) |
| --- | --- |
| Tax Relief* | $288 |
| State and Local Fiscal Relief** | $144 |
| Infrastructure and Science | $111 |
| Protecting the Vulnerable | $81 |
| Health Care | $59 |
| Education and Training | $53 |
| Energy | $43 |
| Other | $8 |

*Tax Relief includes $15 billion for Infrastructure and Science, $61 billion for Protecting the Vulnerable, $25 billion for Education and Training, and $22 billion for Energy, so total funds are $126 billion for Protecting the Vulnerable, $74 billion for Educational and Training, and $65 billion for Energy.

**State and Local Fiscal Relief prevents state and local costs to health and education programs and state and local tax increases.

*Source:* http://www.recovery.gov

❖ Revive the renewable energy industry and provide the capital over the next three years to eventually double domestic renewable energy capacity.

❖ Undertake the largest weatherization program in history by modernizing 75 percent of federal building space and more than one million homes.

❖ Increase college affordability for seven million students by funding the shortfall in Pell Grants, increasing the maximum award level by $500, and providing a new higher education tax cut to nearly four million students.

❖ As part of the $150 billion investment in new infrastructure, enact the largest increase in funding of our nation's roads, bridges, and mass transit systems since the creation of the national highway system in the 1950s.

❖ Provide an $800 Making Work Pay tax credit for 129 million working households, and cut taxes for the families of millions of children through an expansion of the Child Tax Credit.

❖ Require unprecedented levels of transparency, oversight, and accountability.

Expenditures for projects fundable through ARRA were to be made between 2009 and 2011. The Congressional Budget Office (CBO) has estimated several scenarios for ARRA outcomes. Figure 2 shows CBO estimates

**FIGURE 2**  Difference Between Potential GDP in CBO's Baseline and Actual GDP With and Without the Impact of the American Recovery and Reinvestment Act of 2009.

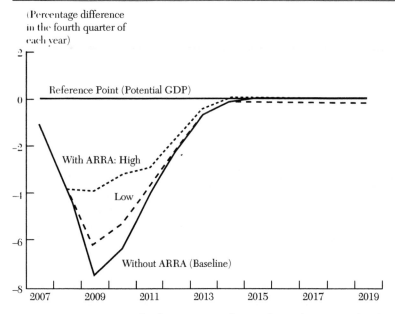

Note: CBO's January 2009 baseline projection of potential gross domestic product (GDP) is set as a reference point. The projection of actual GDP without the effects of the American Recovery and Reinvestment Act of 2009 (ARRA) is CBO's January 2009 estimate, as presented in *The Budget and Economic Outlook: Fiscal Years 2009–2019*. The projections of actual GDP with the effects of ARRA incorporated (the high and low estimates) reflect a range of assumptions.

*Source:* Congressional Budget Office.

for "high" returns from ARRA projects and tax relief, predicting a lower downturn in GDP and a faster recovery, and a "low" estimate, projecting a much greater decrease in GDP (but not as large as the reduction in GDP without ARRA) and a slower recovery. The baseline illustrates the CBO's estimates of the recession without ARRA. Despite this stimulus package, it will take some time for the expenditures and tax policies to have a full effect on the economy.

At the time ARRA was enacted, a number of prominent economists called for a much larger stimulus package to combat the economic downturn. As the economy worsened during 2009 with growing numbers of unemployed workers and increased business failures, more economists called for a second round of stimulus, noting that while ARRA was working, still more was needed.

7. What are the implications of over one-third of the stimulus package targeted at tax relief? Explain by comparing the effects of the tax multiplier to those of the expenditures multiplier.

8. Has a second round of stimulus been requested by the president or passed by Congress? What are the implications of this action or inaction?

## FISCAL POLICY IN AN OPEN ECONOMY

Thus far, we have examined the effects of fiscal policy in our three-sector closed economy of domestic households, businesses, and government. Since international economic activity plays an increasingly important role in U.S. transactions, we need to examine how the foreign sector or net exports (as we are representing the foreign sector) responds to fiscal policy. We can examine two specific effects on net exports: responses to changes in interest rates and responses to changes in currency value. Both affect national income.

Fiscal policy, such as an increase in government expenditures or a tax cut financed by an increase in government borrowing, may cause interest rates to rise in the short run as the government increases its demand for credit. Higher interest rates on government bonds will make U.S. government securities more attractive to both domestic and foreign investors than foreign security offerings with lower interest rates. An increase in the demand for U.S. bonds by foreign investors will create an increased demand for dollars by foreign individuals and institutions and a decrease in the supply of dollars offered by U.S. investors in foreign security markets. This will cause the value of the dollar to increase with respect to other currencies. Each dollar will purchase a larger volume of foreign goods, so imports should increase. On the other hand, U.S. products (exports) will cost more to those desiring U.S. goods, so the demand for U.S. exports should fall because of their relatively higher prices on international markets.

When we account for this effect of fiscal policy actions in an open economy, we see that it acts in opposition to the initial fiscal policy designed to increase levels of income and output. With imports rising and exports falling, net exports $(X - M)$ will fall. In our aggregate expenditure analysis, where $Y = C + I + G + (X - M)$, the increase in $G$ may, through a higher interest rate, cause an appreciation of the U.S. dollar and thus a decrease in net exports. The expenditures multiplier therefore will be less effective in the presence of an international market. In contrast, tax cuts financed by lowered government surpluses rather than by increased government borrowing should stimulate consumption spending. Some of this increased consumption will be spent on imported goods and services, but overall, income $(Y)$ should rise.

A second effect of fiscal policy in an open economy is the effect of output on exchange rates. Here, however, the effects on imports and exports are offsetting, so the total effect is assumed to be zero. As increased government expenditures or tax cuts increase income, those who receive this additional income will be inclined to increase their expenditures on goods and services. Some of this increased demand will be for international products. The demand for imports should increase as incomes rise. This increased demand for imports will yield a greater supply of dollars in the currency markets as U.S. customers exchange dollars for imported goods. The increased supply of U.S. dollars will have the effect of decreasing or depreciating the value of the dollar in the international market. A lower-valued dollar will increase the demand for U.S. exports and decrease the demand for imports in the United States. In this case, fiscal policy in an open economy most likely has a neutral effect. An initial increase in import demand will be followed by a rise in exports and a fall in imports as the dollar depreciates in value, so the original fiscal policy stimulus maintains its effectiveness.

## THE FEDERAL BUDGET

The federal government's fiscal policy is directly related to the federal budget. During the 1980s, 1990s, and after 2002, the public and politicians objected to the size of the federal government, the size of the budget deficit, and its effects. As illustrated in Figure 3, the level of the federal budget deficit increased dramatically in the 1980s, with annual deficits of more than $150 billion and the total accumulated debt of around $1 trillion in 1980 increasing to more than $5 trillion by 1997. Then, between 1998 and 2000, federal surpluses halted the growing debt. After 2002, federal budget deficits sharply increased until faster economic growth and higher tax receipts reduced the deficit level in 2005 through 2007. With the recession that began in late 2007, large deficits resumed; the largest deficit on record was expected in 2009.

In the United States, a few deficit watchers have always been alarmed at prospects of deficits and their implications, but when large deficits were projected to continue throughout the 1990s, deficit reduction became an important political and economic issue. Some have pointed to the large budget deficits incurred by the ARRA as reason not to fund a second stimulus package. A slower recovery, however, would also generate larger budget deficits over a longer period of time.

**FIGURE 3**   The Federal Budget Surplus or Deficit, 1935–2009

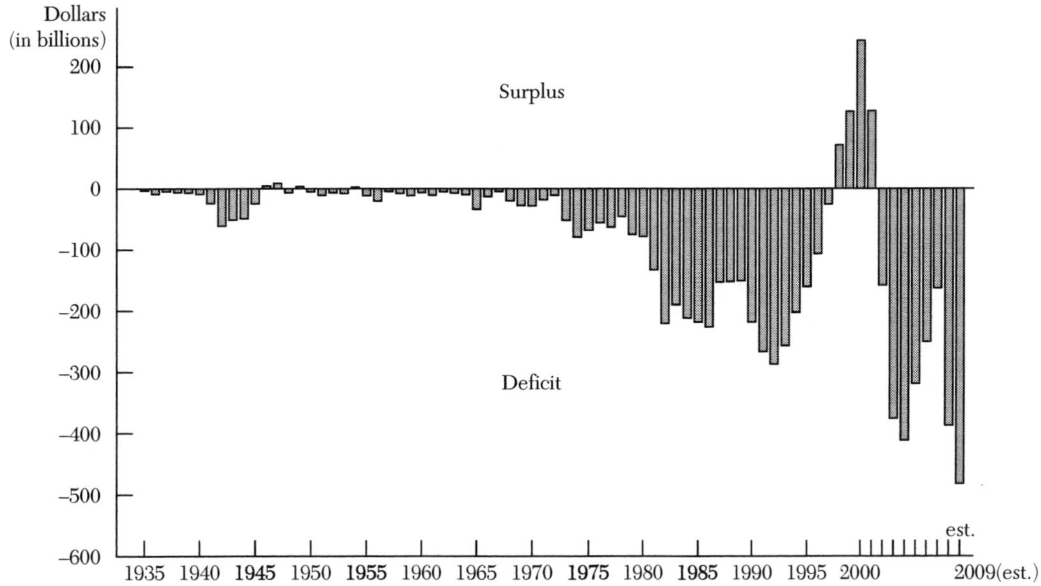

Source: *Economic Report of the President,* CBO, 2009, p. 377.

## The Federal Budget and the Economy

Just as the budget of a family or business determines the direction, priorities, and obligations of that unit, the federal budget determines the direction, priorities, and obligations assumed by the nation. The federal budget consists of expenditures (such as direct purchases of goods and services) and receipts (such as taxes). Elements of fiscal policy are directly reflected in the annual federal budget, which not only indicates a president's view about fiscal and social policy, but also reflects electoral policies and the process of government. The budget that the president proposes and Congress passes, in what is now a yearlong process, reflects what the government will do and what priorities it will set. As is the case with household budgets, receipts are balanced against expenditures. If receipts are greater than expenditures, a surplus results; if expenditures exceed receipts, there is a deficit.

The most obvious source of federal government revenue is tax receipts. Individual income taxes provided 45 percent of the roughly $2.6 trillion collected in 2007. As shown in Figure 4, the importance of individual income taxes has grown since the 1940s. Social Security taxes now provide the next largest single receipt, having increased from only 11 percent in 1950 to 33 percent in 2007.

Corporate income taxes provided a substantial portion of federal receipts during the 1950s and 1960s, but as a result of the Reagan tax cut package of 1981, the corporate share of the total tax burden shrank to 6.2 percent in 1983. The Economic Recovery Tax Act, as it was called, cut personal income tax rates by 23 percent over three years. The measure also accelerated the rate at which businesses could take depreciation deductions, and gave other

**FIGURE 4** Tax Type as a Percentage of Government Revenue, 1940–2007

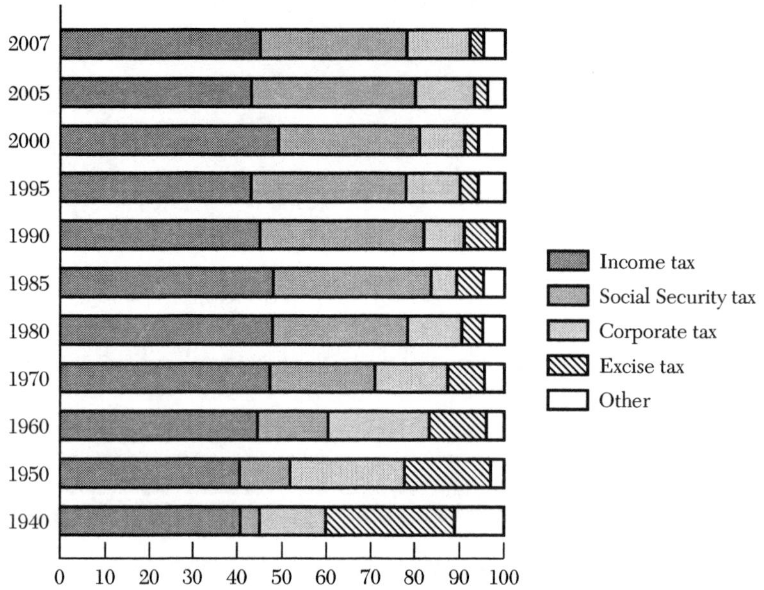

Source: *Economic Report of the President*, 2009, p.380.

deductions and additional loopholes to individuals and businesses alike. The much-heralded Tax Reform Act of 1986 reduced corporate tax rates, eliminated the investment tax credit (which had saved corporations billions in taxes), and made depreciation allowances stricter. The corporate share of taxes increased to 11.4 percent in 1988 and in 2007 corporate taxes contributed 14 percent to total revenues.

The other side of the federal government's budget is expenditures. Table 3 shows federal expenditures both as the proportion of the budget going to selected areas and as a percentage of GDP for selected years. Military expenditures, while not changing dramatically as a percentage of the federal budget, increased dramatically as a percentage of GDP during the 1980s. In 1988 total defense expenditures were $290 billion, or 6.0 percent of GDP. Thanks to the end of the Cold War and the breakup of the former Soviet Union, U.S. defense expenditures were $294 billion, or roughly 3 percent of GDP by 2000. However, the Iraq war has brought additional military expenditures, and substantial increases have occurred in Social Security and Medicare expenditures. At the same time, interest payments on the federal debt have declined as a percent of GDP, thanks to lower interest rates.

Most budgeted programs were, in fact, cut as part of the Reagan and Bush programs to enhance the role of the private sector while reducing the role of government. However, since military, agriculture, Social Security, and interest expenditures increased so significantly in the 1980s, Reagan was unable to keep his campaign promise of reducing government's role. Under his administration, expenditures rose to a peacetime record of 23.7 percent of GDP in 1983.

**Table 3** Government Expenditures as a Percentage of Budget Outlays and GDP, 1975–2009 (Selected Categories)

| Selected Expenditure | 1975 % Budget Outlay | 1975 % GDP | 1980 % Budget Outlay | 1980 % GDP | 1985 % Budget Outlay | 1985 % GDP | 1990 % Budget Outlay | 1990 % GDP | 1995 % Budget Outlay | 1995 % GDP | 2000 % Budget Outlay | 2000 % GDP | 2005 % Budget Outlay | 2005 % GDP | 2007 % Budget Outlay | 2007 % GDP |
|---|---|---|---|---|---|---|---|---|---|---|---|---|---|---|---|---|
| National defense | 26.5 | 5.3 | 23.2 | 4.8 | 26.7 | 6.0 | 23.9 | 5.2 | 18.0 | 3.7 | 16.4 | 2.8 | 20.0 | 4.0 | 21.5 | 4.0 |
| Education/health | 13.2 | 2.6 | 9.2 | 1.9 | 6.6 | 1.5 | 7.7 | 1.7 | 11.2 | 2.3 | 11.9 | 2.1 | 14.2 | 2.8 | 10.3 | 1.9 |
| Social Security (includes Medicare) | | | 26.1 | 5.4 | 26.9 | 6.1 | 27.7 | 6.0 | 29.8 | 6.8 | 33.9 | 6.0 | 20.0 | 3.96 | 22.8 | 4.2 |
| Medicare | — | — | — | | — | | — | | — | | — | | 12.1 | 2.4 | 14.6 | 2.7 |
| Income security | 33.3 | 6.7 | 15.0 | 3.1 | 13.5 | 3.0 | 11.8 | 2.6 | 14.5 | 3.0 | 13.8 | 2.4 | 14.0 | 2.7 | 14.2 | 2.6 |
| Net interest | 9.5 | 1.9 | 9.1 | 1.9 | 13.7 | 3.1 | 14.7 | 3.2 | 15.3 | 3.2 | 12.8 | 2.2 | 7.4 | 1.4 | 9.2 | 1.7 |
| Agriculture | 0.5 | 0.1 | 0.8 | 0.2 | 2.7 | 0.6 | 0.9 | 0.2 | 0.6 | 0.1 | 2.2 | 0.4 | 1.1 | 0.2 | 0.7 | 0.1 |
| **Total budget** | | 20.0 | | 20.7 | | 22.6 | | 21.7 | | 20.9 | | 17.5 | | 19.8 | | 18.6 |
| Surplus/(deficit) | | (2.8) | | (2.1) | | (5.0) | | (3.8) | | (2.2) | | 0.8 | | (4.0) | | (1.3) |

Source: *Economic Report of the President*, 1989, pp. 316, 398, 399; February 1996, p. 369; February 2006, p. 380; February 2009, p. 380.

During the Clinton administration, government expenditures as a percentage of GDP declined to 17.5 percent of GDP. In 2005, the G. W. Bush administration saw government expenditures rise to 19.8 percent of GDP, decreasing to 18.6 percent in 2007.

By grouping these outlays another way, we can see why policy makers had such a difficult time reducing the deficit. Figure 5 shows the discretionary, non-defense–discretionary and nondiscretionary spending as a percentage of the total budget using assumptions based on the 2010 fiscal year budget. Discretionary spending is voted on annually. The government automatically spends money on these mandatory programs. The largest of these entitlements are Medicare and Social Security, which grow as increasingly large numbers of the population reach retirement age.

The combination of tax reductions and expenditure increases led to then-record **budget deficits** between 1980 and 1993. Although the federal budget deficit has been larger when measured as a percentage of GDP, deficits comparable to those registered during the 1980s through the mid-1990s have seldom been recorded during a time of peace or economic growth. In July 2009, U.S. federal debt stood at $11.6 trillion. The United States is the largest debtor nation in the world.

In the early 1990s, in an attempt to deal with large actual and projected deficits, Congress passed the Balanced Budget and Emergency Deficit Control Act (better known as Gramm-Rudman-Hollings), which mandated a balanced budget by 1993 and required automatic spending cuts in military and non-military expenditures if Congress and the president failed to meet annual deficit reduction targets in the federal budget. Those targets were never achieved, in part because of the money spent to bail out failing savings and loan institutions in the late 1980s. In 1990, Congress enacted spending cuts and tax increases to cut the deficit. The Budget Enforcement Act limited discretionary

**FIGURE 5**  Federal Spending by Budget Category (FY 2010 Budget)

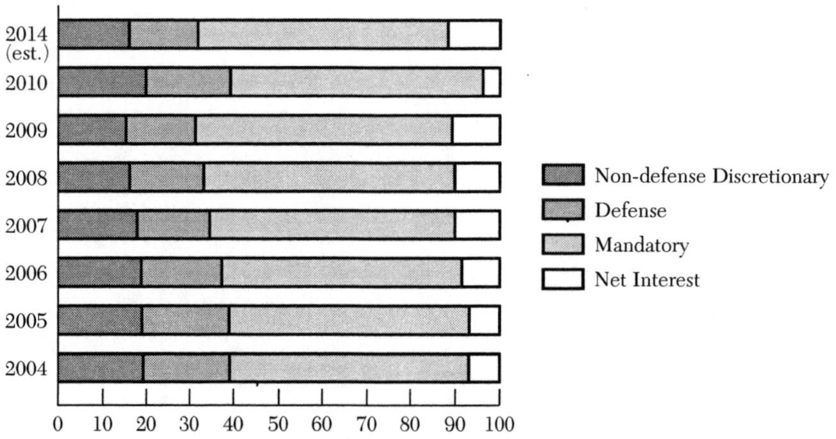

Source: Data from OMB, *Historical Tables, FY 2010 Budget.*

spending and ensured that new entitlement programs would not worsen the deficit. Unfortunately, these were enacted at the same time the 1990 recession began, so tax receipts did not rise as they were expected to and government spending increased to offset the higher unemployment levels generated by the recession. In 1993, Congress passed a five-year deficit reduction plan designed to cut spending and increase revenue. Deficits fell from $290 billion in 1992 to $164 billion in 1995. In 1996, a seven-year plan to balance the budget was passed, and, by 1998, thanks in part to a surging economy resulting in increased tax revenues, the government realized its first surplus since the 1960s. Forecasts were mildly optimistic through 2000 but weakened in 2001 with tax reductions curbing receipts and increases in military and homeland security expenditures. Surpluses turned quickly into deficits as tax cuts continued and military expenditures grew. Economic growth rebounded with these fiscal stimuli until the fourth quarter of 2007, when the economy entered a deep and prolonged recession. The ARRA was implemented to attack the downturn with tax cuts and increased expenditures.

9. Which categories of federal government expenditures have grown most rapidly over the past two decades? Which revenues have seen the greatest growth?

10. What is the forecast for the deficit this year?

## Federal Deficits and Surpluses

Deficits in the federal budget give rise to the **national** (or **federal**) **debt**. The national debt is the debt or obligation of the federal government and is the accumulation of annual budget deficits. When expenditures are greater than revenues, the government must borrow the difference to finance its spending. The government finances its deficits by borrowing from the public through the sale of treasury bills and bonds. Treasury bonds are debt issues of the government that guarantee the repayment of the original investment plus a specified rate or amount of interest. The Treasury Department sells them to the public, to government agencies, and to institutional investors. Surpluses cause some to wonder about the future of treasury bond sales. In the remainder of this chapter, we examine concerns related to federal deficits and federal surpluses.

The national debt has been one of the great conversation topics of Americans concerned with its growth and size. The historical record indicates that all forms of debt increased dramatically after World War II. In the 1960s, the total federal debt was $300 billion, and in 2007 it reached $9 trillion. The debt more than tripled during the 1980s, stabilized in the late 1990s, and has expanded since.

We might ask why the debt is so worrisome to citizens, as well as to economists and policy makers. The government could eliminate it quite simply by assessing every man, woman, and child in the country an additional $37,900 (in 2009), their per capita share of the national debt. But more important facets of the debt need to be examined. The federal debt did not overly concern the majority of U.S. economists until the 1980s. To understand why such an issue is being made of the debt, we need to examine how debt that accumulated before the 1980s differs from debt that accumulated during the 1980s and after.

**The Budget Deficit Through Leakages and Injections.**   One way to examine the federal deficit in terms of the problems deficits bring to our economy is to analyze aggregate expenditures. In equilibrium, all leakages out of the economy must equal all injections into the economy:

$$\text{Injections} = \text{leakages}$$

$$G + I + X = S + Tx + M$$

We can also restate this by subtracting $M$ from both sides of the equation:

$$G + I + (X - M) = S + Tx,$$

where $G$ represents government expenditures, $I$ is investment expenditures, $(X - M)$ is net exports, $S$ is saving, and $Tx$ is taxes. We can rearrange the terms in this equation to show the federal budget deficit or surplus:

$$G - Tx = S - I - (X - M).$$

We know that the deficit or surplus is represented by government expenditures less receipts, or $G - Tx$. If taxes (receipts) are less than government expenditures, there is a deficit.

Reviewing this budget equation clarifies the government's options. If tax receipts are chronically less than government expenditures, the deficit must be offset by one or a combination of factors represented on the right side of the equation just given. The government can fund its expenditures by borrowing savings balances from the private and public sectors. This leaves fewer funds for private investment. Or it can increase borrowing from abroad, thus increasing its obligations to foreign citizens and institutions.*

**What's the Problem with Deficits?**   Before the 1980s, most of the national debt accumulated during war years, especially during World War II and the Vietnam War. Until early 1982 and begining again in 2001, the debt as a percentage of national income continued to fall. As long as GDP was rising faster than the debt each year, there were only three major concerns:

1. Does the debt compete with other uses of credit?
2. Who pays the interest?
3. Who owns the debt and receives the interest?

---

*We can also express this in our national accounting framework, since

$$Y = C + I + G + (X - M),$$

where

$$Y = C + S + Tx$$

Now substitute and simplify:

$$C + S + Tx = C + I + G + (X - M)$$
$$S + Tx = I + G + (X - M)$$
$$G - Tx = S - I - (X - M)$$

The question of alternative financing sources is particularly cause for concern when the economy is operating at close to full employment. The government can increase taxes or borrow. Either action reduces the spending potential of another sector. Tax increases reduce the spending power of consumers and businesses. Borrowing, or enlarging the debt, may force interest rates up because government bond issues will have to be offered at a higher yield to attract enough buyers. Most of these bond issues will be sold to financial intermediaries, corporations, and others, so government spending will tend to take place at the expense of investment (instead of consumption); the financial intermediaries would otherwise lend to corporations for investment purposes rather than buying government bonds. This crowding out of private investment may occur when the economy is expanding. If there were severe levels of unemployment and excess capacity, interest rates would probably not have to rise with the new government bond issues, and businesses would be reluctant to invest anyway, no matter how low the interest rate fell.

Large budget deficits cause concern for future levels of economic growth, which in turn affects wealth and future living standards. While there are many uses for funds made available by businesses and household saving, there is a limit to that saving. National saving consists of private saving and government saving. Government saving is the budget surplus, or the part of its revenues the government does not spend. If the government must borrow from private saving to finance its deficit, it may divert funds from domestic investment. This is a particular problem when savings rates fall markedly. Figure 6 shows that the national saving rate fell from around 8.0 percent of GDP in the 1950s

**FIGURE 6** Net National Saving and Personal Saving as a Percent of GDP (1930–2005), Budget Deficit as a Percent of GDP (1950–2005)

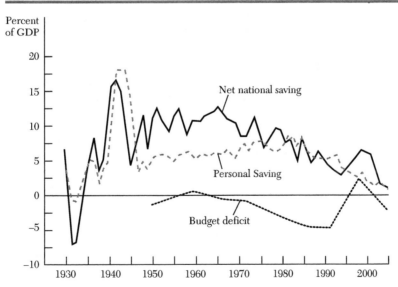

*Source:* GAO analysis of NIPA data from the Bureau of Economic Analysis (BEA). GAO Report, GAO-06-628T.

through the 1970s to 3 percent in the first half of the 1980s and to 2.4 percent in the last half. The national saving rate rose to 5 percent of GDP in the 1990s, only to fall to 2 percent in 2005. Private saving dropped from 9 percent in the 1950–1980 period to 6 percent in the 1980s. Private saving continued to fall through the 1990s, reaching 1 percent in 2004. Government deficits thus consumed many of the resources that had to be parceled out among a variety of credit demands. If interest costs rise, the higher costs can lower the demand for housing and reduce investment. Many economists believe that deficits must remain low if the nation is to achieve long-term prosperity.

The second, more obvious, concern over who owns the debt arises with regard to repayment. It is one thing to pay the interest to ourselves and quite another to owe it to someone else. In 1985, about 11.5 percent of the debt was owned by foreign individuals and governments. By 2007, this figure approached 25 percent.

11. Why did the foreign-held debt increase? Do you think it will continue to do so? Why or why not?

It would be naive to assume that all of us own some of the debt (government bonds) held equally within the U.S. public. Some of us own much more of the debt than others, and the richer we are, the more debt (or bonds) we are likely to own. The poorer among us hold few if any bonds. Institutions and middle- and upper-income individuals use government bonds as a safe and profitable way to hold their savings. Lower-income groups tend not to have substantial savings, since they consume most if not all of their income.

This brings us to the final problem of the interest payments on the debt. In 2008, the debt cost taxpayers more than $253 billion in interest payments. Since the interest payments come from budget receipts, and budget receipts come from taxation, this pattern of interest payments and ownership leads to a redistribution of income in the economy, from bottom to top. Almost everyone pays taxes, some of which are used to pay the interest on the debt. But only individuals who own government bonds receive these interest payments. This is a concern for some economists and politicians.

12. Is ownership of the debt of some concern to you?

13. What groups benefit from the redistributive effects of the debt?

Historically, the debt has financed wars, higher levels of employment and income, and inflation. In the 1980s, it financed additional military and Social Security expenditures and lower taxes. Some argue that the results are a bargain at $37,900 (in 2009) per person! While many economists believe that deficits are an urgent problem, others believe that part of the debt funds much-needed public investments in education, infrastructure, the military, consumer protection, and other public goods.

## Cyclical and Structural Deficits and Surpluses

The Keynesian philosophy toward budgets was that deficits should accumulate during recessions, when additional government expenditures are necessary to boost the economy by stimulating aggregate expenditures, and governments should accumulate surpluses during times of prosperity. The results would be a cyclically balanced budget. Granted, the amounts spent during the recessions might not equal the amounts accumulated during prosperity, but on the whole they would more or less even out. In the United States, however, during the 88 quarters between 1960 and 1981, only four surpluses were recorded. After that, 18 more years passed until the next surplus, recorded in 1999.

When deficits accumulate as a result of economic downturns, they are called **cyclical deficits**, measured by the economic cost of the recession in terms of added expenditures due to unemployment and lost tax receipts. During the recession of the early 1990s, higher levels of unemployment and lower incomes meant that cyclical factors were acting with structural factors to create a much larger than projected federal budget deficit. Cyclical surpluses occur in economic upturns when strong employment and growth yield higher tax receipts. The surpluses of 1999 and 2000 were cyclical surpluses and the 2009 deficit was a cyclical deficit.

Deficits that accrue during times of prosperity or high employment are called **structural deficits**. They result from the structure of federal receipts and expenditures, regardless of the level of economic activity. Between 1960 and 1980, structural deficits averaged less than 2 percent of GDP until 1983, when they reached 2.9 percent of GDP. With economic growth between 1993 and 1995, the cyclical component of the deficit shrank. In 1995, there was a negative cyclical component, since unemployment was below 5.7 percent (the unemployment rate used to calculate "full employment"). With unemployment levels at or below this level in 2005 and 2006, large federal deficits were primarily structural.

The structure of federal receipts and expenditures can also produce structural surpluses. Structural surpluses would occur if the economy were at full employment when the government accrued surpluses. Some economists argue that structural surpluses are detrimental to the economy. According to this argument, surpluses act as a drag on future economic activity by shifting savings from private to public sources. In the 1960s, this phenomenon was called "fiscal drag." Higher tax returns lowered private saving, possibly lowering consumption and limiting loanable funds for private investments.

14. Are cuts in federal expenditures possible? Why or why not?

15. Have any tax cuts or tax increases been passed since 2009? Have new or different types of taxes been proposed? What are they?

16. How large was the federal deficit last year? How large is the federal debt?

17. What would be the effect on income of a decrease in government spending of $0.3 trillion and a tax cut of $0.3 trillion? Is this a balanced budget?

18. Economists have called an unemployment rate of 5.7 percent "full employment." Is there recent evidence that this rate should be changed? If so, what evidence?

# Conclusion

*This chapter has highlighted how fiscal policy works through the tax, transfer, and spending multipliers. For a wide variety of reasons, fiscal policy is not always efficient, but it is most often effective—at least when estimated by Keynesian models. We have also seen the growing concern with structural budget deficits and the desire to balance government receipts against expenditures in periods of economic growth.*

## Review Questions

1. What fiscal policy recommendations would you make to combat unemployment and recession?
   a. What fiscal measures would you recommend if the economy were in the middle of a prolonged period of inflation?
   b. Would you favor a tax policy over a curb on government spending? Why or why not?
   c. What might be the end result of your policy?
   d. How long do you expect the lags to last before your policy would be enacted?

2. What are the differences between automatic stabilizers and discretionary fiscal policy?

3. Would you ever recommend a balanced budget for the federal government? Why or why not? If so, when?

4. Can federal budget deficits be beneficial to the economy?

5. How might deficits limit the productive potential of the economy?

6. Are structural deficits more cause for concern than cyclical deficits? Explain.

7. If MPC = 0.8, what would be the effect of a $10 million tax cut and a $6 million increase in government purchases?

## Note

The body of this chapter dealt only with the effect of injections (government spending, investment, and net exports) on equilibrium income. Now we examine in more detail the effect of leakages or withdrawals in the Keynesian model. We will focus specifically on taxation, although the analysis is similar for other withdrawals, including transfers. In the two-sector model, the only leakage we encountered was saving. When saving increases ($S$ to $S'$) and consumption decreases ($C$ to $C'$), the saving schedule shifts up and to the left, while the consumption schedule shifts down and to the right, and equilibrium income moves to $Y_1$ in Figure A.

Just as all injections— $C$, $I$, $G$, and $(X - M)$—are components of aggregate expenditures and are graphically represented as part of the aggregate expenditures function, all leakages or withdrawals are represented on an aggregate leakage curve. To illustrate our aggregate leakage curve, we

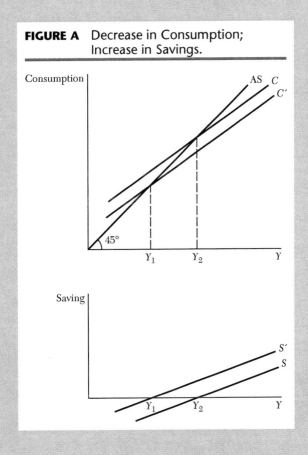

**FIGURE A**  Decrease in Consumption; Increase in Savings.

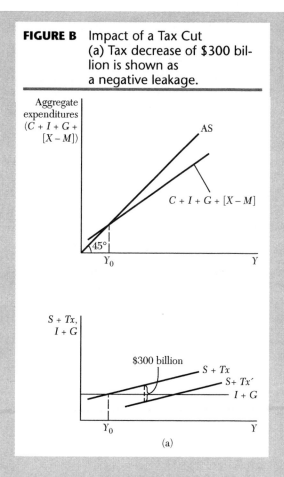

**FIGURE B** Impact of a Tax Cut
(a) Tax decrease of $300 billion is shown as
a negative leakage.

(a)

again expand the model from two to three sectors by adding the taxation leakage to the saving schedule. We add the exogenous tax leakage to the savings function, which in this analysis gives the leakage function its slope (MPS), just as the consumption function gives the injection function or aggregate expenditures curve its slope (MPC). The leakage curve represents positive and negative tax and saving changes. (A tax increase would represent a positive leakage; a tax decrease would represent a negative leakage.) An increase in saving or taxes will shift the leakage curve up and to the left. A decrease in saving or taxes will shift the curve down and to the right; thus, at every level of income, leakages are lower.

Returning to the previous example of a $300 billion tax cut, we arrive at the new equilibrium income after a series of three steps (see Figure B). These three steps occur simultaneously but are shown as a series to clearly demonstrate each part of the

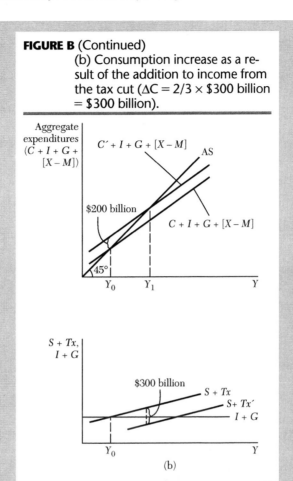

**FIGURE B** (Continued)
(b) Consumption increase as a result of the addition to income from the tax cut ($\Delta C = 2/3 \times \$300$ billion $= \$300$ billion).

(b)

adjustment process. The steps describe how people respond to a cut in taxes. (Note that this is not a cut in the tax rate.) The cut brings an increase in income, but how is that increase allocated? Part of the $300 billion will be consumed, and part will be saved; the MPC and MPS tell us how consumption and saving are allocated. In the first step, Figure B(a), the saving–tax leakage curve shifts down by $300 billion, as taxes are cut by that amount. Second, since income initially rises by the amount of the tax cut, individuals will boost their consumption by MPC times the tax reduction ($2/3 \times \$300$ billion $= \$200$ billion). In Figure B(b), we see the effect of this increase in consumption as the aggregate expenditures curve shifts up by $200 billion. At this point, there is an equilibrium level of income in the

**FIGURE B** (Continued)
(C) Saving increases as a result of the addition to income from the tax cut ($\Delta S = 1/3 \times$ $300 billion = $100 billion).

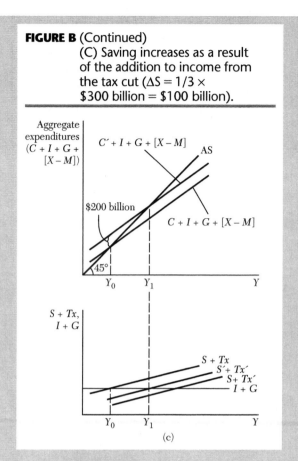

(c)

upper, aggregate expenditures graph, but not in the lower, leakage graph. To arrive at equilibrium in both the upper and lower graphs, we must complete the final step. Just as individuals increase consumption by MPC times the tax reduction, they will increase their saving by MPS times the tax reduction (1/3 × $300 billion = $100 billion). Thus, the saving–tax leakage curve shifts up and to

the left–by $300 billion, as shown in Figure B(c). In the final analysis, income increases from $Y_0$ to $Y_1$, or by $600 billion. To arrive at this result more directly, we can multiply the tax multiplier by the change in taxes:

$$- k_{tx} \times \Delta Tx = \Delta Y$$

$$- 2 \times - \$300 \text{ billion} = \$300 \text{ billion}$$

**108**

# Financial Markets, Money, and Monetary Policy

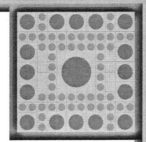

## Introduction

**M**oney *is an asset accepted in exchange for the goods and services we want to purchase. The role of money and the operation of the markets for money and other financial instruments are important in economic decision making and policy making, and economists do not always agree on the way money works through the economy or on its potential impact.*

*Key players in the market for money and other financial instruments are institutions called* **financial intermediaries,** *which hold the funds of savers and make those funds available to borrowers. Financial intermediaries include commercial banks, savings and loan institutions, mutual savings banks, finance companies, credit unions, life insurance companies, mutual funds, and pension funds. They provide financial services demanded by consumers in a changing society. Depository institutions have been more directly linked to Federal Reserve Board (Fed) actions than other financial intermediaries, although the recent financial crisis has expanded the role of the Fed.*

*To begin examining money and a group of financial intermediaries accepting deposits of savers, we will first look at the uses of and demands for money. Next, we will examine the money supply, including the ways the Fed can increase and decrease the money supply and the role of money in the Keynesian model. Finally, we examine monetary policy, and the role of the Federal Reserve and monetary policy in the recent financial crisis.*

### THE USES OF MONEY

Money is important to economics because of its uses. Some say that money is as money does. Few individuals hold dollars for the sheer joy of counting or stacking them.

Money is valued for the goods and services that it buys—for its use as a **medium of exchange**. It is commonly accepted in payment for goods and services.

From Chapter 16 of *Economics: A Tool for Critically Understanding Society*, 9/e. Tom Riddell. Jean Shackelford. Geoffrey Schneider. Steve Stamos. Copyright © 2011 by Pearson Education. Published by Addison-Wesley. All rights reserved.

Before money was institutionalized, barter economies prevailed; people simply exchanged goods and services. Of course, problems arose when two parties could not agree upon objects to trade or when there was no double coincidence of wants. For example, barter fails if one trader desires shoes and has only nuts to offer in exchange, while the shoemaker wants only leather in exchange for shoes. Larger problems would arise if one had only assets that could not be divided, such as a horse to trade for less valuable objects.

Because it is an accepted medium of exchange, money can also be used as a measuring rod for the value of each good or service—in other words, as a **unit of account**. In our economy, goods are measured by a dollar amount. In shopping we observe that a pound of nuts is priced at $4.69, a pair of shoes at $85.98, and a horse and buggy at $5,753. We can use money as our unit of account in measuring the National Income Accounts of GDP and NNP. Firms use money to account for the flow of goods and services produced and sold.

Besides its unique role as a medium of exchange and unit of account, money has two functions that it shares with other assets (things of value that are owned). Money may serve as a **store of value**. To be a store of value, an asset must hold its value into the future. Some other assets that serve this function are stocks, bonds, precious metals, gems, and property. Money may also be a **standard of deferred payment**. Standards of deferred payment are assets accepted by others for future payment.

1. What assets would you accept as payment for your work?

## DEMAND FOR MONEY

The four uses of money are associated with the three categories of demand for money. The **transactions demand**—the only category recognized by the classical economists—indicates the amount of money balances that individuals desire for transaction (purchasing) purposes. This demand corresponds to money's function as a medium of exchange and is often constant with a given level of income and pattern of consumption expenditures.

People also have a **precautionary demand** for money, or a demand for money to hold to meet unforeseen expenses. John Maynard Keynes wrote about this demand as a separate category in *The General Theory*. We observe this precautionary demand as we try to hedge our risks by saving, perhaps for the proverbial "rainy day" or for some other reason.

2. Divide your demands for money into transactions and precautionary balances. What percentage of your money balances do you hold for each?

**FIGURE 1** Precautionary and Transactions Demand for Money

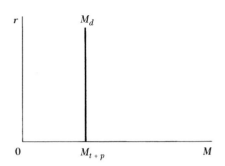

The precautionary demand, like the transactions demand, is generally constant; people at certain income levels will tend to save or keep a relatively fixed proportion of their income for precautionary purposes. Figure 1 shows a demand curve for the transactions and precautionary balances plotted on a price-quantity axis. (This adds money to the array of goods and services for which there is a demand—and later, of course, a supply.) The quantity of money ($M$) is measured along the horizontal axis, and the price of money, represented by the interest rate ($r$),* is measured along the vertical axis. The vertical line $M_d$ indicates that at all rates of interest, the precautionary and transactions demand will be constant for a given individual at a given income level.

The third demand for money (or, as he called it, liquidity preference†) recognized by Keynes is the **speculative demand**. This demand arises from people's desire to maximize their returns on the funds left over after satisfying their transactions and precautionary demands. The speculative demand for funds is inversely related to the interest rate. If the interest rate is high, people will hold relatively few speculative or liquid balances. Instead, they will exchange these speculative money balances for bonds or other assets. If the interest rate is low, individuals may decide to wait and see what happens to interest rates in the future. If interest rates rise, people want to avoid being locked into low-yielding assets, so they prefer to hold (speculative) cash or money balances. One can plot the speculative demand for money with respect to interest and the quantity of money, since $M_{\text{spec}} = f(r)$, as shown in Figure 2.

At extremely high interest rates, the speculative demand for money balances approaches 0, whereas at very low rates of interest, people will desire to hold only money balances. This low-interest range in which the demand for money is perfectly elastic is called the Keynesian **liquidity trap**. Keynes pointed out that at extremely low rates of interest, people believe interest rates can go no

---

*The price of money is the rate of interest, since a person who buys or borrows money pays for it at the prevailing rate of interest. Although there is a wide array of interest rates in the economy at any one time, depending on such factors as risk and time until the asset matures, we will focus on *an* interest rate, assuming that all of them behave similarly.
†Liquidity is the degree of "moneyness." One hundred percent liquid suggests that all of one's assets are in cash and/or demand and checkable deposits. Stocks and bonds and property are assets of somewhat lesser levels of liquidity, since they cannot immediately be converted into cash.

**FIGURE 2**  Speculative Demand for Money

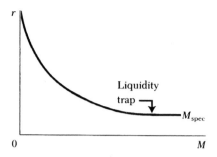

lower and can only rise. To buy bonds would be courting disaster, so people hold on to their cash. This liquidity trap area becomes important when discussing various aspects of monetary policy, a topic we will return to later in the chapter.

If we combine all three demands for money, we obtain the total demand for money, which is plotted in Figure 3. This demand curve for money, like all demand curves, indicates that the quantity demanded varies inversely with price. As the interest rate rises, people will hold smaller money balances, down to the amount needed to satisfy transactions and precautionary demands.

## Changes in the Demand for Money

Like other demand curves, the demand for money may not remain constant over time. Shifts, or changes in demand, are often caused by a change in the level of income. For example, if an individual's income increases from $40,000 a year to $45,000 a year, that person's demand for money will more than likely increase. The reason is that the demand for precautionary and transactions balances increases as income increases. Figure 4 shows how changes in income affect the demand for money.

**FIGURE 3**  Total Demand for Money

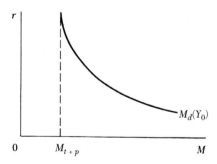

**FIGURE 4**  The Effect of Income Changes on the Demand for Money

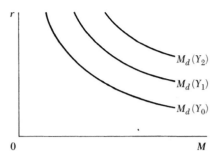

## SUPPLY OF MONEY

Unlike the supply of most goods and services, the total supply of money is controlled not by individual firms, but by the Federal Reserve System, more commonly known as the Fed.

### The Fed

To mend an ailing national banking system by promoting stability in the banking system, the Federal Reserve Act of 1913 established the **Federal Reserve System** (the **Fed**) as the central bank in the United States. The Fed is an independent agency of the government, established by Congress to centralize control over the banking system and the money supply. Figure 5 shows the basic organizational structure of the Federal Reserve System.

Members of the Board of Governors of the Federal Reserve System, appointed to 14 year terms by the president with congressional approval, coordinate and regulate monetary policy in the United States. The chair of the Board of Governors acts as spokesperson for the entire system. The Federal Open Market Committee (FOMC) directs Fed sales and purchases of U.S. Treasury bonds, and the other councils advise. The 12 regional Federal Reserve Banks and their 24 branches throughout the country oversee operations of the member commercial banks in their districts. Figure 6 shows the locations of these regional banks.

The Monetary Control Act of 1980 stipulated that the Federal Reserve can require that *all* banks and depository institutions in the country hold reserves (or a percentage of deposits). The passage of this act gave the Fed control over the reserves placed on money held in commercial banks, savings banks, savings and loan institutions, and credit unions.

3. Congress established the Federal Reserve as an independent agency of the federal government (that is, outside the operational control of Congress or the president). List arguments supporting an independent agency.

4. Who is the current chair of the Fed?

**FIGURE 5**  Federal Reserve System

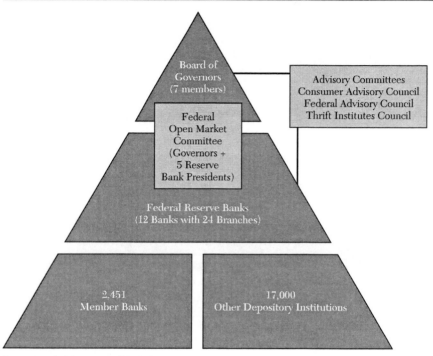

*Source:* Board of Governors of the Federal Reserve System, *The Federal Reserve Today*, p. 2.

**FIGURE 6**  Boundaries of Federal Reserve Districts and Their Branch Territories

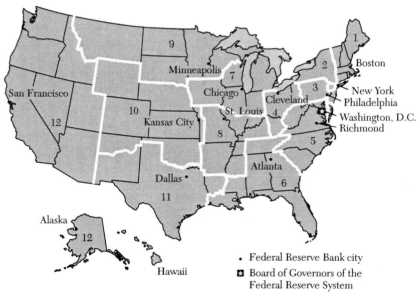

*Source:* Board of Governors of the Federal Reserve System, http://www.federalreserve.gov/otherfrb.htm

## Regulation of Financial Markets

Operating within the U.S. financial markets are many institutional players, all of them subject to some degree of regulation. Commercial banks are the oldest financial intermediaries. Savings banks and insurance companies emerged in the late nineteenth century, while credit unions, real estate trusts, investment banks, bank holding companies, and finance companies developed in the twentieth century. A number of innovations in existing financial institutions occurred in the 1980s, and changes resulting from new regulation and deregulation legislation continued throughout the 1990s.

There is a long history of financial market regulation in the United States. Financial institutions have seen periods of total control and regulation, as well as periods that might be called banking anarchy. The current period of regulation resulted from controls instituted after the Great Depression, as Congress enacted legislation to avoid the recurrence of widespread banking failures. Investors as well as depositors wanted protection from financial market failures. The federal and state governments responded with laws and regulations designed to assure the safety of the financial system. Federal deposit insurance agencies began insuring a variety of deposits, and agencies began to regulate the activities of financial institutions. However, in the 1980s and in 1999, Congress moved to eliminate at least some of the regulations dating from the 1930s.

Regulation limited the kinds of loans and assets each type of financial institution could issue and possess. As a result, the financial industry was segmented into largely different types of institutions with little competition among them. Commercial banks, for example, specialized in commercial loans to businesses, while savings and loan institutions generated home mortgages. Started by builders in the 1870s, savings banks made money available to people wanting to buy the builders' products.

Perhaps the most onerous of the depression-era regulations was **Regulation Q**, which placed ceilings on the interest rate financial institutions could pay for time and savings deposits. The purpose of interest ceilings was to "restrain excessive price competition," which was thought to be one of the causes of the 1933 banking collapse. The interest ceiling was above the market rate of interest through the mid-1960s, so until then it caused no concern. After 1966, market rates rose above the interest ceiling on several occasions. This effectively prevented financial intermediaries from attracting money and then lending it. Instead of depositing their funds in financial intermediaries, people withdrew their dollars and put them into stocks or other assets to get higher returns. Instead of **financial intermediation**, there was **disintermediation**. To avoid interest ceilings, financial intermediaries began creating new financial instruments, since only time and savings deposit accounts were then subject to Regulation Q. But the Federal Reserve was not to be caught short. While Regulation Q covered only two types of accounts in 1965, twenty-four types were covered by 1979.

Because of these rapid financial innovations, Congress came under pressure to deregulate financial markets. The regulation of the 1930s had limited competition and the ability to work within the market system to bid for funds. By the end of the 1970s, the mood toward regulation had substantially changed as described in the 1984 *Economic Report of the President*:

In the 1930s, financial instability was attributed to the natural operation of competitive markets, and this view supported a very substantial extension of regulatory controls over financial markets. More recently, however, a renewed respect for the efficiency of competitive markets has developed, as well as increased recognition of the costs of regulation. Regulation tends to spread in unproductive directions and often causes industries to evolve less efficiently than they otherwise would. For these reasons, the promotion of efficiency by furthering competition is also an important regulatory goal. The purpose of regulation should not be to protect poorly managed individual firms from failure, but rather to prevent such failures from shaking the stability of the financial system as a whole. Regulation should be designed to achieve stability of the system, while individual firms are afforded the maximum possible freedom to compete and innovate.

In the early 1980s, financial deregulation significantly changed the rules of the game in the financial markets. Between 1980 and 1984, most interest rates on federally insured deposits were deregulated, allowing banks and thrift institutions (savings and loan institutions, savings banks, and credit unions) to freely determine the rate of interest they paid on most types of deposits. This added both competition and uncertainty to a vast financial system. The deregulatory activity was started by the Monetary Control Act of 1980 and extended by the Garn–St. Germain Depository Institutions Act of 1982. The Monetary Control Act set lower reserve requirements for all nonmember banks, established the Fed as the lender of the last resort for depository institutions, and eliminated Regulation Q. The Garn–St. Germain Act authorized all financial institutions to offer interest-bearing checking accounts and extended the power of regulators to promote mergers for depository institutions that were failing. It also expanded the lending and deposit powers of thrifts. This permitted some new lending and investing powers, including commercial and real estate loans by savings and loan institutions.

Following deregulation, the rate of bank failures and instability increased, and the savings and loan industry nearly collapsed. Continental Illinois, a major U.S. national bank, paved the way for bank failures in the late 1980s and early 1990s. Unable to arrange a merger for this ailing giant, the Federal Deposit Insurance Corporation (FDIC), which insures deposits of most banks, took over operations. Other failing banks and thrifts were either merged with institutions believed to be more stable or liquidated. Many have therefore questioned the wisdom of aspects of this particular financial deregulation.

Two major reforms in bank regulation took place in the 1990s. In 1994, Congress set nationwide standards for banks wishing to expand or operate branches beyond their home state boundaries. Late in 1999 the Gramm-Leach-Bliley Act was passed by Congress allowing commercial banks to engage in investment banking activities in order to compete more effectively with other financial intermediaries. This legislation revoked part of the Glass-Steagall Act of 1933 designed to protect the public from financiers who might fund some investment activities while denying funds to equally worthy activities. From the late 1990s there was continuing pressure to avoid increased regulation of financial markets and financial instruments. With repercussions from the financial crisis that begun in 2007, there have been increased calls for greater regulation; however, financial institutions have continually resisted further regulation. In late 2009 several measure to regulate financial markets and instruments were under investigation in Congress.

## Banking and Thrift Instability, 1980s and 1990s Style

Deregulation posed enormous problems for the nation's commercial banks and savings institutions. Nearly eight times as many banks closed between 1980 and 1990 as closed during the 1970s. Some 1,570 savings institutions closed their doors or merged with other depository institutions during this period. The government's response to the turmoil in the thrift industry cost U.S. taxpayers an estimated $500 billion or more.

A number of thrifts were in financial difficulty prior to deregulation. Initially chartered to provide mortgage funds to the housing market, savings and loan institutions were legally restricted to holding only mortgages as assets. After World War II, amidst a large upswing in purchases of single-family homes, the demand for mortgages rose, and savings institutions prospered despite the long-term, low-interest nature of these mortgages. Thanks to Regulation Q limiting the interest rate that could be paid to depositors, tax benefits to the industry, and federal insurance guarantees to depositors, savings institutions could thrive as long as interest rates remained low. However, interest rates rose markedly in the 1970s, and savings institutions had to pay higher interest rates to attract deposits. Their profits were squeezed, since the long-run returns on the mortgages already in their portfolios remained fixed at low rates, even though new mortgages reflected the higher rates. Furthermore, the institutions faced geographic restrictions on

their customer base, so institutions in agriculture and oil-producing states were especially fragile. Energy and agricultural prices plunged in the 1980s, and increasing numbers of firms in the Midwest and Southwest failed, rendering many loans worthless. Deregulation freed these institutions to engage in potentially more lucrative but riskier areas of investment. Thrifts diversified into office buildings, commercial loans, and some direct purchases of franchises. At the same time, federal depository insurance was increased from $40,000 per account to $100,000 per account, so thrifts sought out larger deposits by offering more attractive rates of return. They hoped the new channels of investment open to them would more than offset the higher interest rates they were paying for funds. The risk for bankers (and depositors) was limited, since most deposits were insured.

During this same period, federal budget cuts, combined with a spirit of deregulation, reduced the number of bank examiners hired to oversee these more risky (and sometimes fraudulent) activities. The reduction in regulation and inspection, along with an overextension of risky loans, left many institutions with deposit liabilities in excess of the value of their assets. These ingredients completed a recipe for widespread thrift failure.

With the mounting failures draining federal deposit insurance funds, Congress in 1989 enacted the Financial Institutions

Reform, Recovery and Enforcement Act (FIR-REA). This law provided funds to merge or liquidate failing thrift institutions and prevent the thrift failures of the eighties from recurring. FIRREA created the Resolution Trust Corporation (RTC) to manage a bailout of the savings and loan industry through the early 1990s. Among its charges, the RTC was to sell houses, apartment buildings, golf resorts, office buildings, and other assets of failed thrifts. Much of the real estate sold at bargain-basement prices, recouping only a small fraction of the moneys lost. These massive sales depressed real estate markets and new construction in communities with the highest levels of RTC sales.

FIRREA also eliminated other thrift regulatory agencies and established several new agencies in their place. The law established more stringent capital standards, requiring thrifts to meet the higher capital requirements of banks. Regulators continued to examine bank and thrift capital requirements through the 1990s.

Economists estimated that in the early 1990s, closing or selling insolvent thrifts cost taxpayers some $10 million for each day the S&Ls stayed open.

5. List some of the opportunity costs of the thrift bailout. (What could have been purchased with these amounts?)

6. Some economists argue that markets function more efficiently without regulation. Explain why deregulation of the S&L industry worked so poorly.

## Measures of the Money Supply

Besides controlling the amount of credit in the system of depository institutions (which is often referred to as the banking system), the Fed also regulates the money supply. Because a number of financial assets are "used" as money, economists measure the money supply in broader terms than currency used for exchange. They use measures of the money supply called **monetary aggregates**, which include measures for $M_1$ and $M_2$. Figure 7 details the components of each measure.

The most narrowly defined monetary aggregate includes most of the "money" that we use for our day-to-day transactions and is called $M_1$. $M_1$ includes coins and currency plus demand deposits (checking accounts), traveler's checks, and other checkable deposits (including NOW and ATS accounts*) held by the public. In 2009, currency and coins accounted for about 51 percent of $M_1$, demand deposits for 26 percent, other checkable deposits for 21 percent, and traveler's checks for 0.3 percent. The total

---

*Negotiable order of withdrawal (NOW) accounts are interest-bearing checking accounts. They became legal throughout the United States on November 1, 1980, with an initial maximum interest rate of $5^1/_4$ percent. NOW accounts may be issued by all depository institutions. ATS accounts are automatic transfer service accounts.

**FIGURE 7** Components of the Monetary Aggregates, July 2009

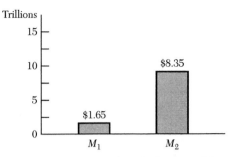

$M_1$ includes currency, traveler's checks, demand deposits, and other checkable deposits.
$M_2$ includes $M_1$, small-denomination time deposits, savings deposits and money market
deposit accounts, money market mutual fund shares (noninstitutional), overnight
repurchase agreements, and overnight eurodollars.
*Source:* Board of Governors of the Federal Reserve System, *Statistical Release,* May 28, 2009.

money supply measured as $M_1$ stood at $1.6 trillion in mid 2009. $M_1$ has
historically grown at an annual rate of around 5 or 6 percent. In 1990,
the growth rate of $M_1$ was only 4 percent, but it increased to 14 percent in
1992 as the economy slowed. After 1995, the annual change in $M_1$ averaged a
2 percent increase.

An expanded monetary aggregate $M_2$ includes $M_1$ and adds other short-term
accounts that are easily converted into money. $M_2$ equals $M_1$ plus short-term
time and savings accounts and other interest-bearing accounts, including
money market deposit accounts, noninstitutional money market mutual funds,
and some other very liquid assets.* In 2009, $M_2$ was $8.3 trillion—over five
times the value of $M_1$.

Some economists believe that the use of the $M_2$ definition better explains
consumption and other decisions made in the economy. Other economists,
however, believe that the Federal Reserve—when reflecting on policy actions
that will result in changes in the money supply—really looks at the availability
of credit in the economy rather than any precise $M_1$ or $M_2$ definition. For example, if the Fed concludes that credit is too tight, it will take measures to increase credit availability by increasing the money supply.

Although the Fed is responsible for initiating changes in policies to alter the
money supply, individual depository institutions allocate the money to the
public. To a large extent, their allocation reflects the interest rates in the economy. If interest rates are low, depository institutions are reluctant to lend large
quantities of money and risk being locked into low-yielding assets. On the
other hand, if interest rates are high, the depository institutions will be more

---

*Money market mutual funds (MMMFs) and money market deposit accounts (MMDAs) are
funds issued to savers and backed by holdings of high-quality short-term assets. MMDAs are
federally insured bank deposit accounts.

**FIGURE 8**  The Money Supply

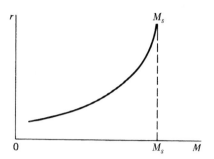

willing to lend money *if it is available to them* (or if the Fed has allocated additional money by implementing policies that increase the money supply). We can illustrate this by constructing a money supply curve. The interest rate is on the vertical axis, and the quantity of money is on the horizontal axis, as in Figure 8.

When we combine the supply and demand curves for money, the intersection of the two curves signifies equilibrium in the money market, as shown in Figure 9. At point $E$ the quantity of money demanded equals the quantity supplied at an interest rate of $r_0$. In equilibrium, there is no excess demand or supply. If the Fed allows the money supply to increase, then the $M_{s0}$ curve will shift to the right ($M_{s1}$) usually resulting in a lower interest rate ($r_1$) as in Figure 10. A decrease in the money supply will shift $M_{s0}$ to the left ($M_{s2}$) and increase the interest rate ($r_2$) Later in this chapter, we will look at the tools with which the Fed changes the money supply. First we will examine the process by which commercial banks "create" money and how this money works within the Keynesian model.

## Suppliers of Money

All financial intermediaries facilitate the exchange of money, but commercial banks and other depository institutions also have the power to "create"

**FIGURE 9**  Equilibrium in the Money Market

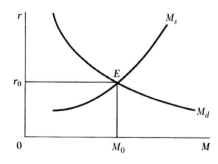

**FIGURE 10** Changes in the Money Supply

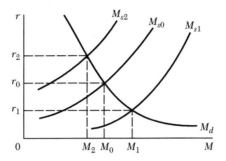

money. They create money on the basis of a **fractional reserve system** of deposit balances. The Fed requires that every depository institution hold reserves, setting aside a certain percentage of its total deposits in its vault or in the nearest Federal Reserve Bank to ensure safety and the ability to meet deposit withdrawals. The **reserve requirement** (the percentage of reserves that must be held) varies according to the asset size of the depository and the type of account. Table 1 lists the most recent reserve requirements mandated by the Fed.

 7. Why isn't there a 100 percent reserve requirement?

An example of the money creation process should help clarify what happens to a deposit in a commercial bank or other depository institution. For simplicity's sake, we shall use a 10 percent reserve requirement for demand deposits and begin with a newly created $1,000 deposit. With this deposit, new deposits in the depository or banking system increase by $1,000, and required reserves increase by $100. This leaves the commercial bank with $1,000 minus $100, or $900. The prudent (profit-maximizing) banker would use the $900 to generate loans and investments of an equal amount.

**Table 1** Reserve Requirements of Depository Institutions

| | Requirements | |
|---|---|---|
| **Type of Liability** | **Reserve Percentage (%) of Liabilities** | **Effective Date** |
| **(Net Transaction Accounts)** | | |
| $0 to $10.7 million | 0 | 12/31/09 |
| More than $10 million to $55.2 million | 3 | 12/31/09 |
| More than $55.2 million | 10 | 12/31/09 |
| Nonpersonal time deposits | 0 | 12/27/90 |
| Eurocurrency liabilities | 0 | 12/27/90 |

*Source:* www.federalreserve.gove/monetarypolicy/reservereq.htm

**`121**

Perhaps you are in the market for a $900 loan. If our friendly neighborhood banker decides you are creditworthy, you may receive the "extra" $900. If you spend the $900 on new stereo components, there is a good chance that the full $900 will enter the banking system when the Stereo Shack deposits its daily balances. The banking system then has another deposit, this time one of $900. It must hold 10 percent of $900, or $90, as the reserve requirement on the *new* $900 deposit. Total new deposits are now $1,900, and total new required reserves are $190 in the banking system. And what will happen to the $900 minus $90, or $810, left in the bank? Of course, it becomes a potential source for increases in loans and investments. Table 2 shows the final result of the initial $1,000 demand deposit.

Rather than carrying this process to its final result, we can more easily find the total amount of money "created" by using the following formula:

$$\Delta R \times 1/r_{dd} = \Delta DD,$$

where $\Delta R$ is the original change in reserves, $r_{dd}$ is the reserve requirement on demand deposits, and $\Delta DD$ is the total change in demand deposits. We can substitute numbers from our example:

$$\$1,000 \times 1/(1/10) = \Delta DD$$

$$\$1,000 \times 10 = \Delta DD$$

$$\$10,000 = \Delta DD$$

**Table 2** Money Creation: Example

| Position of Depository Institution | New Deposits | New Loans and Investments | Required Reserves |
|---|---|---|---|
| Original depository institution | $ 1,000.00 | $ 900.00 | $ 100.00 |
| 2nd depository institution | 900.00 | 810.00 | 90.00 |
| 3rd depository institution | 810.00 | 729.00 | 81.00 |
| 4th depository institution | 729.00 | 656.10 | 72.90 |
| 5th depository institution | 656.10 | 590.49 | 65.60 |
| 6th depository institution | 590.49 | 531.44 | 59.05 |
| 7th depository institution | 531.44 | 478.30 | 53.14 |
| 8th depository institution | 478.30 | 430.47 | 47.83 |
| 9th depository institution | 430.47 | 387.42 | 43.05 |
| 10th depository institution | 387.42 | 348.68 | 38.74 |
| 11th depository institution | 348.68 | 313.81 | 34.87 |
| 12th depository institution | + 313.81 | +282.43 | 31.38 |
| Sum of 12 depository institutions | $ 7,175.71 | $ 6,458.14 | $ 717.61 |
| Sum of remaining depository institutions | + 2,824.29 | + 2,541.86 | + 282.39 |
| Total for system as a whole | $10,000.00 | $9,000.00 | $1,000.00 |

Note: Totals may not be accurate due to rounding.

From $1,000, with the stroke of a pen, depository institutions can "make" $10,000—representing $9,000 of *new* money.

Before we accept this fountain pen magic, however, we must take note of several conditions. The first is that an individual bank or depository institution acting alone cannot create money. The process must operate throughout the whole system. To more easily understand this, imagine that a single depository institution tried to expand or create money on its own. Based on the $1,000 increase in its reserves with the $1,000 deposit, the institution loaned $9,000. What happens to that depository institution when someone comes to withdraw or use the funds the depository institution has just lent? As you might imagine, many problems can result, one being that the bank cannot maintain its reserve requirement.

8. What other difficulties might this depository institution run into?

A second point to remember is that the simplified money creation process as described works only if there are no leakages in the system. Leakages can occur in several places. Individuals may decide to place their funds elsewhere, either outside the depository institutions or in hoards. If they do not deposit the funds, then there are no reserves to expand upon. Consumers may place some funds in time accounts. These funds have lower reserve requirements, so the money multiplier is larger. Consequently, such deposits will lead to an even greater expansion of the money supply.

Another leakage may appear within the financial system itself. Bankers and other deposit managers may decide that they can earn greater profits by holding assets other than loans or securities. Perhaps they believe their liquidity is too low and desire to place their remaining funds (or excess reserves) in more short-term assets, such as government bonds. In either case, there is a leakage of funds that do not reenter the demand deposit flow for an indefinite period of time. Indeed, the amount of assets that depository institutions hold in loans or securities is approximately 60 percent of their total portfolio.

Caution should therefore be the byword when examining the money creation process. Nevertheless, the process does suggest that commercial banks and other depository institutions can expand the money supply by "creating" demand deposits. In addition, the simple formula $\Delta R \times r_{dd} = \Delta DD$ approximates the amount of money that the system can create from a new deposit.

9. What happens to the money supply when people take $1,000 out of their depository institution deposits?

## The Myth and Mystique of Money

In the following excerpt from "Commercial Banks as Creators of Money," Yale economist James Tobin tries to steal our thunder in explaining the multiple money creation process in a principles text:

Perhaps the greatest moment of triumph for the elementary economics teacher is his [her] exposition of the multiple creation of bank credit and bank deposits. Before the admiring eyes of freshmen [s]he puts to rout the practical banker who is so sure that [s]he "lends only the money depositors entrust to him [her]." The banker is shown to have a worm's-eye view, and his [her] error stands as an introductory object lesson in the fallacy of composition. From the Olympian vantage of the teacher and the textbook it appears that the banker's dictum must be reversed: depositors entrust to bankers whatever amounts the bankers lend. To be sure, this is not true of a single bank; one bank's loan may wind up as another bank's deposit. But it is, as the arithmetic of successive rounds of deposit creation makes clear, true of the banking system as a whole. Whatever their other errors, a long line of financial heretics have been right in speaking of "fountain pen money"—money created by the stroke of the bank president's pen when she approves a loan and credits the proceeds to the borrower's checking account.

In this time-honored exposition two characteristics of commercial banks are intertwined. One is that their liabilities—well, at least their demand deposit liabilities—serve as widely acceptable means of payment. Thus, they count, along with coin and currency in public circulation, as "money." The other is that the preferences of the public normally play no role in determining the total volume of deposits or the total quantity of money. For it is the beginning of wisdom in monetary economics to observe that money is like the "hot potato" of a children's game: one individual may pass it to another, but the group as a whole cannot get rid of it. If the economy and the supply of money are out of adjustment, it is the economy that must do the adjusting. This is as true, evidently, of the money created by bankers' fountain pens as of money created by public printing presses.

The commercial banks possess the widow's cruse [an expression implying unending supply]. And because they possess this key to unlimited expansion, they have to be restrained by reserve requirements.

Excerpt from J. Tobin, "Commercial Banks as Creators of Money," in BANKING<br>AND MONETARY STUDIES, D. Carson, ed. © 1963 Irwin.

# THE BIG PICTURE

## Money and the Keynesian System

Increases in spending—whether by businesses (as investment) or the government (as expenditures or taxes) work through the multiplier to increase income by amounts greater than the original spending increases or tax cuts. Similarly, decreases in investment or government spending or increases in taxes reduce income by more than the original spending cut or tax increase through the multiplier. In the sections just above we saw how equilibrium in the money market, where the supply of money $M_s$ equals the demand for money $M_d$ is at an interest rate $(r)$. In Figure BP.1 we see that this interest rate is at $r_0$.

With just one more piece of information we can see how increases in the money supply will—in our Keynesian analysis—impact investment decisions and thus income. Increases in investment work through the multiplier to increase income by more than the original investment. (Decreased investment will have the opposite effect on income.)

The key to linking monetary policy and the money supply to investment decisions is the interest rate. In Figure BP.2 we see a demand for investment graph, with interest rates $(r)$ on the vertical axis and the quantity of investment $(Q_I)$ on the horizontal axis. This demand curve is downward sloping, illustrating that at high interest rates, the cost of investment funds is high and managers will need to earn very high returns from any investment made—thus the demand for investment is low at high rates of interest. As interest rates fall, investment demand increases as money to fund investment activities becomes cheaper.

When the Federal Reserve increases the money available and interest rates fall, businesses will find investment opportunities more attractive at these lower interest rates. As they undertake these additional investments—these new investment expenditures work through the Keynesian multiplier to increase income—by more than the initial investment expenditure. Thus we have another possible policy aid to expand income.

Figure BP.3 illustrates the effect of this additional investment.

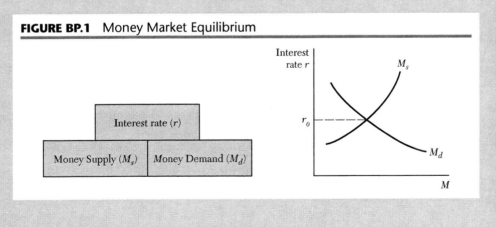

**FIGURE BP.1** Money Market Equilibrium

**FIGURE BP.2** Investment Demand

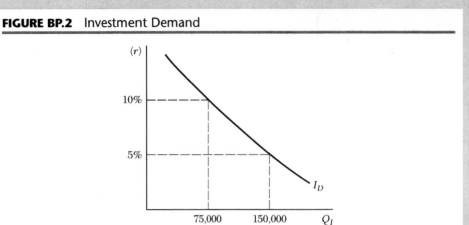

Suppose that owners of a golf course decide that lower interest rates make it possible for them to install a watering system that costs $150,000. When interest rates were high, the cost of the system was too high and the returns to making such an investment decision too small. So this additional investment is triggered through lower interest rates. This generates $150,000 in income for the firm manufacturing the automatic watering systems. Using a multiplier of 4, the watering system manufacturer will spend three-fourths of the $150,000, or $112,500 on purchases of components, equipment rental, labor, and other goods or services. Again, the component suppliers and workers will continue the spending cycle, with three-fourths of $112,500 or $84,375 worth of purchases—perhaps on vacations, rent, travel, food, and so on. And the spending cycle continues until the total increase in income generated by the $150,000 investment in watering equipment generates increased income of $600,000, which equals the multiplier (4) times the initial investment ($150,000).

If the Federal Reserve contracts the money supply, interest rates will rise (*cet. par.*) and investment will drop—and thus income will fall.

**FIGURE BP.3** Money, Interest Rates, Investment, and the Keynesian Multiplier

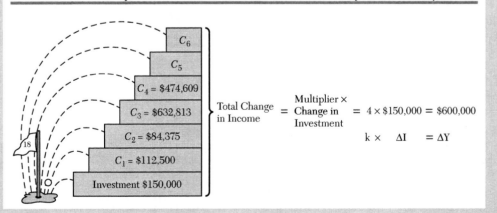

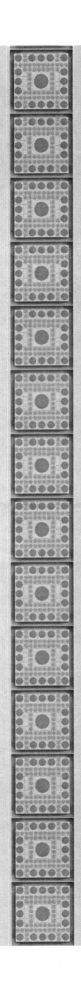

# MONEY AND THE KEYNESIAN SYSTEM: THE DETAILS

Money can be an integral part of the Keynesian system. The gist of the Keynesian system is that changes in consumption, investment, and government spending can effectively be used to expand or lower the level of income in the economy. Money can and most often does work within the Keynesian sphere to allow income changes as well. Changes in the money supply often directly influence both the business and household sectors in their investment and consumption decisions.

An increase in the supply of money will lower the interest rate (see Figure 10), just as (*ceteris paribus*) any increase in supply will decrease the price of a product. As Figure 10 shows, an increase in $M_s$ from $M_{s0}$ to $M_{s1}$ lowers interest rates from $r_0$ to $r_1$. These interest rates and the demand for investment are shown in Figure 11. As money becomes "cheaper," investors reconsider their present levels of investment. Low interest rates will encourage businesses to borrow from commercial banks and to spend these funds on new buildings and equipment (i.e., investment); high rates, on the other hand, deter investment decisions. This is expressed graphically in Figure 11 as an inverse relationship between the rate of interest ($r$) and the level of investment ($I$, or $I = f(r)$. As the interest rate falls from $r_0$ to $r_1$, investment (in housing, equipment, or plants) will expand from $I_0$ to $I_1$.

Returning to the Keynesian model developed in the last two chapters, we can again examine the effect of an increase in investment. This time, however, the investment increase is stimulated by a reduction in the interest rate, generated by an increase in the money supply (see Figure 10). As the money supply increases from $M_{s0}$ to $M_{s1}$ in Figure 10, the interest rate decreases from $r_0$ to $r_1$. As this occurs, investment increases from $I_0$ to $I_1$ (see Figure 11). Finally, this increased investment, working through the multiplier, generates a new higher income level, $Y_1$ as in Figure 12. (Remember, $I_1 - I_0 = \Delta I$, $Y_1 - Y_0 = \Delta Y$, and $\Delta Y = k \times \Delta I$.)

 10. When the Fed decreases the money supply, what happens to interest rates? The level of investment? The level of income? Employment?

**FIGURE 11**  The Interest-Investment Relationship

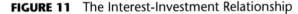

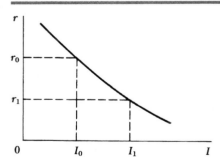

**FIGURE 12**   Income Response to a Change in Investment

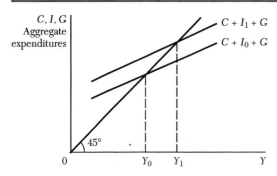

## The Liquidity Trap

Keynes relied more on fiscal policy for the stimulation of aggregate expenditures because he expected that during times of depression the economy would operate in the area of the liquidity trap. In this area, no matter how much the money supply increased, the rate of interest would fall no lower. And the business community's grim expectations of the future would discourage any further investment activity, even with low rates of interest. As we can see in Figure 13, changes in the money supply within the range of the liquidity trap will have no effect on interest rates. And if interest rates are unchanged, the levels of investment and income also will remain the same, yielding no effect on aggregate expenditures. For example, as interest rates in Japan fell to almost zero in 2001, some characterized Japan as experiencing a liquidity trap at that time.

Keynes also believed that business and consumer expectations could change during depressions, thereby thwarting the effect of monetary policy. For these reasons, economists often say that increasing the money stock to increase investment is much like pushing on a string. In *The General Theory*, Keynes expressed substantial doubt about the ability of monetary policy—a policy that changes the money supply—to rescue the economy from a severe depression. Yet, during the past four decades, we have seen the power of monetary policy to affect the levels of aggregate expenditures in the economy. During this period, the Fed has played an active role in determining aggregate expenditures, a practice that has

**FIGURE 13**   Money Supply Increase in the Liquidity Trap

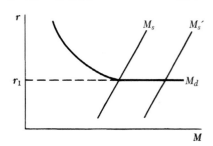

drawn frequent criticism. Still, monetary policy has continued to be an important tool for economic stabilization.

# MONETARY POLICY

Some critics have argued that the Fed is too powerful, too independent, and too business-oriented. Others believe that the money supply is much too important to be left to the discretion of mere mortals. In this section, we shall examine the tools that enable the Federal Reserve to control the supply of money and credit in the economy and outline effects of international markets. After a review of the Greenspan years, we shall examine recent Federal Reserve policy and the interaction between monetary and fiscal policy.

## Tools of the Trade

To affect the level of income in the economy, the Fed has at hand several tools. The two primary tools are (1) reserve requirement changes and (2) open-market operations. On occasion—for example, during World War II—the Fed has implemented several selective credit controls on home mortgages and consumer credit. The only credit control that it regularly uses is the margin requirement for stocks, which stipulates the percentages of payment that must be in cash on any security purchase. In March 1980, the Fed responded to President Carter's request for tighter credit to help quell the inflationary trends by announcing new controls on consumer and business credit. It quickly withdrew these controls when evidence showed they were dramatically worsening the recession of 1980. In 2008 and 2009 the Fed extented its power considerably, introducing a number of new tools to stem the growing financial crisis and ensure the stability of the financial system. The Fed can also use moral suasion in pursuit of its economic goals; that is, it can attempt to persuade relevant economic actors to engage in or refrain from certain activities. Since 2003, changes in another tool, the discount rate, have been pegged to the fed funds rate (see below).

**Reserve Requirements.** As we saw earlier in Table 1, each depository institution must keep a reserve requirement at the Federal Reserve or as cash in vault. The Board of Governors of the Federal Reserve can change the levels of reserves required at any time. In general, the central bank views its ability to change reserve requirements as its most powerful tool and uses this tool with utmost discretion. Since a change in reserve requirements of only 1 percent alters the monetary situation geometrically, changes in reserve requirements have been infrequent since 1935, when this tool became available. In more recent years the Fed has altered the size of liabilities on which reserves are held.

Critics claim that this tool works like an ax rather than a scalpel. An example shows why. Assume the Fed wants to restrict economic activity by reducing the money supply (e.g., to fight inflation). If banking assets are at $400 billion with 10 percent reserve requirements, some $40 billion is being held as reserves. If reserve requirements are increased by 1 percent, to 11 percent, some $44 billion must be held. This takes $4 billion out of the money supply immediately, as loans and investments are called in to increase reserves to the new level. More would be taken out of the system later through multiple deposit contraction—the reverse of the multiple deposit expansion explained previously.

---

11. In the example just given, what might happen to interest rates? Why?

12. What would happen if reserve requirements were lowered by 1 percent? How much would member banks be required to hold? What would happen to the "extra" money (or excess reserves)?

---

An increase in reserve requirements can absorb large changes in *excess reserves*, or additional moneys held by depository institutions, such as those that occurred during the 1930s when substantial amounts of gold flowed into the country. A reduction in the reserve requirement may offset a large loss in reserves. In either case, a change in reserve requirements announces a change in Fed policy to the public as well as to the banks and other depository institutions. Critics of the Fed suggest that other means are more appropriate for the announcement of policy changes.

**Open-Market Operations.** The Fed is engaged daily in **open-market operations** through the activities of the Federal Reserve Open Market Committee. Activities in the open market involve purchases and sales of government bonds, bills, and notes at the Federal Reserve Bank of New York. These actions affect the money supply as well as interest rates. To increase the money supply and economic activity (e.g., to combat recession), the Fed actively buys bonds (Treasury issues). Buying bonds takes them out of the hands of the banks and other depository institutions and increases the money supply by exchanging the bonds for money (in the form of a check or cash from the Fed). If, on the other hand, the Fed wants to reduce the money stock, it will step up bond *sales* to commercial banks and other depository institutions, this time increasing the holding of bonds at banks and decreasing their holding of reserves.

As discussed in the box below titled "Interest Rates, Bond Prices, and the Money Supply," the effect on interest rates of these bond sales and purchases is inversely related to the money supply. When bond sales reduce the money stock, interest rates must increase in order to attract businesses as well as households to purchase the bond offerings. Otherwise, investors would place their funds elsewhere. Bond sales, then, encourage interest rates upward as they compete with other assets for the public's cash balances. Once the sales have been made, the interest rate will also rise because of the shortage of money.

Open-market operations are the Fed's most important tool. They take place on a day-to-day basis, and the Fed's Open Market Committee meets regularly to decide how open-market operations should affect the money supply and interest rates.

---

13. How do bond purchases by the Fed affect interest rates in the economy? Why?

---

## Interest Rates, Bond Prices, and the Money Supply

We can use an example to illustrate how the interest rate is related to the price of bonds and to the purchase of a bond by the Federal Reserve. First, assume you receive a $100 government bond for your birthday. In the fine print on this bond, the U.S. government promises to pay you $100 at the end of ten years. Obviously, the people who gave you the bond did not pay $100 for something that is worth $100 at the end of ten years; they paid less.

To find the price they paid, we can examine a present-value table such as Table 3. The *present value* of your $100 bond payable in ten years is the amount it is worth today; more generally, present value is what a dollar at the end of a specified future year is worth today. Examining the abbreviated present-value table in Table 3, we find that the present value depends on the interest rate. At an interest rate of 10 percent, the present value is $38.50; if the interest rate were 15 percent, the price of the bond would be $24.70. As the interest rate rises (from 10 to 15 percent), the price of the $100 bond falls (from $38.50 to $24.70). There is an inverse relation between the rate of return (interest rate) and the price of the bond. In essence, the bondholder earns interest on the bond every year it is held.

When the Federal Reserve purchases bonds (not $100 savings bonds, but $100,000 and larger denominations of U.S. Treasury bonds, notes, and bills) in the open market in order to increase the money supply, the demand for bonds increases, so the price of bonds rises (Figure 14). The interest rate is inversely related to price, so the interest rate falls. Thus, as the Fed buys bonds, increasing the money supply, interest rates fall.

**Table 3** Present Value of $100.00

| | Interest Rate | | | |
|---|---|---|---|---|
| Year | 3% | 7% | 10% | 15% |
| 1 | 97.10 | 93.50 | 90.90 | 87.00 |
| 2 | 94.30 | 87.30 | 82.60 | 75.60 |
| 3 | 91.50 | 81.60 | 75.10 | 65.80 |
| 4 | 88.90 | 76.30 | 68.30 | 57.20 |
| 5 | 86.30 | 71.30 | 62.00 | 49.70 |
| 6 | 83.80 | 66.66 | 56.40 | 43.20 |
| 7 | 81.30 | 62.30 | 51.30 | 37.60 |
| 8 | 78.90 | 58.20 | 46.60 | 32.60 |
| 9 | 76.60 | 54.40 | 42.40 | 28.40 |
| 10 | 74.40 | 50.80 | 38.50 | 24.70 |

*Note*: The formula for finding the present value entries in the table is $P = R/(1 + r)^t$. The present value, $P$, equals the future return, $R$ (in this case, $100), divided by $(1 + \text{rate of interest})^t$, where $t$ is the number of years to maturity. (In our example, $t = 10$ years.)

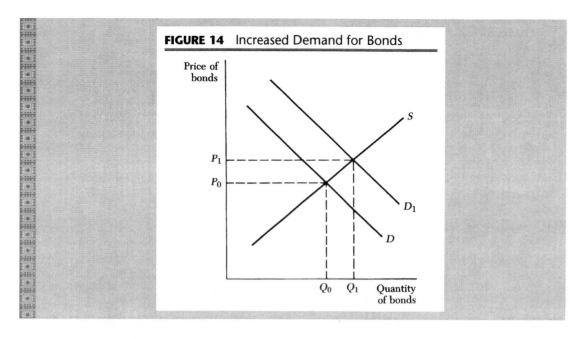

**FIGURE 14** Increased Demand for Bonds

**The Discount Rate.** The Federal Reserve also establishes the **discount rate**—the rate at which a bank or depository institution can borrow from the Fed. Often, institutions borrow from the Fed to protect their reserve position. They typically present collateral consisting of bonds, which the Fed discounts for short-term borrowing purposes. In 2003 the Fed adopted a policy that "tied" the discount rate to the fed funds rate (see below). If the Fed increases the fed funds target rate, for most banks and other depository institutions the discount rate will be 1 percent greater than the fed funds target. This will ensure that funds are available when there might be a shortage of liquidity within the banking system. This rate is called the *primary credit rate*.

In "emergency" situations, the Fed may serve as "the lender of last resort," with the discount rate historically providing liquidity. The Fed stood ready in this capacity immediately after the stock market crash of October 1987. Alan Greenspan, then chairman of the Fed's Board of Governors, issued the following statement on the day following the crash: "The Federal Reserve, consistent with its responsibilities as the nation's central bank, affirmed today its readiness to serve as a source of liquidity to support the economic and financial system." This brief statement seemed to reassure financial markets, particularly as the Fed took necessary actions to ensure adequate liquidity to the financial system. To calm the uncertainty accompanying the terror attacks of September 11, 2001, Greenspan issued a similar statement, again ensuring liquidity.

**The Fed Funds Rate.** For more than two decades, the interest rate on federal funds (fed funds) instruments has played an important role in Federal Reserve monetary policy. The fed funds instruments are overnight or very short-term loans in which one bank lends another some of its deposits at the Fed. (Typically, these deposits are at the Fed to meet reserve requirements.) If a bank has deposited more money at the Fed than is necessary to meet its reserve requirements, the bank may lend those excess deposits to banks needing additional reserves. The **fed funds rate** is the interest rate that banks charge when they lend these reserves for short periods of time. The Fed can "target" the fed funds rate by using its reserve requirement and open-market operations tools. In recent years, the Federal Reserve Open Market Committee has voted to raise or lower targets for the fed funds rate. The Fed usually uses open-market operations to meet the fed funds target rate.

## Lags in Monetary Policy

As is true with fiscal policy, lags or delays are inherent in monetary actions. Economists have classified these lags into two major types: the *inside lag* and the *outside lag*. The inside lag comprises a *recognition lag* (the time it takes for the Federal Reserve authorities to recognize there is a problem in the economy) and an *action lag* (the time of recognition until the time some policy is implemented). These lags are usually a function of measurement and forecasting.

After the action takes place, there is an outside lag before the impact of the policy (either partial or total) is felt in the economy. The length of impact lags is a subject of dispute among economists and economic models. Monetarists—economists who favor monetary policies over fiscal policies—argue that the impact lag with monetary actions is much shorter than the one estimated by their Keynesian counterparts.

## Monetary Policy in an Open Economy

Monetary policy has two types of effects on international markets in an open economy. One is an interest effect, similar to but not the same as that experienced in fiscal policy in an international environment. The second is an effect on prices due to monetary changes.

If the Fed takes some policy action to increase the money supply (to expand the economy), interest rates will fall. In international financial markets, demand for U.S. assets, which yield a return attached to this lower interest rate, will decline. This will decrease the demand for dollars, shifting the dollar demand curve to the left, such as the shift from $D_0$ to $D_1$ in Figure 15. At the same time, because of the lower interest rates, U.S. investors will seek higher-yielding securities in the international arena. As U.S. citizens trade their dollars or dollar-denominated securities for higher-yielding foreign securities, the supply of dollars in the international market will increase, shifting the dollar supply curve to the right (the shift from $S_0$ to $S_1$ in Figure 15). These changes in the demand for and supply of dollars in the international financial markets will depreciate the value of the dollar (bid the value of the dollar down with respect to other currencies currently in demand).

This lower-valued dollar will create a demand for U.S. exports, since they are now cheaper to foreign citizens. At the same time, imports into the United States will decline, since imports now cost more of the lower-valued dollar. Net exports

**FIGURE 15** Demand and Supply of Dollars in the International Market

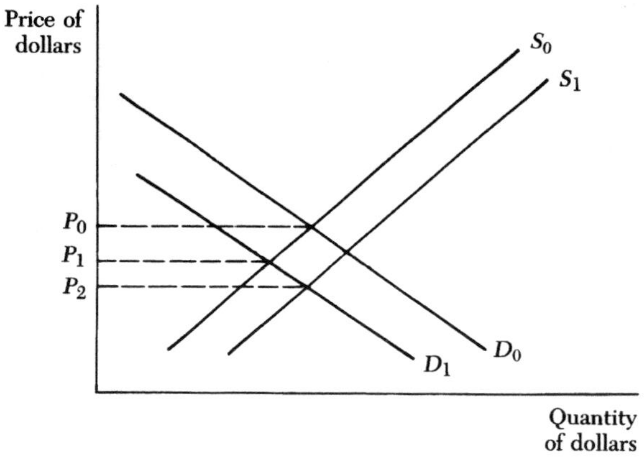

(X – M) will rise. This increases aggregate expenditures and income, thus reinforcing the monetary expansion also designed to increase aggregate expenditures.

Monetary policy will also produce a long-run price effect in the international financial markets. To the extent to which increases in the money supply lead to increases in domestic prices, foreign exchange markets of U.S. trading partners will be affected. If the increase in the money supply brings about a 5 percent increase in prices of domestic products, this price increase will be felt in both domestic and international markets.

Let's look at the effect of this type of policy on trade between the United States and Japan. A 5 percent increase in the price of U.S. products will decrease the demand for or purchase of U.S. products by the Japanese (assuming an elastic demand for U.S. exports). This will cause a decrease in the demand for dollars, since the Japanese are purchasing fewer U.S. goods. This decrease causes the demand curve for dollars to shift to the left (from $D_0$ to $D_1$ in Figure 15). At the same time, a 5 percent increase in domestic prices makes Japanese products relatively less expensive in the United States. As U.S. consumers increase their demand for Japanese products, they supply more dollars to the international market, thus shifting the supply curve for dollars to the right, as in Figure 15.

Both of these actions serve to lower the value of the dollar and appreciate the value of the yen. From here on out, consumer reactions are reversed. The Japanese will resume purchasing U.S. products. Although prices did increase, the yen appreciation offsets this price increase. Likewise, demand for Japanese products will fall back to previous levels. Despite the price effects produced by monetary policy, after currency adjustments, the level of exports and imports should remain about the same.

14. After income has increased due to monetary expansion, what will be the reaction in international markets?

## A Brief History of Monetary Policy

The Fed has powerful tools, and its independence gives it the authority to carry out the monetary policy it views as best. During the 1950s and 1960s, the Fed followed its collective instinct in managing money matters. After economists severely criticized this policy in the mid-1960s, the Fed began to target interest rate levels in adjusting the nation's money supply. This type of policy, despite outcries from monetarists, continued until the fall of 1979. Monetarists believe that control of the nation's money supply is far more important than control of interest rates. In contrast, the Keynesians rely heavily on interest rates to transmit the effects of monetary policy to the economy.

In 1982, amidst low inflation and economic recession, the Fed, under chairman Paul Volcker, began increasing the monetary growth rate and paid more attention to interest rate targets. Low inflation continued and, coupled with economic growth, left the recession of the early 1980s behind. By 1987, when Alan Greenspan assumed the chairmanship of the Fed's Board of Governors, the economic recovery was into its fifth year.

## Greenspan's Fed: 1987–2005

Looking for a conservative Republican to replace Paul Volcker as chairman of the Federal Reserve Board of Governors, the Reagan administration in 1987 turned to Alan Greenspan. Greenspan had served as chair of the Council of Economic Advisors beginning in 1974 under President Nixon and continuing through the Ford administration. Known as a meticulous observer and student of statistical data of all economic markets, Greenspan played a more activist role in fine-tuning the economy, carefully watching leading indicators that might suggest greater levels of inflation. Indeed, the first Bush administration criticized his tolerance of higher interest rates at the expense of slower economic growth and argued that the Fed did not do enough to lower interest rates to ward off the recession of the early 1990s.

Fed policy actions during the Greenspan years were often credited for bringing economic stability in the late 1980s and setting the stage for economic growth between 1995 and 1999. As illustrated in Figure 16, Greenspan's Fed

**FIGURE 16**  Federal Open Market Committee (FOMC) Intended Federal Funds Rate, and Discount Rate, and Primary Credit Rate

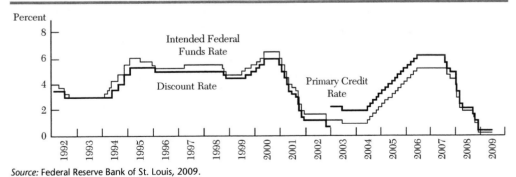

*Source:* Federal Reserve Bank of St. Louis, 2009.

raised the fed funds and discount rates to reduce inflationary tendencies during the late 1980s. During the recession of 1990–1991, the Fed lowered these rates. The series of prolonged reductions in the fed funds targets and discount rates helped the economy to rebound into a period of prolonged economic growth, which continued into 2001. Fear of inflation began to spread in the mid-1990s, and between 1994 and 2000, the Fed responded by increasing the fed funds targets and discount rates several times. The Fed continued to monitor for potential inflationary activity until early 2001 as the technology bubble collapsed, when it abruptly lowered the discount rate and fed funds targets, hoping to avert a serious economic downturn, and continued lowering the targets until mid-2004, when growth expanded and inflationary pressures returned in the form of higher oil prices. The Fed quickly targeted a higher fed funds rate.

15. Why can't the Fed target both the money supply and interest rates?

16. Plot what has happened to the general level of interest rates and to $M_1$ and $M_2$ since this book has been published. (This information is published monthly in the *Federal Reserve Bulletin*.) What does the Fed appear to have been targeting?

In the mid-1990s, the press portrayed Greenspan as the "poster boy for the new economy." Economic growth was exploding at a rate of 6.5 percent. The Fed helped the U.S. economy maintain growth in spite of currency crises in Mexico, Asia, Russia, and Latin America, as well as fears of a "Y2K" meltdown of computer systems at the turn of the millennium in the United States and abroad. During this period, a hedge fund called Long Term Capital Management made massive money-losing speculative transactions in financial instruments of the Russian, Asian, and Latin American markets.[*] The New York Fed helped to avoid panic by orchestrating a bailout of the fund by private companies.

By early 2001, however, many who had sung Greenspan's praises were wondering whether he had lost his touch and reacted too slowly. Greenspan's Fed tried to engineer a "soft landing" for the economy, which would see continuing growth, albeit at a slower rate. The stock market, as described in the next section, declined dramatically and the economy abruptly slowed, with unemployment rising to 6 percent in 2003. Monetary policy kept interest rates low and while business investment lagged, consumer spending continued. Housing construction and mortgage refinancing led some to conclude that a "bubble" might have developed in the housing sector—as housing "wealth" fueled consumption expenditures and consumer borrowing. Economic growth rebounded and in late 2004 the Fed initiated policies to target higher interest rates as raw material and oil prices increased inflationary expectations. Through all of this, Greenspan, initially appointed to chair the Fed by President Reagan in 1987, ended his career at the Fed on January 31, 2006, and was succeeded by Ben Bernanke.

---

[*]Hedge funds engage in very speculative trades (or "bets") for wealthy individuals. They remain largely unregulated.

### Bernanke's Fed

In the fall of 2005, President George W. Bush announced his choice of Ben S. Bernanke to replace Alan Greenspan as chairman of the Board of Governors of the Fed and President Obama has recommended renewal of his appointment. The former Princeton University professor has held many Federal Reserve roles and his nomination was easily approved by Congress. Before his appointment, Bernanke favored a program of "inflation targeting," which has been adopted by both the European Central Bank and by the Bank of England. Time will tell if inflation targets become part of U.S. Federal Reserve policy making. Bernanke's Fed continued to target higher fed funds rates through the end of 2007.

The financial crisis that emerged at the end of 2007 sent the fed funds rate plummeting. It reached a 0.5 to zero percent target by the end of 2008 and remained at that target through 2009.

17. Are you convinced that there is a relationship between the money supply and prices? Why or why not?

18. Have inflation rates increased? What is the current inflation rate?

19. What Federal Reserve policies helped the United States avoid a recession since 2009? Were there two consecutive quarters of negative growth in the economy?

## Stock Markets Bubble Trouble in the Greenspan Era

In early October 1987, the Dow Jones Industrial Average (one measure of U.S. stock market performance) was at 2,700 points. On October 19, 1987, two months after Greenspan was sworn in as chairman of the Federal Reserve Board of Governors, the Dow dropped 508 points, losing $1 trillion in (paper) wealth and 20 percent of its value. By the end of the month, the Dow stood at just 1,700.

The Greenspan Fed moved to ensure liquidity of financial intermediaries and reassured the stumbling financial markets with a simple one-line statement reinforcing the Fed's role as a lender of last resort. This was enough to steady markets and begin an era that often characterized Greenspan as legendary—an almost mythical figure who steps in at exactly the right time to reassure the financial system.

Between 1991 and 1996, U.S. productivity boomed, reflecting growth in the high-technology "New Economy" sectors. The Dow Jones Industrial Average and the then-fledgling NASDAQ Composite Index (an index for the NASDAQ, an exchange for smaller, often high-tech companies' stocks) galloped to all-time highs. With the Dow reaching 10,000 points, Greenspan on December 5, 1996, tried to moderate the growth by referring to it as "irrational exuberance." Nevertheless, money continued to pour into the stock market, which reached a peak on March 10, 1999.

By many accounts, the rapid increases in stock prices during the late 1990s represented a "bubble" in the stock market. Bubbles are nothing new. In the late 1500s and early 1600s, speculation in tulip bulbs drove prices of some bulbs to exorbitant levels. Prices eventually crashed, and many speculators were left penniless. Similarly, as graphed in Figure 17, a bubble in the

Dow grew and burst between 1924 and 1932, and Japan's Nikkei stock average experienced a bubble between 1982 and 2001. The NASDAQ's bubble also burst. Between the end of 2000 and beginning of 2001, investors in U.S. stock markets lost more than $5.2 trillion of (paper) wealth. Some critics blamed Greenspan for the accompanying slowdown in the economy. We must be careful, however, not to confuse stock market performance with economic performance. The stock market is just one part of the U.S. economy.

Between 2001 and March 2004, the NASDAQ and Dow recovered from their 2001 lows. But, as the Federal Reserve prepared to pare the growth of the money supply and increase interest rates, stock market volatility resumed. As interest rates began to rise, concern arose that the developing housing bubble might crash and dampen the longer-run future of an economic recovery as consumers faced the repayment of high debt levels and potentially lower home values. By the end of 2006, housing prices began to fall and inventories of unsold housing grew significantly. The housing market did crash with an estimated $7 trillion in lost house wealth due to lower prices. The Dow also suffered a more than 50 percent decline between October 2007 and March 2009.

**FIGURE 17**   Stock Market Bubbles

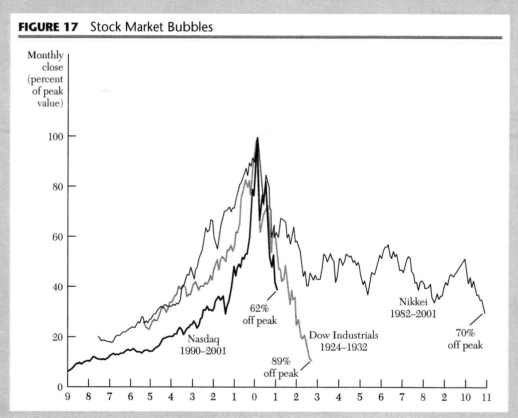

Source: Data from *Investor's Business Daily*, Vol. 17, No. 240, 2001 and Dow reports. Copyright © 2001 Investor's Business Daily, Inc. Reprinted with permission.

# ENTERING THE GLOBAL FINANCIAL CRISIS: THE COLLAPSE OF THE HOUSING BUBBLE, 2007–2009

After the technology, or .com bubble burst in 2000, the Federal Reserve began increasing the supply of money to ensure enough liquidity to avoid a recession, as people with stock wealth lost an estimated $7 trillion. The Fed continued to lower the fed funds target rate through 2004, also responding to the economic downturn after the terror attacks of September 11, 2001 (see Figure 6). Earlier in this chapter we noted that as the money supply increases interest rates fall, and as interest rates fall there is more borrowing for investment and for consumer spending. Since the Federal Reserve made funds widely available, financial intermediaries (such as banks) lent to customers wanting to purchase consumer goods, as well as build and purchase homes. Shortly thereafter, some economists warned of a housing bubble that was building in the United States and in several European countries. Rising house prices helped homeowners feel wealthier, and those who lost wealth as stock prices crashed after the technology bubble regained wealth as they watched equity in their houses increase. Between 2002 and 2006, home prices rose far faster than the historical average and were rising faster than the cost of rental homes as well—indicating that the price increase was not because of a limited supply of housing. As house prices rose, some homeowners increased their consumption, often borrowing funds based on their increased home value; others opted to purchase larger homes, while others entered a housing market that had heretofore eluded them because of low income or poor credit. This increased borrowing by individuals who might not be able to repay these loans, and financial intermediaries lending to these borrowers, contributed to the global financial crisis that began in late 2007, but other factors were even more important.

Banks try to lend to the best customers first. There is less risk that these borrowers will default on loan payments. These are individuals with a good credit rating, who pay bills on time, and who have an income stream large enough to ensure loan repayment. After the "good borrower" market is saturated and if funds are still available to lend, banks lend to higher-risk borrowers. Between 2000 and 2007, an abundant money supply and low interest rates ensured that financial institutions had ample funds for lending. Banks and mortgage companies began to lend to "subprime" borrowers—those with a poor credit rating or without a wage or income stream that would suggest with certainty that the borrowed funds could be repaid. Most of these subprime loans had variable interest rates; that is, the interest rate on the loan changed as interest rates changed in the economy. While interest rates remained low, subprime borrowers could more than likely make loan payments. When interest rates rose, however, the amount owed on these loans increased, making it harder for people who had taken on larger mortgage obligations to make monthly payments on the loan. As long as housing prices continued to rise and interest rates remained low, loan payments were made. Homeowners were participating in the "American Dream" of owning their own home, or owning an even larger home, and some speculators were hoping for quick profits from rising house prices.

But why would banks and mortgage institutions lend to subprime, high-risk borrowers? First of all, financial institutions had a lot of funds to lend. A low fed funds target rate generated increased liquidity through the money supply, and, at the same time Asian countries and Middle East oil-producing countries transferred surplus funds from international trade into the United States. A second reason was *securitization*: the bundling of various kinds of loans (mortgage loans, credit card loans, auto loans, etc.) and "repackaging" them into instruments with characteristics borrowers might want. The repackaged loans are then resold as bonds or collateralized mortgage obligations (CMOs) to investors, who are often other financial intermediaries. A bank that lent funds to a subprime borrower might quickly sell that loan to another financial intermediary (perhaps an investment bank) for repackaging. Thus, despite having made the loan, the bank would no longer hold any risk from that loan. With securitization there was little reason for mortgage lenders to care whether a loan they made would be repaid or not. After all, the loan is very quickly moved out of the lender's portfolio.

Still, the effects of the housing market collapse on the economy would have been much milder if it was simply high-risk or subprime borrowers not repaying loans on houses. The economy would have experienced a mild downturn rather than a great recession. Indeed, other financial innovations (besides securitization) caused the deepening and widening of the crisis that propelled not only the United States but other economies of the world into the deepest recession since the Great Depression.

Some financial intermediaries (such as investment banks Goldman Sachs, Lehman Brothers and Bear Sterns, and the insurance giant AIG) created a financial instrument called a credit default swap (CDS). Credit default swaps were sold to institutions purchasing bonds or CMOs that were based on mortgages (some subprime) as the underlying asset. These CDSs basically "insured" purchasers if there was a default on the instrument (the bond or the CMO), or if the institution issuing the bond or the CMO went out of business. These CDSs were complex (often running hundreds of pages) and were ultimately "bets." Purchasers of CDSs were betting that if there were defaults on the subprime mortgages that comprised the securitized loans they purchased (as bonds and CMOs), the CDSs would pay off. Issuers of the CDSs were "betting" that the subprime mortgages would be paid. CDS issuers were also firms that bundled and sold securitized loans. To attract buyers to purchase a bundle of loans (as a bond or CMO), financial institutions such as Bear Stearns, Lehman Brothers, and Citibank would also offer to sell a CDS to the purchaser. This certainly made purchasing bonds or CMOs containing subprime loans more attractive because of the risk. A default on the estimated $1.3 trillion of subprime loans would have caused a setback for the U.S. economy, but with an estimated $600 trillion of unregulated CDSs sold worldwide, a financial crisis ensued, followed by the Great Recession.

In early 2007 there were some signs (including financial institution failures) that something might be amiss in financial markets, but authorities didn't seem to recognize the potential severity of the problem until late in 2008. In March 2008, investment bank Bear Stearns suffered great losses from the sale of CMOs and CDSs. The Fed agreed to absorb $30 billion in Bear Stearns liabilities before JP Morgan Chase purchased the company at a fire sale price. By September, other Wall Street and Main Street financial institutions were also under pressure. Lehman Brothers went into bankruptcy, while Merrill Lynch sold itself to Bank of America and Wachovia sold itself to Wells Fargo. By the end of the month, all remaining major investment banks in the United States had reorganized as bank holding companies, making them eligible for Federal Reserve loans. The Fed also bailed out the insurance giant American International Group (AIG), as its losses in the CDS market continued to mount.

Between 2008 and mid-2009, some 87 bank failures were reported. This compares to no failures between 2003 and 2004 and three in 2007.

*Source:* Toles © 2009 The Washington Post. Reprinted by permission of Universal Uclick. All rights reserved.

# FEDERAL RESERVE RESPONSE TO THE FINANCIAL CRISIS

Financial institutions in the United States (and throughout the world) responded to the growing crisis in late 2008 by refusing to lend—thus freezing credit markets. Loans dried up—even to the best borrowers. This meant that businesses relying on loans for investments or inventory purchases could not make those investments or replace depleted inventories. The Federal Reserve immediately reduced the fed funds rate (see Figure 6), hoping to unfreeze credit markets by pouring liquidity into the financial system. By the end of 2008, the Fed had more than doubled the funds on which the money supply is based. It had extended loans to banks and other financial institutions and purchased commercial paper (IOUs issued by one firm and purchased by another). It had expanded the monetary policy tools beyond open market operations, the discount rate, and reserve requirements. The list now includes the tools below.

Each of the tools listed in the box below were created by the Federal Reserve to add additional liquidity into the financial system and to reduce the possibility of a system collapse. Figure 17 illustrates the size of Fed actions through these tools in nominal dollars.

---

## Federal Reserve Monetary Tools Created in Response to the 2007–2009 Financial Crisis

- ❖ *Interest on Required Reserve Balances and Excess Balances*—Interest that eliminates an implied tax on required reserves and excess reserves.
- ❖ *Term Auction Facility*—Allows the Fed to auction term funds to depository institutions.
- ❖ *Primary Dealer Credit Facility*—Allows the Fed to give overnight loans to primary bond dealers to facilitate the operation of financial markets.
- ❖ *Term Securities Lending Facility*—Promotes liquidity and aids the functioning of financial markets by offering to loan Treasury securities held by the Fed against eligible collateral.
- ❖ *ABCP MMMF Liquidity Facility*—The asset-backed commercial paper money market mutual fund liquidity facility provides additional liquidity by allowing the Fed to lend to depository institutions and bank holding companies for the purchase of high-quality commercial paper from money market mutual funds if certain conditions are met.
- ❖ *Commercial Paper Funding Facility*—Another measure for the Fed to provide liquidity to the commercial paper market.
- ❖ *Money Market Investor Funding Facility*—Allows the Fed to provide liquidity to investors in the U.S. money market.
- ❖ *Term Asset-Backed Securities Loan Facility*—A funding facility supported by the Troubled Asset Relief Program (see below) designed to help depository institutions meet the credit needs of households and small businesses.

*Source:* http://www.federalreserve.gov/monetarypolicy/ abcpmmmmf.html. For a more complete description of these new monetary policy tools, go to the web site.

# THE **BIG** PICTURE

## Financial Crisis 101

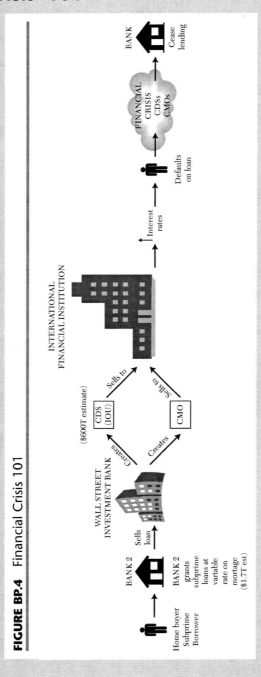

**FIGURE BP.4** Financial Crisis 101

**FIGURE 17** Bailout Costs vs Big Historical Events

Bear Stearns

Asset-Backed Commercial Paper

Term Discount Window Program

Money Market Mutual Fund Liquidity Facility

Primary Dealer Credit Facility

Money Market Investor Funding Facility

Fannie Mae, and Freddie Mac

Expansion of Swap Lines

Term Auction Facility

$50 billion

Term Securities Lending Facility

AIG bailout

Commercial Paper Funding Facility

Term Asset-Backed Securities Loan Facility

Race to the Moon

S&L Crisis

Korean War

Marshall Plan

Louisiana Purchase

Invasion of Iraq

Vietnam War

The New Deal

**Occured over 12 months**　　　　**Occured over 206 years**

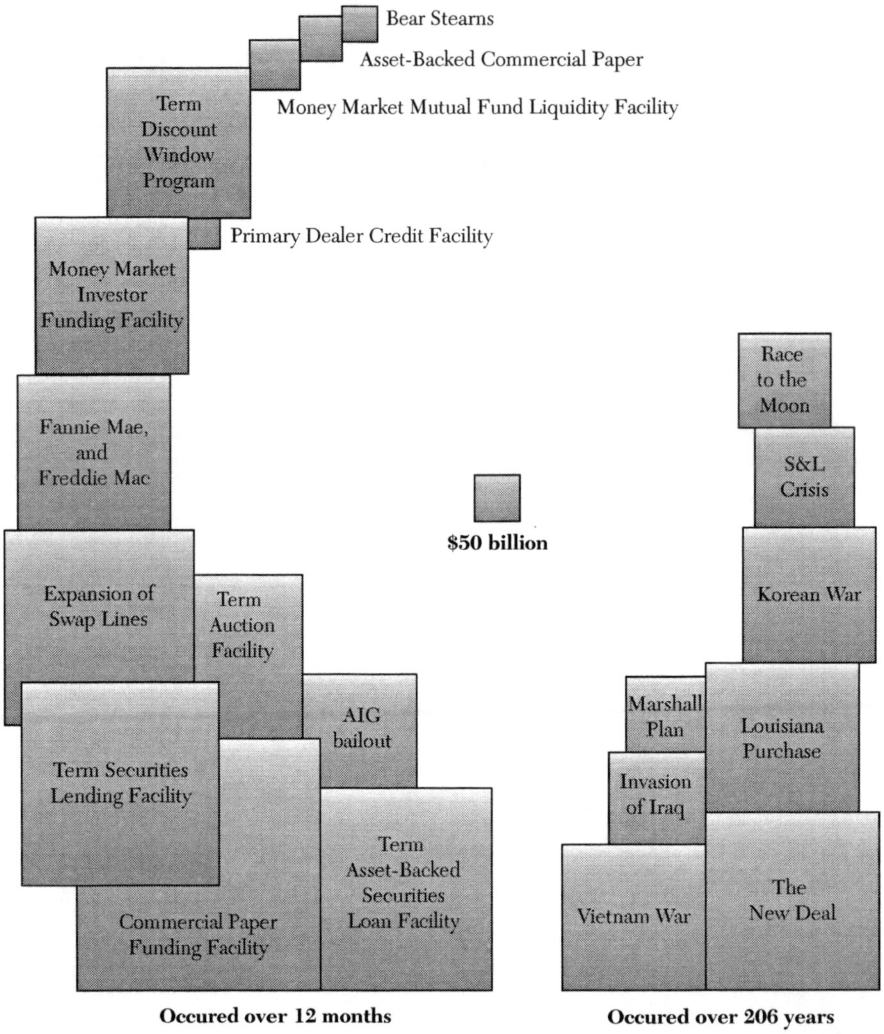

*Source:* http://www.ritholtz.com/blog/2009/06/bailout-costs-vs-big-historical-events/, Barry Ritholtz–June 18th, 2009.

# THE TREASURY BAILOUT PLAN—EESA AND TARP

As uncertainty continued throughout the world, financial markets and officials at the U.S. Treasury also responded to the growing financial crisis. In early October, Congress passed the Emergency Economic Stabilization Act (EESA) of 2008. The EESA authorized the Treasury to spend $700 billion under the Troubled Asset Relief Program (TARP). The first TARP funds were aimed at unfreezing credit markets by injecting funds into the largest banks in the United States chiefly through the purchase of preferred stock in those banks. The Treasury continued to purchase shares in large and smaller banks as well. Despite this infusion of funds, credit was slow to expand. Initially the program was set up to purchase "troubled" or so-called "toxic" assets and sell those assets in private auctions, but as of mid-2009 the details for that program were still being worked out. TARP funds were also used as loans to ailing auto companies General Motors and Chrysler and to AIG. Additional programs have emerged under TARP to help homeowners refinance mortgages, unfreeze credit markets for student and small business loans, and continue investment in institutions the Treasury deems important to U.S. financial stability.

# MONETARY AND FISCAL POLICY

Models constructed to measure the effectiveness of monetary and fiscal policy yield different results if underlying assumptions used in the models differ. Monetarists emphasize velocity as the mode of transmission, and the Keynesians stress the rate of interest.

Monetarists assume that there can be no effective expansion of fiscal policy unless it is accompanied by an increase in the money supply. Why? The government *must* finance its expenditures with increases in taxes or by debt issue. Either method transfers money from one sector of the economy to another. As government spending proceeds and GDP increases, if the money supply has not grown, consumers and investors will find themselves short of cash and will begin to try to increase their liquidity by selling their financial holdings. This will increase bond sales even further, driving the price of bonds down and the interest rate up. As the interest rate rises, business investors are crowded out of financial markets by the government, so GDP doesn't change. Spending is just transferred from one sector to another.

For Keynesians, however, the reason for government spending is to stimulate an economy in which neither business *nor* households are spending. The government at least gets the process started. Expansionary fiscal policy increases economic activity. This encourages spending by consumers and businesses in the future.

In practice, monetary policy is very effective at slowing the economy but not very effective when used to stimulate economic activity. The presence of an international sector tends to reinforce the income and output effects of monetary policy.

## Coordination of Monetary and Fiscal Policy

We have seen how monetary and fiscal policy may provide a powerful punch when used together to stimulate economic recovery. However, coordinating the two policies at times other than an economic and financial crisis may be problematic. Since the Fed determines monetary policy, and fiscal expenditures are in the hands of Congress and the president, policy decisions sometimes offset one another or are not complementary. For example, the Fed reacted to the high inflation rates of 1980 by attempting to reduce the money supply in order to decrease aggregate expenditures. On the other hand, Congress decreased taxes, which increased aggregate expenditures. High interest rates created by the tight money supply tended to counteract the desired investment effects from lower tax rates. The chairman of the Federal Reserve Board now regularly informs Congress of impending Fed action so that there are no surprises, but policies may still offset one another.

Some people have called for a reduction in the Fed's independence in order to achieve greater coordination of monetary and fiscal policies. Critics of this suggestion argue that to have either the legislative or the executive branch of the government control the Fed would make the money supply a political tool—as surely as many fiscal expenditures and taxing decisions already are. They argue that we could expect regular increases in the money supply in election years and decreases after elections. Whatever the solution, an effective economic policy clearly requires that monetary and fiscal policy at least be aimed in the same direction.

20. What is the Fed doing today to defeat the forces of inflation? Is its policy being coordinated with the executive branch?

21. What kinds of "political mischief" might occur if the monetary authority were controlled by the executive branch?

# Conclusion

*By examining the institution of money and the institutions that extend and regulate monetary instruments in the economy, we have discovered rather powerful tools by which the economy has been regulated over the past several decades. This regulation has focused on monetary ease during economic downturns and monetary restraint during periods of inflation. While monetary policy may have strong economic effects, changing institutions, financial instruments, lags, velocity changes, and internal financing of corporate investment may at times offset or thwart an intended monetary policy action.*

## Review Questions

**1.** Explain the differences among the transactions, precautionary, and speculative demands for money. List five factors that influence your demands for money.

**2.** Why is a barter economy unsuitable for today's world?

**3.** What is the difference between $M_1$ and $M_2$? Is it important to distinguish between them? Does it really matter what the money supply is? Discuss.

**4.** Suppose you discovered $50,000 of old dollars stuffed in a mattress in your dorm.
   a. What would be the effect of the $50,000 of "new money" on the banking system? Explain.
   b. What would be the effect if you spent the money on a new BMW?
   c. What if you stuffed the money back into the mattress?

**5.** How do the demands for money relate to Keynesian income and employment theory?

**6.** Which of the monetary policy tools is used most actively by the Fed? Under what situations would the Fed use another tool?

**7.** Why do monetarists argue that fiscal policy is ineffective in adjusting the economy?

**8.** What are some of the factors that inhibit the successful implementation of monetary policy?

**9.** In what kinds of situations is fiscal policy more effective than monetary policy? In what kinds of situations is monetary policy more effective than fiscal policy?

**10.** What would be some of the complications of finding the proper mix of monetary and fiscal policy?

**11.** If the economy were experiencing high unemployment and moderate inflation, what would be the appropriate monetary policy? Why?

# Aggregate Demand and Aggregate Supply

From Chapter 17 of *Economics: A Tool for Critically Understanding Society*, 9/e. Tom Riddell. Jean Shackelford. Geoffrey Schneider. Steve Stamos. Copyright © 2011 by Pearson Education. Published by Addison-Wesley. All rights reserved.

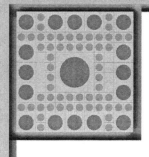

# Aggregate Demand and Aggregate Supply

## THE **BIG** PICTURE

***Introduction*** The building blocks of Keynesian macroeconomic theory include the multiplier, the components of aggregate expenditure, and financial markets. In this chapter we add another building block to our macroeconomic theory: the analysis of prices using a model of aggregate demand (AD) and aggregate supply (AS).

Although Keynes himself pointed out limitations to his theory of aggregate expenditures, the shortcoming of the Keynesian analysis that has most bothered modern economists is the lack of an analysis of prices. In the "real world" economy, since the 1960s, the United States has experienced price changes sometimes larger, sometimes smaller. These changes have occurred not just on certain goods and services, but across the whole economy. In this chapter, we will develop an analysis of aggregate demand and aggregate supply that allows us to illustrate how changes in economic policy or changes in other economic variables affect aggregate prices and output. From this analysis, we will be better able to examine the potential stabilizing effects of policy changes, an issue central to the ongoing debate over stabilization policy.

**Aggregate demand** is the total quantity of goods and services demanded by households, businesses, government, and the international sector at various prices. The aggregate demand curve illustrates the sum of these sector demands, showing the negative relationship between the aggregate output of goods and services, or real GDP demanded, and the overall price level. **Aggregate supply** is the total quantity of goods and services firms are willing to supply at varying price levels. The aggregate supply curve illustrates the relationship between the aggregate output supplied by all firms and the overall price level. The aggregate demand curve for the economy is downward sloping, while the aggregate supply curve generally illustrates a positive relationship between the price level and GDP, depending mostly on the time frame we choose to examine. Both Figure BP.1 and Figure 1 show the relationship between aggregate demand and aggregate supply. Equilibrium is the point where aggregate demand equals aggregate supply.

**FIGURE BP.1** Aggregate Demand and Aggregate Supply

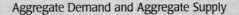

## AGGREGATE ANALYSIS

We will save derivation of the aggregate demand curve for a more advanced course in macroeconomic theory, but we will show logically why the curve is downward sloping and examine economic variables that are reflected by shifts in the aggregate demand curve. Recognizing that in macroeconomic theory, an analysis of supply has historically accompanied one of demand, we will then turn our attention to factors important to aggregate supply. We will also attempt to understand why supply policies are often precarious in their outcome. We will discuss the views of supply-side economists in the 1980s and the results of supply-side policies during the Reagan administration.

Aggregate demand has served as the center of economic theory and policy for the past four and a half decades, and Keynesian solutions have remained at the helm of economic thought and have often been preferred by policy makers. Our analysis of aggregate demand and aggregate supply will allow us to understand the role of economic policy variables as well as of supply shocks and productivity changes on real income and prices.

## AGGREGATE DEMAND

The aggregate demand curve relates the price level to real output (or real GDP) in the overall economy. It shows how the demand for goods and services varies with the price level. This is possible since all points on the aggregate demand curve are equilibrium points in both the money (financial) market and the market for goods and services. Exogenous changes in both the money and goods markets affect the aggregate demand curve and thus prices and real GDP.

Although this particular aggregate demand curve looks like a demand curve in microeconomics, it is very different. A price rise is not analogous to a jump in the price of butter that prompts us to switch to margarine

**FIGURE 1** Aggregate Demand and Aggregate Supply

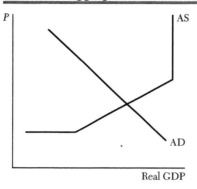

Real GDP

or some other substitute. A price increase signals that *all* domestic prices are rising, including the prices of domestically produced substitutes.

## Conditions for Goods and Money Market Equilibrium: A Review

Equilibrium positions in the goods market are found at every point on the aggregate demand curve. The components of the goods and services market are

$$C + I + G + (X - M) = \text{aggregate expenditures,}$$

where $C$ is consumption expenditures, $I$ is investment expenditures, $G$ is government expenditures, and $X - M$ is net foreign expenditures (net exports). This market is at equilibrium when aggregate expenditures equal aggregate output of goods and services.

In the money market, equilibrium is achieved when money supply equals money demand. The aggregate demand curve is derived from equilibrium conditions in both markets. Therefore, at any point on the aggregate demand curve, aggregate expenditures are equal to aggregate output, and money supply equals money demand.

Prices are measured by some weighted price index such as the GDP deflator, and are represented by $P$ on the vertical axis in Figure 2. Real income and output changes are represented by real GDP on the horizontal axis. We have assumed that the aggregate demand curve is downward sloping, showing an inverse relation between prices and real GDP. While we do not have all the tools necessary to derive this relationship here, we can intuitively show that this relationship is plausible by asking ourselves what happens to aggregate demand when there is a general rise in prices. If we aren't careful, however, we are likely to arrive at an answer that would yield a downward-sloping aggregate demand curve, but for the wrong reasons. Since our experience has been more as consumers rather than as economists, we are likely to conclude that a general rise in prices will decrease the real income of consumers, thus reducing consumption expenditures. Aggregate

**FIGURE 2** Aggregate Demand

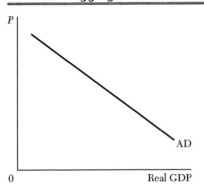

expenditures for goods and services would decline, leading to a decrease in GDP. But price increases yield additional revenues for producers, which they may share with the household sector through wage increases or higher dividends. If production is unchanged, then income would stay the same, so our assumption about the effect of an increase in the general price level on the goods market is a bit premature.

If, however, we look to the money or financial market, we will arrive at a better answer to our question about the slope of the aggregate demand curve. If there is a rise in prices, and if the Federal Reserve does not increase the growth rate in the money supply, the demand for money will increase, since consumers will need more money to keep their levels of consumption if velocity is constant. (With $M$ constant and $P$ rising, the demand for money increases.) As the demand for money rises, interest rates will rise. (Figure 3 shows that in response to an increase in the overall price level, money demand increases from $M_{D0}$ to $M_{D1}$ and with $M_s$ constant, interest rates rise from $r_0$ to $r_1$.) This means that less money is available at every interest rate for investment by the business sector (see Figure 4) and for expenditures by consumers. So, with everything else remaining the same, a rise in prices means that the same amount of (nominal) money balances must be used to purchase goods and services at higher

**FIGURE 3** Money Demand with a Price Increase

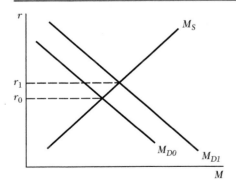

**FIGURE 4**  Demand for Investment Funds

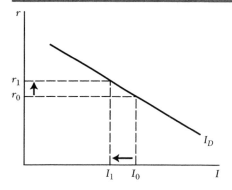

prices. Interest rates will be bid up, demand for funds for investment and consumption purposes will fall, and thus aggregate expenditures will fall. This analysis logically gives us the downward-sloping aggregate demand curve and the inverse relation between prices and real GDP. On the graph in Figure 5, we can see that a price increase from $P_0$ to $P_1$ decreases real GDP from $\text{GDP}_A$ to $\text{GDP}_B$, a movement from point $A$ to point $B$ on the aggregate demand curve.

Two other relationships explain the inverse relationship between prices and real GDP. As prices rise, the real wealth of people holding money balances declines. Those who are holding money balances cannot purchase the same quantity of goods and services as they did at lower prices, so the demand for goods and services falls, as does real GDP. Secondly, when prices increase in the United States, we can expect net exports $(X - M)$ to decline, since the prices of domestic goods have increased relative to foreign goods. U.S. exports are relatively more expensive, so the international market will demand fewer U.S. exports. Again, price increases will lower GDP—hence the movement from point $A$ to point $B$ in Figure 5.

Conversely, a decrease in the price level will raise the aggregate quantity of goods and services demanded. Three reasons account for this: The real interest rate falls due to a greater availability of money balances, since the real money

**FIGURE 5**  Movement Along the Aggregate Demand Curve

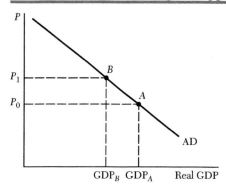

supply increases as prices fall. The real wealth of persons holding money balances increases when prices fall. Net exports increase as prices of domestic goods fall relative to prices of foreign goods.

## Shifts in the Aggregate Demand Curve

The analysis of aggregate demand allows us to observe how exogenous changes affect aggregate demand and thus the overall price level *and* the level of real GDP. The aggregate demand curve describes the economy in equilibrium in both the market for goods and services and the money market. Any exogenous or induced change that results in a shift in the aggregate expenditures curve or in the demand or supply curve of money will by definition cause a shift in the aggregate demand curve. With prices remaining constant, increases in government expenditures ($G$), investment expenditures ($I$), exogenous consumption expenditures ($C$), and net exports ($X - M$), as well as tax cuts and an increase in the money supply, will increase income in the goods market and will cause the aggregate demand curve to shift outward to the right. In Figure 6, the aggregate demand curve $AD_0$ shifts to the right to $AD_1$. At every price level, real GDP is higher on $AD_1$. Tax cuts or increases in $G$, $C$, $I$, net exports ($X - M$), and the money supply cause the aggregate demand curve to shift to the right, away from the axis, as shown by $AD_1$ in Figure 6. With this shift, at every price level, GDP is higher.

We can now envision the effects of monetary policy and fiscal policy and changes in autonomous spending on price levels as well as on real income and output. Table 1 summarizes the effects of policy changes on aggregate demand.

1. The 2010 federal budget called for income tax reductions, with the less wealthy receiving greater returns from these cuts. The budget proposal also included increased spending. Using the preceding analysis of aggregate demand curves, illustrate and explain what these curves predict would happen to aggregate demand.

**FIGURE 6** Shifts in the Aggregate Demand Curve

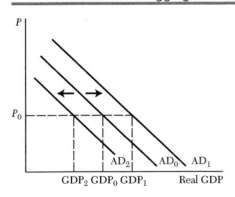

**Table 1** Effects of Monetary and Fiscal Policy on Aggregate Demand

| Policy | Effect of Policy | Effect on Aggregate Demand (AD) |
|---|---|---|
| Monetary Policy | Increase in money supply | AD curve shifts to the right. |
| | Decrease in money supply | AD curve shifts to the left. |
| Fiscal Policy | Increase in G | AD curve shifts to the right. |
| | Decrease in Tx | AD curve shifts to the right. |
| | Decrease in G | AD curve shifts to the left. |
| | Increase in Tx | AD curve shifts to the left. |

While we are primarily interested in policy changes that can shift the aggregate demand curve, several non-policy-related factors can cause a shift in the aggregate demand curve. An increase in real wealth will cause an outward shift. When stock market prices rose dramatically in 1999, holders of corporate stock increased their wealth, and their demand for goods and services increased. The increase in housing prices produced the same result. The increased equity in their homes caused homeowners to increase their borrowing and thus increase their demand for goods and services. Decreases in wealth due to the dramatic downturn in house prices in 2007 caused the aggregate demand curve to shift to the left.

Expectations also influence shifts in the aggregate demand curve. If consumers and investors become increasingly optimistic about the economy, aggregate demand may shift to the right. An expectation that the inflation rate will rise will produce the same result, as consumers and investors purchase durable goods now while prices are lower than those they predict in the future. On the international front, if real income rises abroad so that foreign citizens have more to spend, we can expect an increased demand for domestic goods and services. Again, the aggregate demand curve will shift to the right. All of these shifts indicate that real GDP is higher at every level of prices, as shown in Figure 6.

2. List the conditions unrelated to economic policy that would cause the aggregate demand curve to shift to the left, indicating lower real GDP at all price levels.

## SHORT-RUN AGGREGATE SUPPLY

The short-run aggregate supply shows the relationship between the output that is hypothetically supplied by the nation's producers of goods and services in response to changes in the price level. In the short run, producer responses will be restrained by the level of plant or factory capacity available for producing additional output and by the speed at which the prices of inputs or factors of production respond to the increase in the overall price level. Many economists believe that there is a delay between a rise in the general price level and resulting increases in prices for raw materials and labor. We will assume that in the short run, input prices do not change. Our examination of long-run aggregate supply will account for increases in resource prices in response to increases in overall prices.

Producers respond to increases in demand by increasing production, since increases in demand tend to bid output prices up and, with factor costs stable, to increase producer profits. Thus, we must examine the level of plant capacity available in the economy to trace the level of real output (GDP) that can be supplied at various price levels, given increases in demand. Tracing these responses will give us a curve that represents short-run aggregate supply.

If the economy is in a severe recession or depression, plenty of plant capacity will be available for producing additional products. Excess labor and capital will be available for the production process, since by definition, high levels of unemployment and low levels of output mean that greater increases in output (GDP) can be made available without producers incurring large costs. Thus, if the economy were operating at a point such as point $A$ in Figure 7, a small increase in demand—to point $B$—would increase real GDP without an overall price increase or with only a very small increase.

At the other extreme, if the economy is operating near or at full capacity, large quantities of output are already being produced. By definition, at full capacity, no new output can be produced. Producers are literally using every available machine, worker, and plant as much as is possible. At point $C$ in Figure 7, an increase in demand—to point $D$—can only bid up the level of prices. Little or no additional output will be forthcoming.

Most often the economy is operating somewhere between these two extreme possibilities of short-run aggregate supply responses. More normally the economy might be at point $E$. At this point, if demand is increased—to point $F$ —there will be increased GDP in the form of goods and services, and there will be a modest increase in the overall price level.

The upward slope of the aggregate supply curve is partly due to diminishing returns and partly due to resource and factor costs (particularly fixed wages) rising less rapidly than prices when demand for additional output increases. Moving along the aggregate supply curve illustrates the effect of increased aggregate demand at different levels of output and different price levels. Thus, the aggregate supply curve shows us the price level associated with each level of output, where firms will produce a profit-maximizing output at a fixed wage rate and a given level of productivity.

**FIGURE 7** Short-Run Aggregate Supply

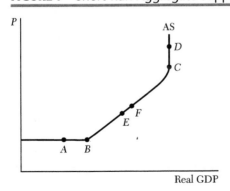

157

## Causes of Shifts in the Short-Run Aggregate Supply Curve

The short-run aggregate supply curve may shift for many reasons, including changes in the labor market, supply shocks, and government policies that affect supply. Positive factors that cut costs, such as technological innovations, will cause the aggregate supply curve to shift to the right. Negative factors, such as rising costs, will cause a shift to the left. Let's examine some conditions that will cause such shifts.

Labor market forces have had and continue to have effects on the aggregate supply curve. Increases and decreases in the labor force are obvious causes of a shift. Over the past four decades, women have entered the U.S. labor force in record numbers. Increases in the labor supply will, of course, increase aggregate supply and shift the curve to the right. Any factor that makes people want to work less—such as attending school, avoiding higher taxes, or pursuing more leisure activities—will cause a shift to the left.

Expectations also cause the short-run aggregate supply curve to shift. If producers expect higher inflation in the future, they will adjust short-run production levels to reflect the expected price hikes. Expected crop failure or surplus will also be reflected in the short-run aggregate supply curve as drought or perhaps freezing weather affects the production level of various crops.

3. If most producers expected prices to rise in the near future, which way would the short-run aggregate supply curve shift? Why? Illustrate with an example.

Most of us are familiar with price changes for domestic and imported resources, another factor affecting the aggregate supply curve. The oil price increases of the 1970s created supply shocks throughout the world, causing a leftward shift in the short-run aggregate supply curve. **Supply shocks** are unexpected events that cause increases in prices. They occur when the cost of producing a wide variety of products increases dramatically, causing the aggregate supply curve to shift to the left and thus push prices upward. During the 1970s, the United States and the world economy experienced a variety of supply shocks, which sent prices soaring. The most noteworthy supply shock occurred in 1973 and 1974, when the powerful OPEC nations placed an embargo (restriction on the import or export of a good) on oil exports. The reduced supply of oil products to many nations of the world severely curtailed production and increased prices, as shown by the shift from $AS_0$ to $AS_1$ in Figure 8. The price level on $AS_1$ is raised for each level of real output.

Other, less noteworthy supply shocks have affected the prices and output of many goods and services throughout the world. Price increases of raw materials and/or agricultural products have often been the cause of these shocks. The price increases may be caused by weather—from drought to floods, earthquakes and hurricanes—and by wars, both of which are beyond the control of policy makers. Large, rapid, and perhaps unexpected currency depreciations may also

**FIGURE 8** A Supply Shock

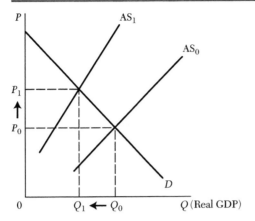

result in dramatic price increases or a supply shock for a nation heavily reliant on imported goods.

During the 1998–2000 U.S. economic expansion, low prices of imported goods affected the aggregate supply curve. In the late 1990s, many Asian economies, weakened by recession and its accompanying high unemployment, produced and exported goods very cheaply. A strong dollar and weakening Asian currencies ensured that exports to U.S. markets would be priced even lower. These cheap imports pressured U.S. producers to keep prices low so that their products could remain competitive in international markets. The low prices in an increasingly global marketplace served, in effect, as a "reverse supply shock." In contrast, from 2004 through mid-2007 as the U.S. economy grew, price pressures on the supply side were felt in some commodities markets, including copper and oil.

4. List other possible shocks to a nation's aggregate supply.

5. List some other factors that would be the reverse of shocks and would increase the nation's supply.

6. List five ways that the government might increase production of the supply of goods and services to the public (i.e., shift the AS curve to the right).

## Long-Run Aggregate Supply

Many economists believe that in the long run, the aggregate supply is a vertical line at the full-employment level of output; as new resources and technologies develop, this vertical line shifts to the right. According to this view, in the long run, economic policy will have only price effects unless productivity or technology improves. Before we examine these factors that cause shifts in long-run aggregate supply, we will illustrate how equilibrium is reached using the short- and long-run aggregate supply curves with the aggregate demand curve.

## Arriving at Equilibrium

Now that we have introduced the concept of aggregate supply, let's see how changes in aggregate demand will lead first to equilibrium with short-run aggregate supply and then move to an equilibrium on a long-run aggregate supply curve. (In Figure 9 the entire multiplier effect is seen on the horizontal part of the short-run aggregate supply curve AS.) Under normal economic conditions, the short-run aggregate supply curve slopes upward. As aggregate demand increases from $AD_0$ to $AD_1$, perhaps due to increased government expenditures or decreased taxes, the effect of the expenditure increase is shown as increased real income, GDP, or output; GDP rises from $GDP_0$ to $GDP_1$. Moving along the short-run aggregate supply curve $AS_0$, real GDP increases (from $GDP_0$ to $GDP_1$) as do prices (from $P_0$ to $P_1$). Equilibrium is found where $AS_0 = AS_1$ at point $B$. Equilibrium moves from point $A$ to point $B$. As the economy reaches its capacity to produce additional goods and services, further increases in aggregate demand push up prices.

Is this a stable equilibrium? No. Firms may be happy with this adjustment, but workers will not be. Prices have increased from $P_0$ to $P_1$, so workers' real wages have fallen. Workers will not be satisfied with a reduction in their real wages and will insist on a nominal wage increase during the next round of wage negotiations. Since the short-run aggregate supply curve was derived within the context of a model that assumed nominal wages were set and unchanged, any increase in the nominal wage, which increases producers' costs of production, will cause the short-run aggregate supply curve to shift. Responding to the increase in nominal wages, the short-run aggregate supply curve shifts from $AS_0$ to $AS_1$ in Figure 9. Now we find our short-run equilibrium position at $D$, where GDP has fallen from $GDP_1$ to $GDP_0$ and $P$ has increased from $P_1$ to $P_2$.

If there are no additional exogenous changes, there will be no more tendency for movement in the economy. We can see that the long-run aggregate supply

**FIGURE 9** Equilibrium with Aggregate Demand and Long-Run and Short-Run Aggregate Supply

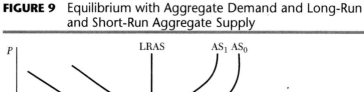

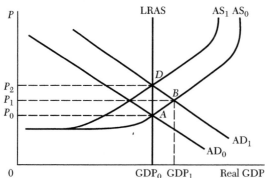

curve (LRAS) is vertical at $GDP_0$. (If, as we will see later, technology improves in the long run, LRAS would shift to the right, and so would real GDP.)

We examine the short-run aggregate supply curve to see the effect immediately after some fiscal, monetary, or other stimulus to aggregate demand has been introduced, before the economy has time to adjust to these changes in the long run. Firms will adjust their production levels based on the changes in aggregate demand. They will try to increase output to meet the increased demand at a higher price level, since supply is a function of price. Short-run effects are particularly important to economists who see stabilization policy as important to fine-tuning the economy, and to an understanding of the economy that we face from day to day. Perhaps Keynes expressed the concerns of those economists interested in the short run best when he remarked, "In the long run, we are all dead."

## Shifts in the Long-Run Aggregate Supply Curve

Since the long-run aggregate supply curve is not responsive to price changes, it is vertical. Any shift in the long-run aggregate supply curve will reflect a change in the quantity of resources available, a change in the productivity of resources, a change in technology, or perhaps some institutional change that affects resource efficiency or productivity. Each of these will increase or decrease output at all price levels and thus cause the LRAS curve to shift. These factors are mostly insensitive to price changes and are not *immediately* affected by short-term macroeconomic policy.

## Productivity

An important source of shifts in the long-run aggregate supply curve comes from increases and decreases in labor **productivity**, or the amount of output produced by a unit of input, in this case, a laborer. Increased productivity shifts the LRAS curve to the right, indicating more output at each price level. The importance of productivity growth is that it allows for noninflationary increases in real GDP, as shown in Figure 10.

**FIGURE 10**   Impact of Productivity Increases on Long-Run Aggregate Supply

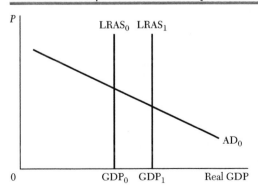

**Table 2**  Growth of U.S. Output per
Person-Hour Worked, 1973–2007

| Period | Average Annual Growth |
|--------|------------------------|
| 1973–1980 | 0.6% |
| 1980–1981 | 0.7% |
| 1981–1990 | 0.9% |
| 1990–1995 | 2.2% |
| 1995–2000 | 3.1% |
| 2000–2007 | 2.3% |

*Source:* Bureau of Labor Statistics, 2000, 2008.

Productivity is difficult to measure. One problem is the measurement of actual output. As the nation's labor force has shifted from industrial production to service activities, physical output is more difficult to measure. Approximately 18 percent of the nation's nonagricultural workers produce a tangible product. The rest produce services that can be measured in dollars only by examining the number of hours worked. Furthermore, the lack of accounting for quality improvements in manufactured goods has in the past understated U.S. productivity figures. Increases in the numbers of temporary workers paid by temp agencies rather than firms tends to overstate productivity increases.

In the 1970s and 1980s, economists and politicians were concerned with the apparent decline in the growth rate of U.S. productivity. Gains in labor productivity, measured as output per person-hour worked, appear to have been sluggish until the 1990s. While the average annual growth of output per worker was 1.9 percent between 1950 and 1973, Table 2 shows it grew 0.6 percent annually between 1973 and 1980, and it averaged less than 1 percent until the 1990s. In contrast, between 1960 and 1973, productivity increased by more than 4 percent annually in Germany and by more than 5 percent in Japan. Since 1979, productivity increases have averaged between 2 and 3 percent in Germany and 3 and 4 percent in Japan (see Figure 11).

Recent trends in the United States show productivity gains have slowed after averaging 3.1 percent annually between 1995 and 2000. Productivity normally increases during a recession, so this increase would have been expected in the early 1990s. During the second half of the 1990s, increases in investment spending, particularly in information and communications technology, are believed to have sparked further increases. Historically, productivity increases as labor has more capital to work with, more education, and more training. Despite rapid growth rates in output per worker in Japan and Germany, U.S. workers remain the most productive in the world, with the average worker producing some $28 worth of goods and services per hour and more than $49,000 worth of goods and services annually.

Economists often attribute slowdowns in worker productivity to a slowdown in innovation and technological change. Other culprits that have been cited as contributors to slowdowns in productivity growth include slower growth

**FIGURE 11** Output per Manufacturing Employee in Selected Countries

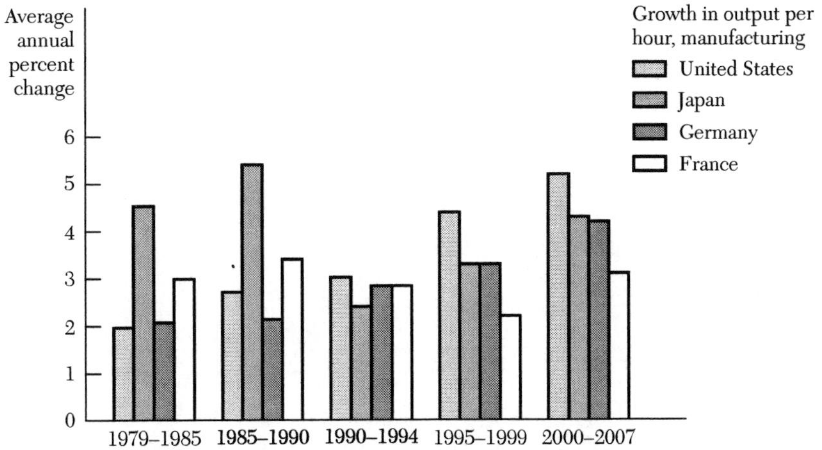

Average annual percent change

Growth in output per hour, manufacturing
- United States
- Japan
- Germany
- France

| | 1979–1985 | 1985–1990 | 1990–1994 | 1995–1999 | 2000–2007 |
|---|---|---|---|---|---|

*Source:* Bureau of Labor Statistics "International Comparisons of Manufacturing Productivity" 1950-2005, BCS 2009.

of private and public investment expenditures, flagging funding for research and development efforts, increased costs of health and safety regulations, and high energy prices during the 1970s. In 2006, slowing productivity rates were partly attributed to cost-cutting options. Aggressive cost-cutting after 2001 sparked productivity increases, but further cost reductions are limited. A reduction in investment in high tech has also been linked to a slowing of productivity growth.

7. Why would slower growth of investment expenditures contribute to decreases in productivity growth rates? How would increased energy costs contribute?

Labor and capitalists, however, sometimes hold different views of policies to increase productivity. Corporations would suggest tax cuts for business to stimulate capital investment and other incentives for research and development and thus shift the aggregate supply curve to the right, providing lower prices at each level of output. Labor, on the other hand, would argue for training programs and higher wages to improve productivity growth. That approach requires that output increase faster than the costs of training and pay increases.

Princeton economist William Baumol and his associates have argued that while productivity is a concern, it should be viewed in a long-run rather than a short-run context, and that increases in U.S. and U.K. productivity growth over the past decade must be sustained to have a long-run impact, since rising productivity and resulting economic growth can help rising debt levels. In discussing recent trends in productivity in their article "Pause Stirs Concern That Growth in Productivity May Be Flattening," Mark Whitehouse and Tim Aeppel write:

Productivity matters for everyone, because it provides the essential ingredient that makes nations rich. When companies produce more for each hour their employees work, they can pay higher wages or reap bigger profits without having to raise prices. Annual productivity growth of 2 percent would more than double inflation-adjusted wages over 40 years, all else being equal. Add another percentage point in productivity growth, and wages would more than triple.

—*The Wall Street Journal*, November 3, 2006, p. 1.

## Aggregate Supply and Economic Growth

Thus far in our examination of macroeconomics we have seen how changes in aggregate demand and in aggregate supply affect real GDP, our primary measure of economic performance. Economic growth, remember, is defined as the change in real GDP from one year to the next and is in part determined by the growth in the labor force (or quantity of labor), by physical and human capital accumulation, and by advances in technology. Politicians and policy makers often discuss plans to increase the economy's growth rate, but even a seemingly slow rate of growth has a profound impact over the long term. Compounded over many years, growth at a rate of just 1 or 2 percent contributes greatly to the size of a nation's economy.

Figure 12 shows real growth in the U.S. economy over the past century. Over that period, real GDP per person grew on average at about 2 percent annually. Between 1960 and 1973, GDP growth per person averaged 4.2 percent, but between 1975 and 1985, the growth rate fell to 1.1 percent per year. It then rebounded a bit, averaging 2.1 percent between 1990 and 2004.

Factors that cause changes in medium and long-term economic growth are the same factors that cause shifts in the long-run aggregate supply curve: changes in labor productivity and discoveries of new technologies or innovations. What is responsible for these? Often, investment (funded from saving) in new capital or public investment in a nation's infrastructure will increase worker productivity. Investment in human capital has historically improved productivity as well. This investment may take the form of public-sector expenditures on education and training or private expenditures on worker training.

New technological innovation may be fostered by investment expenditures on research and development—for instance, Defense Department research and development expenditures that led to the Internet*—or simply "learning by doing." Once a technical innovation that may improve productivity occurs, investment in capital (perhaps through equipment expenditures) employing this technology or innovation makes it available to the labor force. There is a crucial link between technology, science, and knowledge; advances in one serve as a catalyst for advances in another.

*Internet technology is a product of Department of Defense expenditures during the Cold War. The Advanced Research Projects Agency (ARPA), set up by the Eisenhower administration in 1957, began exploring computer communication, and in 1969 ARPAnet linked four research universities. During the 1970s ARPAnet expanded, and other networks were established—again, mostly linking universities. Research reports and articles were read and discussed on e-mail (electronic mail) and electronic discussion groups. In the 1980s, establishment of a communication standard, or protocol, allowed for the development of the Internet.

**FIGURE 12** Economic Growth in the United States, 1895–2005

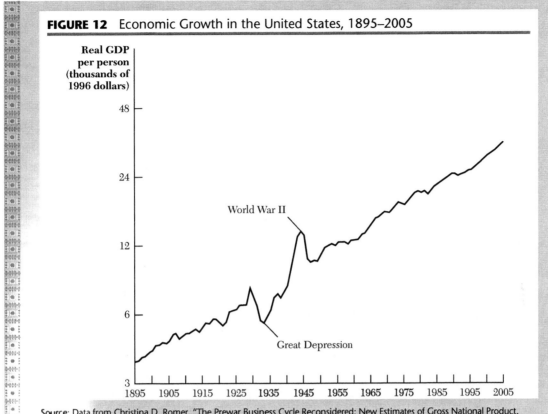

Source: Data from Christina D. Romer, "The Prewar Business Cycle Reconsidered: New Estimates of Gross National Product, 1869-1908," *Journal of Political Economy* Vol. 97(1989); *National Income and Product Accounts of the United States; Historical Statistics of the United States Colonial Times to 1957* (U.S. Department of Commerce, 1960); *Economic Report of the President,* 1999; Michael Parkin, *Economics,* 5th ed., Addison Wesley, 2005. p. 463; and www.gov/fls/flsgdp.pdf, 2006.

Productivity, along with increases in the labor force, increases in capital, and changes in technology, has a powerful effect on aggregate supply and on the nation's standard of living. Therefore, now that we have developed the theory of aggregate supply and understand how various factors influence it, we must examine how our theory of supply relates to economic policy.

## SUPPLY-SIDE ECONOMIC POLICY

In 1975, a handful of academic economists, together with politicians and journalists, began to reexamine the problems of the U.S. economy from a different perspective than mainstream Keynesian economics. The focus of the reexamination was on the "supply side." As we have seen previously, the orthodox Keynesian approach to the problems of inflation and unemployment focused on the demand side of the economy. If the economy showed signs of recession or depression, the verdict was that the economy was suffering from insufficient aggregate demand. If there were inflationary trends, then aggregate demand was too robust. Supply-side economists argued that those policies tended to be inflationary; once the government had initiated spending for particular programs, spending was hard to reduce.

## Rationale for Supply-Side Economics

Neither Keynes nor the classical economists totally ignored the supply side of the market in their economic analysis, but the policies Keynesians designed were predominantly aimed at either shoring up a weak aggregate demand or calming one that was excessive. To them, income or output was a function of aggregate demand.

Proponents of the supply-side approach argued that federal, state, and local governments had stifled production and incentive in the United States with their emphasis on policies leading to increased spending, taxation, and regulation. They argued that higher tax rates (particularly progressive taxes) and increased government regulation reduced incentives, while spending fueled inflation.

Supply-side advocates argued that increased tax rates inhibited production and reduced output as people substituted leisure activities for productive activity and did more work in which they had less skill. This would reduce the time spent in more productive economic activities, which because of higher taxes were less financially rewarding, and lead to an inefficient allocation of economic resources. Further inefficiencies would occur if tax-deductible goods became less desirable than those that were nondeductible. Finally, advocates of a supply-side approach pointed to the declining productivity in the United States and argued that lower corporate tax rates would generate more business investment and thus increase productivity.

This theory also predicted increased saving and perhaps increases in the rate of saving. Supply-side economists argued that lower tax rates would induce more saving in the private sector; the tax reductions would leave people more income from which to consume and save. If the government also reduced its spending, additional investment funds would become available. Greater investment should lead to lower interest rates and economic growth.

In summary, advocates of the supply-side approach to economic policy saw tax rates as extremely important in determining total output in the economy. They believed that decreases in tax rates caused individuals and businesses to substitute such productive activity as work, investment, and specialization for nonproductive activities. This would result in a more efficient allocation of resources. Total economic output would rise with lower tax rates.

 8. How do taxes directly affect supply? Illustrate on a graph of aggregate supply and aggregate demand how a tax cut works.

## Supply-Side Critics

Some economists sympathized with the notions put forth by advocates of the supply-side approach but noted that policies to stimulate supply-side increases take long periods of time before having noticeable effects on the economy. Indeed, they added, some of those policies might increase aggregate demand at the same time.

Another supply-side argument that came under fire was the assertion that lower tax rates would provide incentives for people to work more, since they could "keep" more of their income. Critics of this notion argued instead that higher tax rates had forced some people to work more than they would like to simply to maintain their standard of living. These people already had two jobs or worked overtime to keep the same level of income in the face of high tax rates. It was hard to conceive of them working more, yet easy to envision their working less if the tax rate fell.

Tax cuts for businesses had critics as well. Although in theory the cuts should stimulate investment, the critics questioned whether these funds would in fact be spent on new, productive activities. They cited corporate mergers in the 1980s, such as the purchase of Montgomery Ward by Mobil Oil, and Nabisco by R. J. Reynolds, as examples of corporate spending that created no new jobs or productive output for the nation.

Finally, the supply-side aspects of 1980s economic policies tended to shift the distribution of income. Wealthy individuals benefited far more than middle- and lower-middle-income groups. In absolute-dollar amounts, the benefit to those earning less than $10,000 a year was minimal, if not negative.

The Federal Reserve set the recovery of 1983–1984 in motion by pumping up the growth rate of the money supply in 1982, at the same time Congress increased military spending and enacted tax cuts. This stimulated a *demand-led*, rather than a supply-led, recovery, although business tax cuts did kick in somewhat higher levels of investment as the recovery mounted. The effects of supply-side policies of the early 1980s had decreased economic growth rates while increasing unemployment and budget deficits. Tax incentives to individuals and businesses had unexpected outcomes: decreases in the personal saving rate and investment expenditures as a percentage of national income.

# THE BIG PICTURE

## And the Big Picture Concluded

In this chapter we have completed the construction of the aggregate supply–aggregate demand model that allows us to analyze and show the effects of prices when economic policies are implemented. While the aggregate demand–aggregate supply graphs resemble market supply graphs, this resemblance is where the similarity stops. Information about money markets, goods and services markets, and economic policy is reflected in the aggregate demand–aggregate supply analysis, telling us how those markets respond to economic events, including policy decisions. We can now assess aggregate output and price levels for the economy. Figure BP.2 outlines the path we have taken to develop this model to this point.

**FIGURE BP.2** Construction of the Aggregate Demand–Aggregate Supply Model

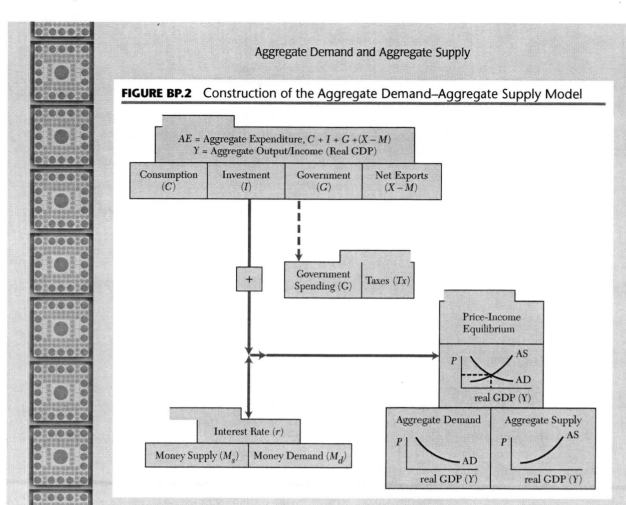

# ❖Conclusion

*Because price stability is one of the three macroeconomic goals, we need to be aware of price changes that may result from supply shocks—such as oil or energy shortages and productivity changes.*

## Review Questions

**1.** How is monetary policy related to aggregate demand?

**2.** What incentives do supply-side policies attempt to improve? Are incentives important in economic analysis?

**3.** Explain the relationship between supply-side tax policies and "demand-side" policies. Are the two interrelated? Explain.

4. Why is it difficult to increase output and thus expand economic growth through supply-side policies?

5. What was the last supply shock to occur in the United States? Explain its significance.

6. What were some of the reasons for the slowdown in productivity in the late 1970s and early 1980s? Increases in the 1990s?

7. Does it matter whether productivity is viewed in the short or long run? How does one increase productivity?

# Unemployment, Inflation, and Stabilization Policy in a Global Economy

From Chapter 18 of *Economics: A Tool for Critically Understanding Society*, 9/e. Tom Riddell. Jean Shackelford. Geoffrey Schneider. Steve Stamos. Copyright © 2011 by Pearson Education. Published by Addison-Wesley. All rights reserved.

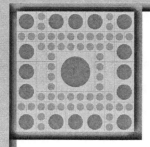

# Unemployment, Inflation, and Stabilization Policy in a Global Economy

## ❖ Introduction

**A**s the United States entered the twenty-first century, it was experiencing the longest period of sustained growth on record. But as the economic slowdown in 2001 was exacerbated by the terror attacks on the World Trade Center and the Pentagon, policy makers began again to reconsider policies concerning unemployment and inflation. During the years of economic growth in the 1960s, some economists declared the business cycle "dead," only to have it roar back in the 1970s and 1980s. From the economic experiences of those decades, economists not only learned about trade-offs, but they also discovered how economic variables might respond to policy.

There is some conflict between the monetarists and the Keynesians about solving these problems, and there might be other contending opinions. Conservatives, liberals, and radicals see different sorts of problems and different sets of solutions. One issue, which we shall focus on in the first part of the chapter, is the trade-off between the macroeconomic goals of unemployment and inflation. An even more troublesome situation happens when inflation and unemployment occur at the same time, resulting in what economists call **stagflation**.

We will begin by examining unemployment and inflation, the trade-off between the two, and the implications for stabilization policy. From there we will outline the views of several competing schools of economic thought to see how (or, in some cases, if) we can effectively use macroeconomic policy to reach societal goals.

### THE TRADE-OFF: UNEMPLOYMENT AND INFLATION

Given the economic goals of price stability, full employment, and growth, Keynesian macroeconomic policy prescriptions advise us that increased spending and/or increases in the money supply may be necessary to attain full employment, with price increases as a side effect. On the other hand, if policy makers attempt to curb inflation through monetary and fiscal measures, income will fall—and so will employment. We seem to be between a rock and a hard place. But an even more difficult problem emerges when the economy develops high inflation as well as high unemployment rates.

## The Phillips Curve

At one time, economists believed they had a rather simple answer to questions dealing with the trade-off between full employment and price stability. Economist A. W. Phillips studied the British economy for 100-plus years and found a rather stable relationship between increases in the wage rate and the rate of unemployment. High rates of unemployment were associated with low wage increases, and wage increases appeared to be related to the general rate of inflation. In the 1960s, U.S. economists Paul Samuelson and Robert Solow related rates of price increase to rates of unemployment and found that inflation and unemployment were inversely related. High inflation rates were associated with low unemployment rates and vice versa. When plotted, this downward-sloping relationship between the inflation rate and the unemployment rate came to be known as the **Phillips curve**.

If the Phillips curve is valid, then the matter of priorities seems to be rather straightforward. Economists could present a menu of the various trade-offs that were possible—perhaps a 4 percent inflation rate with a 5 percent unemployment rate, or a 2 percent inflation rate with a 6 percent unemployment rate. Through the democratic process, the electorate would establish which combination it desired, and the policy makers would fine-tune the economy to obtain this trade-off. If the economy had 5 percent inflation and 4 percent unemployment but the electorate and policy makers desired 4 and 4.5 percent rates, then economic policy should be ever so slightly more restrictive.

During the 1960s, the United States had one of its longest periods of uninterrupted economic growth, inflation averaged around 2 percent (although it accelerated to over 5 percent by the late 1960s), and the unemployment rate declined from 6.7 percent in 1961 to 3.5 percent in 1969. (Figure 1 graphs these rates, which are listed in Table 1.) But the 1970s and early 1980s presented a vastly different picture. In 1971, the unemployment rate climbed above 5.9 percent while the inflation rate rose to nearly 5 percent. By 1981, the unemployment rate reached 7.6 percent, and inflation was 10.3 percent. As inflation dropped to between 3 and 4 percent, unemployment peaked at 9.6 percent in 1983 and declined somewhat to 7.5 percent in 1984. The idea of a simple trade-off between inflation and unemployment had broken down. It took increasingly higher levels of unemployment to reduce inflation by increasingly smaller amounts.

Despite the generally inverse relationship between unemployment and price pressures, the trade-off appeared to worsen, leading some economists to suggest that the Phillips curve had shifted. By "connecting the dots" between the annual points plotted between 1960 and 1968 and between 1969 and 1974 on Figure 1, we show a shifting Phillips curve. After that time, connecting the

**FIGURE 1** The Phillips Curve and the U.S. Economy, 1960–2008

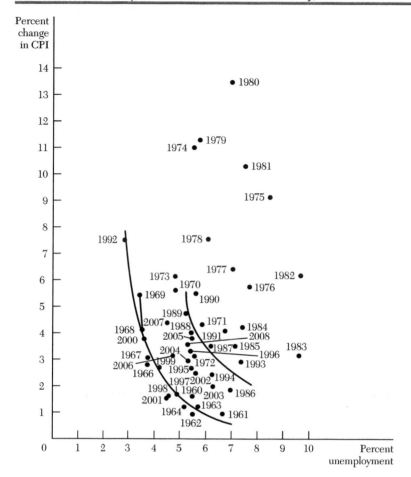

dots creates an upward and then a downward spiral, indicating a longer upward movement in the 1970s and early 1980s, followed by a more recent downward trend in the late 1980s and the 1990s, renewing the idea of a trade-off.

Some economists attributed shifts in the Phillips curve in the 1970s to supply shocks the economy received during those years. These included the very high increases in oil prices caused by the OPEC embargo, increased prices of agricultural products, and the increased prices of foreign goods brought about by the fall in the dollar's value in 1973. This period generated critiques of the Phillips curve, with Edmund Phelps and Milton Friedman arguing that inflationary expectations might be generating the higher levels of inflation and unemployment.

The 1990s brought the U.S. economy low levels of unemployment and inflation, accompanying a record number of months of sustained economic growth. As economic activity slowed in 2001–2003, higher unemployment levels peaked at 6 percent in 2003 while prices remained low. As the recovery gained momentum in 2004, job growth was initially sluggish and inflationary pressures

**Table 1** Inflation and Unemployment in the U.S. Economy, 1950–2008

| Year | Inflation | | Unemployment Rate | Year | Inflation | | Unemployment Rate |
|------|-------------------------|---------------------------|-------------------|------|-------------------------|---------------------------|-------------------|
| | Consumer Price Index* | Year-to-Year Change | | | Consumer Price Index* | Year-to-Year Change | |
| 1950 | 24.1 | 1.3% | 5.3% | 1980 | 82.4 | 13.5% | 7.1% |
| 1951 | 26.0 | 7.9 | 3.3 | 1981 | 90.9 | 10.3 | 7.6 |
| 1952 | 26.5 | 1.9 | 3.0 | 1982 | 96.5 | 6.2 | 9.7 |
| 1953 | 26.7 | 0.8 | 2.9 | 1983 | 99.6 | 3.2 | 9.6 |
| 1954 | 26.9 | 0.7 | 5.5 | 1984 | 103.9 | 4.3 | 7.5 |
| 1955 | 26.8 | −0.4 | 4.4 | 1985 | 107.6 | 3.6 | 7.2 |
| 1956 | 27.2 | 1.5 | 4.1 | 1986 | 109.6 | 1.9 | 7.0 |
| 1957 | 28.1 | 3.3 | 4.3 | 1987 | 113.6 | 3.6 | 6.2 |
| 1958 | 28.9 | 2.8 | 6.8 | 1988 | 118.3 | 4.1 | 5.5 |
| 1959 | 29.1 | 0.7 | 5.5 | 1989 | 124.0 | 4.8 | 5.3 |
| 1960 | 29.6 | 1.7 | 5.5 | 1990 | 130.7 | 5.4 | 5.5 |
| 1961 | 29.9 | 1.0 | 6.7 | 1991 | 136.2 | 4.2 | 6.7 |
| 1962 | 30.2 | 1.0 | 5.5 | 1992 | 140.3 | 3.0 | 7.4 |
| 1963 | 30.6 | 1.3 | 5.7 | 1993 | 144.5 | 3.0 | 6.8 |
| 1964 | 31.0 | 1.3 | 5.2 | 1994 | 148.2 | 2.6 | 6.1 |
| 1965 | 31.5 | 1.6 | 4.5 | 1995 | 152.4 | 2.8 | 5.6 |
| 1966 | 32.4 | 2.9 | 3.8 | 1996 | 156.9 | 3.3 | 5.4 |
| 1967 | 33.4 | 3.1 | 3.8 | 1997 | 160.5 | 1.7 | 4.9 |
| 1968 | 34.7 | 3.7 | 3.6 | 1998 | 163.0 | 1.6 | 4.5 |
| 1969 | 36.7 | 5.5 | 3.5 | 1999 | 166.6 | 2.7 | 4.2 |
| 1970 | 38.8 | 5.7 | 4.9 | 2000 | 172.2 | 3.4 | 4.0 |
| 1971 | 40.5 | 4.4 | 5.9 | 2001 | 177:1 | 1.6 | 4.7 |
| 1972 | 41.8 | 3.2 | 5.6 | 2002 | 179.9 | 2.4 | 5.8 |
| 1973 | 44.4 | 6.2 | 4.9 | 2003 | 184.0 | 1.9. | 6.0 |
| 1974 | 49.3 | 11.0 | 5.6 | 2004 | 185.9 | 3.3 | 5.5 |
| 1975 | 53.8 | 9.1 | 8.5 | 2005 | 195.3 | 3.4 | 5.1 |
| 1976 | 56.9 | 5.8 | 7.7 | 2006 | 201.6 | 2.5 | 4.6 |
| 1977 | 60.6 | 6.5 | 7.1 | 2007 | 207.3 | 4.1 | 4.6 |
| 1978 | 65.2 | 7.6 | 6.1 | 2008 | NA | 3.1 | 5.1 |
| 1979 | 72.6 | 11.3 | 5.8 | | | | |

*The Consumer Price Index (CPI) measures changes in the "cost of living" (1982 – 1984 = 100). The inflation rate is the percent change in CPI.

*Source: Economic Report of the President,* 2009, pp. 334,353,357.

edged prices upward. The economy continued to grow at an accelerated rate through 2005 and early 2006. Growth slowed to modest levels in late 2006 as prices continued to rise. In addition to concerns about levels of employment and price stability, significant concerns about trade deficits and other structural problems remained. In a nation with one of the world's highest standards of living, homelessness persists, and the infant mortality rate remains among the highest of the industrial nations. Continuing increases in poverty levels, especially among the young, are particularly troublesome, as are the growing numbers of workers without health insurance. Even in periods of low inflation and unemployment, these troubling economic issues remained unsolved.

# INFLATION

We have defined inflation as a rise in the general price level. We can expect price increases to accompany a growing, viable economy, but if these price increases are larger than increases in productivity or real output would dictate, they are inflationary. Table 1 indicates what has happened to prices in the past half century, measured as changes in the Consumer Price Index (CPI). These numbers reflect revisions that government economists have made to the way they measure inflation, beginning in 1995. The revisions lowered the level of inflation from earlier years by about 0.68 percentage points per year. The purpose of these changes was to provide a more accurate measure of inflation experienced by consumers. Note the lower rates of inflation in recent years.

1. On the average, how much would something that cost $200 in 1967 cost in 2007? How much have prices increased since you were born?

2. Does any information in the table surprise you? If so, what surprised you? (If not, what met your expectations?)

We can see that any action that shifts the aggregate demand curve to the right or the aggregate supply curve to the left causes price increases and possibly inflation. We can classify the prevailing types of inflation according to the possible cause of each: demand-pull inflation, cost-push inflation, and expectations-generated inflation. These types of inflation can occur simultaneously or independently.

**Demand-pull inflation** is a rise in the price level attributed to excessive aggregate demand. Aggregate demand can increase for a number of reasons, including increases in autonomous consumption, investment, government spending, net exports, and the money supply or decreases in taxes or saving. We can view this graphically in Figure 2, where AS represents the aggregate

**FIGURE 2**  Demand-Pull Inflation

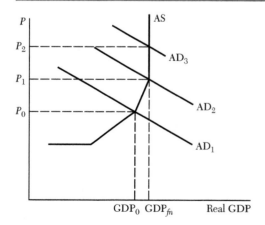

supply curve, and AD represents aggregate demand. All are plotted with respect to real output (real GDP) and the general price level ($P$). A rightward shift of the aggregate demand curve from $AD_1$ to $AD_2$ increases both prices and real output in the short run as real GDP increases from $GDP_0$ to $GDP_{fn}$ and prices increase from $P_0$ to $P_1$. As income levels increase, the demand for goods and services will rise. Initially, as demand increases, prices are bid up, output increases, and more laborers are hired to produce products. If resources are fully employed and aggregate demand continues to rise, as illustrated by a shift from $AD_2$ to $AD_3$, there is no increase in GDP, only an increase in prices. We know that the higher aggregate demand in the face of limited supply will cause shortages of goods and services and the need for additional labor to increase production. The increased demand for goods and services, raw materials, and labor may even exceed the capacity to generate new output.

A simple remedy for inflation generated by increased aggregate demand is to cut back on spending and the money supply. The same technique can thwart inflationary expectations. Reductions in the growth rate of the money supply are particularly effective (and painful).

**Cost-push** (or supply) **inflation** puts the responsibility for price increases on rising costs of production. As production costs increase, the supply curve shifts to the left, leading to higher prices. A few of the cost factors that might cause a shift in the supply function are wages, raw material prices, interest rates, and profits. In Figure 3 higher costs bring about increases in price as well as a reduction in output. In the long run, producers will be able to reduce wages because of higher levels of unemployment, and output will return to the original level ($GDP_{fn}$).

Cost increases can come from many places, including increases in raw material prices, labor costs, and higher profits. As market structures have become more concentrated, some large corporations have gained more ability to administer prices for their own benefit—which in most cases means to increase prices and profits. During the 1970s, resource shortages pushed the prices of some goods upward. The lack of supply created a bottleneck in the

**FIGURE 3** Cost-Push Inflation

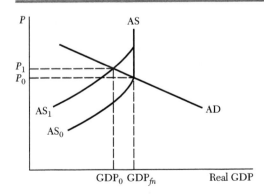

production process, with limited amounts of raw materials forthcoming, even at higher costs.

Unlike aggregate demand inflation, cost-push or supply inflation has no simple remedy. Resource shortages are difficult to prevent. Cartels that withhold raw materials are hard to bargain with. Controls placed on wages and prices, and other types of incomes policies, do not seem to work very well, when viewed in a historical context. Indeed, controls often lead to contrived shortages, as suppliers hesitate to continue production when they cannot recoup rising costs.

If businesses respond to higher output and profits sparked by an increase in aggregate demand by hiring additional workers, more jobs become available, and unemployment falls. If the current rates of inflation are expected to continue, *expectations-generated inflation* may occur. Workers, trying to restore the purchasing power of their wages, press for increases based on inflationary expectations. Once workers attain higher wages, the aggregate supply will decrease to reflect the increased costs to firms. With these higher costs, profits fall, and firms cut back on output. Now real GDP falls back to its original level, but prices are now at a higher level.

While expectations may seem an unlikely candidate for economic analysis, inflationary expectations are at times important in explaining inflation. Each time we expect inflation, we tend to generate inflationary price increases. Yale economist William Nordhaus stated this well:

> Inflation is a highly inertial process. It will go along to whatever rate it has been going at until it is shocked to a different level.... From 1973 to 1980 we had 6 to 9 percent inflation built into the wage and price system. It [higher inflation] was built into contracts. It was built into expectations. The recession [1980–1982] beat it down to 5 percent and now we have lower inertial rates.

Inflationary expectations directly affect aggregate supply. As wages increase because workers expect inflation, costs to firms increase. Firms then pass on these increased costs to consumers in the form of higher prices. On the demand side, expectations of higher interest rates generate consumer and business borrowing and expenditures. These activities increase aggregate demand and drive up prices.

When inflationary expectations are low, inflation is easier to moderate with monetary and fiscal policy. In the 1970s, when inflationary expectations were high, the fiscal policies employed were largely ineffective. They resulted in increased unemployment without significantly lower inflation. From the late 1980s through the late 1990s, expectations remained low and thus aided in maintaining stable prices. As the U.S. and industrial economies expanded from 2004 through 2006, inflationary expectations increased as rising oil and commodity prices and consumer demand pushed prices upward.

## THE IMPACT OF UNEMPLOYMENT AND INFLATION

Although policy makers and politicians would prefer to have the low inflation *and* low unemployment characteristic of the late 1960s and late 1990s, when unemployment or prices begin to rise, policy makers must respond to those changes. Decisions must be made about which goal, full employment or price stability, is preferable. Economists studying this question have found that higher unemployment and higher inflation affect different groups in different ways.

According to a study by Princeton economist Alan Blinder, former member of the Federal Reserve Board and Council of Economic Advisors, and Northwestern University economist Rebecca Blank, the unemployment rate for teens increases at two times the base rate, and unemployment for the elderly increases at about half the base rate. Blinder and Blank also made the following observations:

> The burden of unemployment is distributed unequally across age, race, and sex groups. In particular, nonwhite and young workers are more severely affected. On the other hand, female and older workers—who are also typically low-wage workers—are not as sensitive to changes in general unemployment levels.

They conclude, "The business cycle is not neutral in spreading the burden of unemployment. Certain workers experience much larger increases in unemployment when the general economy turns down than others." Blank and Blinder also found that whites, males, and the middle-aged receive a larger share of unemployment compensation than do unemployed workers in other categories.*

Inflation particularly hurts creditors and those on fixed incomes, while borrowers in general benefit. The poor seem to be hurt less by inflation than the rich. Prices generally rise for consumers at all income levels, but so do wages and salaries. However, the income from and worth of wealthy people's assets are more readily eroded by inflation.

3. What effect will supply shortages have on the trade-off between inflation and unemployment when unemployment is increasing?

4. How might inflation benefit a person who borrows money? Is this always so?

## STABILIZATION POLICY: AN INTERNATIONAL PERSPECTIVE

Unemployment and inflation concern policy makers throughout the world's industrial and developing nations. The 1990s brought generally low rates of unemployment and inflation in the United States, Germany, and Japan, but several other industrial nations experienced substantially higher unemployment. Table 2 shows recent unemployment and inflation rates in some of the nations that actively compete with the United States in international markets.

Many of the European nations listed in the table have chosen more aggressive social programs than those in the United States for dealing with the effects of unemployment. These more generous programs have at least partially resulted in higher taxes. The United States, along with

---

*Rebecca M. Blank and Alan S. Blinder, "Macroeconomics, Income Distribution and Poverty," in Sheldon H. Danziger and Daniel Weinberg, eds., *Fighting Poverty: What Works and What Doesn't* (Cambridge, MA: Harvard University Press, 1986), p. 191.

**Table 2** Unemployment and Inflation Rates in Selected Countries, 2007

| Country | Unemployment Rate | Change in Consumer Price Index |
|---|---|---|
| United States | 4.6% | 2.9% |
| Australia | 4.4 | 2.3 |
| Canada | 6.0 | 2.1 |
| France | 8.3 | 1.5 |
| Germany | 8.4 | 2.1 |
| Italy | 6.1 | 1.8 |
| Japan | 3.9 | 0.1 |
| Sweden | 6.1 | 2.2 |
| United Kingdom | 5.3 | 4.3 |

*Source: Statistical Abstract of the United States, 2009, Tables 1321 and 1311.*

Japan and Korea, has a relatively lower tax burden than the other industrialized nations. At the same time, many of these nations have also experienced higher government deficits.

# MACROECONOMIC SOLUTIONS: THE ALTERNATIVES

While the Keynesian aggregate expenditures model we have explored commends the use of monetary and fiscal policy in stabilization efforts, other economic models and theories question the effectiveness of intervention. The dilemma is what to do—not so much about inflation and unemployment but about government budgets, trade deficits, economic and productivity growth rates, and the myriad of other economic problems that surround us in the context of a complex and increasingly interdependent world economy. Traditional Keynesian remedies, declared deficient during the stagflation of the 1970s, returned with renewed vitality to the New Keynesians by the end of the 1980s, and attained even greater importance in 2008 and 2009.

Ever an evolutionary theory, Keynesianism is becoming more eclectic, encompassing some of the better ideas presented by other schools of macro-economic thought in the 1980s. These include a larger framework on which consumers base their expectations of the future and a reaffirmation that, along with fiscal policy, monetary policy is important to stabilization efforts. As Keynesians returned to the limelight, popular movements of the 1970s and 1980s lost favor. To better understand the status of stabilization policy, we will briefly summarize some of the theories and policies of contending schools of thought and review their standing in the early twenty-first century.

## Monetarist Solutions

Monetarists believe that growth rates of money control inflation and business cycle activity. Monetary policy, therefore, is the most effective way to stabilize the economy, although most monetarists prefer a nondiscretionary rule rather than small changes in policy that aim to fine-tune the economy. Monetarists contend that only money matters, since increases in money allow fiscal policy to be effective in the long run. (Actually, it is monetary policy that is effective.) The monetarists focus on the long run and avoid short-run solutions.

Boosted by the failures of Keynesian theory and policy to explain and counter the stagflation of the 1970s, the monetarists entered the 1980s with their theories at the top of the hit parade. But even the 1970s and certainly the following two decades dealt monetarists a cruel blow. Predictions fell by the wayside. Velocity was unstable, as was the demand for money. The money supply proved hard to target. Inflation of the 1970s proved not to be a monetary phenomenon, and inflation predicted in the 1980s failed to materialize. The monetarists fell from favor.

## Supply-Side Solutions

Although supply-siders fell from favor at the end of the 1980s, the election in 2000 of George W. Bush helped them regain some power in policy-making circles. In the 1980s, wishful thinking proved no match for the economy that resulted from supply-side policies. Marginal tax rate policies designed to stimulate investment and incentives brought about increased unemployment, decreased saving and investment, large budget deficits, and increased income and wealth inequality. Economists accept the supply-side idea that marginal tax rates can help to increase incentives and investment, but most economists see them having a rather small effect on overall economic activity. Supply-side stabilization policies should not be disregarded, but their stabilization effect is small.

## New Classical Solutions

The New Classical or Rational Expectations school of macroeconomic thought gained support and prestige during the 1970s and early 1980s. Its abstract theoretical and mathematical model, based on classical assumptions of pure and perfect competition, appealed to a number of academic economists. New Classical economists argue that firms and workers acquire, assess, and utilize information very quickly and rationally. For example, in our prior discussion of inflation, economists subscribing to the New Classical view would argue that as soon as laborers realized policy makers were trying to stimulate demand, they would adjust their consumption and wage demands, making the "short-run" Phillips curve trade-off even shorter and making the long-run aggregate supply and vertical Phillips curves the only appropriate ones for examining policy actions. Short-run stabilization policy would be useless, since rational people would react immediately and "outguess" the policy. Only policy "surprises" would be effective. Rational individuals would use all information, not just past data about prices or income. Policy makers could introduce or curb inflationary expectations simply by appointing a new Federal Reserve chair known to be easy or tough on inflation. New Classical economists would rely on perfectly competitive markets—ones without collusion, price fixing, or monopoly—to chart the best course for the economy.

When economists examined the evidence from the late 1970s and 1980s, New Classical theories fell short. According to the theories, inflation could be reduced without an increase in unemployment. With the Federal Reserve decreasing the growth rate of the money supply, economic actors should have adjusted their inflationary expectations downward, avoiding high levels of unemployment. But that period showed the short-run Phillips curve to be alive and well, and Rational Expectations remains a theory without an accompanying reality.

## Post-Keynesian (Managed Capitalist) Solutions

Post-Keynesians, distrustful of solutions that rely solely on market activity, and the long-run timing of such solutions, and relying heavily on the role of demand in the economy, recommend adoption of an incomes policy to determine an annual noninflationary rise in all types of income. This would involve controls over the rates of increase in personal and business income. Tax incentives would assure compliance. The post-Keynesians believe that government and business should jointly make decisions for long-run public and private investment, and that employment and growth policies are central to a recovery and economic restructuring.

In the 1980s, post-Keynesian alternatives such as wage and price controls faded from sight as means to combat inflation or reduce unemployment. In the postwar era, however, every president until Ronald Reagan at some point flirted with controls or guidelines. Nevertheless, outside of the political machismo derived from controls, there has been little evidence that the particular types of controls instituted have been effective.

## Feminist Economists' Solutions

Feminist economists note the failure of present economic models to predict and address real-world concerns of women, children, and men. They seek to go beyond formal economic models based on what they see as oversimplified assumptions about human behavior. For example, feminist economist Nancy Folbre has pointed out that while Adam Smith noted the role that competitive markets play in our lives, the expanding role of the market has sometimes come at the cost of care for others. Smith considered this problem but, according to Folbre, "didn't take it seriously, because he optimistically assumed that people were not all that selfish". He considered love of family, duty to others, and loyalty to country the hallmarks of an advanced civilization. The book that launched his career was entitled *The Theory of the Moral Sentiments*. In it he wrote:

> However selfish soever man may be supposed, there are evidently some principles in his nature, which interest him in the fortune of others, and render their happiness necessary to him, though he derives nothing from it, except the pleasure of seeing it.

Folbre, too, considers a more caring macroeconomics, where societal goods other than wealth are factors:

> Extending family values to society as a whole requires looking beyond the redistribution of income to ways of strengthening cultural values of love, obligation, and reciprocity....
>
> We could encourage greater civic participation, offering tax credits and other incentives for the provision of care services that develop long-term relationships between individuals and communities. We could discourage residential and cultural segregation by class and ethnicity. We could defend and enlarge our

public spaces. Our educational institutions could encourage the development of caring skills and community involvement. Among other strategies, we might invite young people to repay the money invested in them through national service rather than simply through taxes.

Policies designed to promote care for other people appear unproductive only to those who define economic efficiency in cramped terms, such as increases in GDP. The weakening of family and social solidarity can impose enormous costs, reflected in educational failures, poor health, environmental degradation, high crime rates, and a cultural atmosphere of anxiety and resentment. The care and nurturance of human capabilities has always been difficult and expensive. In the past, a sexual division of labor based upon the subordination of women helped minimize both the difficulties and the expense. Today, however, the costs of providing care need to be explicitly confronted and fairly distributed.

—Nancy Folbre, *The Invisible Heart: Economics and Family Values,*
New Press, 2001, pp. 229–230.

Feminist perspectives on economics, such as the one seen here, often expand the scope of the traditional meaning of stabilization policy, pushing it beyond indicators such as inflation and unemployment rates.

## Radical Solutions

Radical economists argued that the stagflation of the 1970s was symptomatic not only of a failure of Keynesian theory and policy but also of a fundamental breakdown of U.S. capitalism. Radicals viewed U.S. capitalism as experiencing a long-term structural crisis, explained not by factors external to the economy but by the business cycle. A radical critique of Keynesian theory and policy challenges the "theory of the state," with the state as the legitimate arbiter of societal conflicts resulting from interest groups' political behavior and lobbying. Arguing that the state consciously guides the economy and cyclical instability in order to serve the needs of the dominant economic class, Raford Boddy and James Crotty summarize the functional analysis of a recession in the business cycle:

It is the economic function of the recession to correct the imbalances of the previous expansion and thereby create the preconditions for a new one. By robbing millions of people of their jobs, and threatening the jobs of millions of others, recessions reduce worker demands and end the rise of labor costs. They eventually rebuild profit margins and stabilize prices. During recessions inventories are cut, loans are repaid, corporate liquidity position is reversed. All the statements of Keynesian economists to the contrary notwithstanding, recessions are inevitable in the unplanned economy of the United States because they perform an essential function for which no adequate substitute has thus far been available.

—Raford Boddy and James R. Crotty, "Who Will Plan the
Planned Economy?" *The Progressive,* February 1975.

Radicals see increases in concentration and specialization of production by domestic and multinational corporations as expanding both their political and their economic power. An increasingly symbiotic relationship between government and business explains the structural transformation of U.S. capitalism since World

War II, prohibits the possibility of genuine democracy in the United States, and clearly depicts an underlying class character of government functions and policies. Radicals view stabilization policies as outside the interests of workers and the democratic process.

5. What are the top five macroeconomic issues today? Select one of those issues and explain how conservatives, liberals, and radicals respond. How might a feminist economist respond to that issue?

# Conclusion

*We must increasingly adapt our theory and policy within the context of the existing U.S. and world economies, finding solutions that are effective within this context. The U.S. economy is far different from what it was in the post–World War II era. The workforce is changing, and the economic base, which was continually regenerated through economic growth, is no longer industrial. Additionally, policy decisions must reflect the fact that the U.S. economy in this century is greatly dependent on the other nations of the world. As government leaders plan for economic growth in the United States, they must do so within a world context. Today around 10 percent of the products made in the United States are exported to other nations. Exports plus imports made up about 20 percent of the U.S. GDP in 2004, compared with 12.4 percent of GDP in 1970 and less than 10 percent in the 1960s. If the economies of U.S. trading partners are unhealthy, we cannot expect the U.S. economy to remain vigorous.*

*The Keynesian approach to economic policy has carried us a long way from the classical approach. Yet problems still exist, and new approaches may be needed to deal with future problems. Many of these issues are increasing our attention toward macroeconomics and the functioning of specific markets. Before we look further at policy, however, we need to broaden our perspective and see what is happening in international economics. An understanding of the global arena is necessary to appreciate the full complexity of macroeconomic problems.*

## Review Questions

**1.** What is the basis for the trade-off or inverse relationship between inflation and unemployment? Why can't there be zero unemployment and zero inflation?

**2.** Do you think fighting inflation is more important than fighting unemployment? Why or why not?

**3.** What competing theories explain inflation in the economy?

**4.** What structural elements in the economy limit the effectiveness of fiscal and monetary policies?

**5.** How does avoiding a boom avoid a recession? What is the resulting impact on inflation?

**6.** What are the main schools of thought with respect to macroeconomic stabilization policy? What are the main issues of contention? Does the recent macroeconomic performance of the U.S. economy suport the ideas of one school more than another?

# THINKING CRITICALLY

## SPEND ME TO THE MOON

In examining macroeconomic theory and policy, we have seen how and why both monetary and fiscal policies are important to economic growth and stabilization. While at times complicated by the increasing globalization of economic activity and fluctuations beyond U.S. borders, stabilization policies, when employed, have had some success in calming national and international markets. As you might expect, opinions about macroeconomic goals and the policies the government or the Fed should pursue to accomplish them are often linked to belief systems. We understand how monetary and fiscal policy works. We understand the limitations and the strengths of monetary, spending, and taxation policies. But one of the most often asked questions is, What should U.S. or Fed policy be? In answering this question, conservative, liberal, and radical perspectives play an important role in establishing the dialogue and the parameters of discussion.

Between 1999 and 2000, economists representing every perspective applauded the Fed's use of monetary policy to sustain a buoyant and growing economy (although some believed even higher growth could have been generated with lower interest rates). However, economists from each paradigm criticized the Fed's failure to recognize hints of recession in early 2000 and its tardy response. While many questioned whether or not the Fed once again was slow to recognize inflation expectations in 2004, neither monetary or fiscal authorities recognized the extent of the housing bubble or the effects of tax regulation of financial institutions since the 1980s. While there is some agreement among economists about the effect that expenditures have on GDP (and on employment and prices) there is little agreement about who should do the spending—businesses, consumers, or the government—or just whose taxes should be cut or increased. There is also disagreement about the priority of economic goals and objectives. Some prefer targeting full employment, while others would rather focus on inflation, with these inflation fights continuing through the economic recession and financial crises that began in 2007. Some economists, including Jamie Galbraith at the University of Texas, focus on links among factors, such as how increased income inequality tends to signal economic downturns in the overall context of unemployment and inflation. (For more information about this linkage, visit the Utip Inequality Watch Web site at utip.gov.utexas.edu.) Some conservatives have resisted surpluses, arguing that politicians would spend any excess revenues on new programs or expansion of existing programs. Over past decades, persistent and ongoing deficits have effectively squelched serious public policy discussions about new spending programs—after all, when can nations "afford" to discuss innovative policies focusing on public goods?

Over the years, one group of economists has as a goal continued reduction of structural deficits and paying down the accumulated federal debt. They focus on the short- and long-run effects of lower interest rate costs on the federal budget and the economy. To them, the opportunity cost of a large deficit is high.

Other economists, such as the late Robert Eisner, a past president of the American Economic Association who taught at Northwestern University, have argued that part of the federal deficit amassed from government spending can be seen as a good thing when viewed in the context of public investment expenditures. Eisner argued, "Much of the debt goes to pay for physical assets—roads, buildings, schools, the defense system—which ought to be separated, as is done by corporations, into a capital budget." He further argued that "budget deficits not only do not inhibit real growth but also that deficit spending is what promotes national growth, prosperity and savings."

So after the dust settles on the Great Recession of 2007–2009, what should a macroeconomic policy aimed at long-term growth look like? As you might expect by now, economists (and politicians) are of at least three different minds on this question. One group, favoring tax cuts, argues that by putting funds into the pockets of taxpayers, greater consumer spending will stimulate business investment, innovation, and long-term growth. Yet even among those favoring tax cuts there are disagreements over who exactly should receive the tax advantages. Should the benefit fall to wealthier taxpayers, in middle or lower income groups? Certainly tax cuts will stimulate economic activity, but is it the best way to stimulate long-term growth?

Certainly not, argues another group, pointing out that tax cuts and spending used separately or together are fine to reverse cyclical downturns in economic activity—but they note that until 2009, structural, not cyclical, deficits have left the United States burdened with a large public debt that may slow down long-term growth. Interest payments must be made on the debt and deficits potentially generate higher interest rates from government borrowing in times when monetary authorities are restraining monetary growth. Critical of the advocates of tax cuts, this group argues that the resulting reduced government revenues simply add to structural deficits. Tax cuts may not have expiration dates and may not be changed after the cycle has reversed. (They also remind us that the political leaders in the United States have shown little fiscal or budgetary restraint in curbing expenditures despite the reduction in revenues.) Their argument, then, is that minimizing or eliminating structural deficits and "paying down" or repaying cyclical deficits during economic upswings (or booms) leads to lower interest rates—thus stimulating long-term economic growth.

A final group argues that neither deep tax cuts nor "buying" lower deficits will ensure long-term growth. They argue that government spending in areas such as education, science, and technology inspires innovation producing long-term investment payoffs. Indeed, in his book *The Internet Galaxy*, Manuel Castells writes about ARPANET, the predecessor of the Internet:

However, to say that ARPANET was not a military oriented project does not mean that its Defense Department origins were inconsequential for the development of the Internet. For all the vision and all the competence these scientists displayed in their project, they could never have commanded the level of resources that was necessary to build a computer network and to design all the appropriate technologies. The Cold War provided a context in which there was strong public and government support to invest in cutting-edge science and technology, particularly after the challenge of the Soviet space program became a threat to U.S. national security.

In excerpts from the article, "Forget Bush and Gore; Our Economy Needs Another Khrushchev," Barry Bluestone, professor of political economy at Northeastern University, continues the debate in the tradition of Professor Eisner—but with a twist. Bluestone argues that the great growth in technology generating the productivity surge in the late 1990s was initiated not by Reagan, Clinton, or Greenspan, but by government expenditures that started during the Cold War era. (The Cold War began at the conclusion of World War II and ended in 1989 with the fall of the Berlin Wall and the collapse of the Soviet Union.) These expenditures resulted in defense projects and a space program, which brought miniaturization, computer technology, Teflon, and the Internet, among other innovations. Bluestone argues that the vast expenditures on research and development necessary to fund such projects can be generated only through the deep pockets of the government. Research and development budgets of individual companies—while large when added together—are simply too shallow and unfocused to yield impressive and prolonged results. He also argues that emphasis on education and training in science and mathematics had an enormous impact on today's economic expansion, and that too little interest in these areas bodes ill for the future. So, argues Bluestone, it is not tax cuts or deficit repayments but investment expenditures in science and technology, that stimulate long-term economic growth.

David Leonhardt is also concerned about long-term economic growth as the economy emerges from the 2007–2009 recession. In "The Big Fix," a February 1, 2009, *New York Times Magazine* article Leonhardt raises questions about "where sources of real growth will come from." While Bluestone points to the "deep pockets" of the government, Leonhardt focuses on areas President Barak Obama has outlined that "lay a new foundation for growth," outlining the short-term costs and long-term benefits of public investment in green technology, health care, and education.

## Exercises

Read the excerpts from the Bluestone and Leonhardt articles, and answer the following questions.

1. In what ways are Bluestone's arguments similar to Schumpeter's analysis of long waves of economic cycles? How long are the time lags in cycles as predicted by each economist? How would each economist stimulate the economy to yield such technical advances? List the ways macroeconomic policy can stimulate growth. Are any of these policies consistent with Leonhardt's concerns?

2. Look at recent articles or information about the telecom industry, which after explosive growth and huge investments in capital during the late 1990s faced grave economic difficulties when the tech bubble crashed. Contrast this to the development of the first telephone network by AT&T—a government-protected monopoly. Could different government policies in these two eras have yielded different outcomes? Explain.

3. Explain the policies Bluestone and Leonhardt might recommend be used to stabilize the economy. Can the concerns highlighted by Leonhardt be dealt with using Bluestone-type recommendations? Explain.

4. Use the Keynesian-cross diagram and the model of aggregate demand and aggregate supply to show the effects on GDP and prices of spending of the sort Bluestone and Leonhardt recommend. How would the multiplier effects work?

5. Bluestone believes that an emphasis on math and science education during the Cold War advanced today's developments in science and technology. Are you a science or a mathematics major? Are you planning on enrolling in a number of science and mathematics courses during your undergraduate years? Why or why not? What is currently happening to math and science enrollments? Who is receiving Ph.D.s in the sciences and mathematics? What jobs are available for scientists and mathematicians?

6. Eisner and Bluestone seem to think that if the government accumulates deficits to fund expenditures that advance society, we should simply consider the future return to the private sector (and perhaps resulting surpluses) to be a cost of "doing the public's business." Others, particularly groups such as the Concord Coalition, see deficits as bad at all times. Examine Bluestone's arguments, and take a look at information from the Concord Coalition (www.concord.coalition.com), then assess your own position on deficits.

7. In the debate over government tax and expenditure policies, what underlying assumptions of conservatives, liberals, and radicals inform their positions, as detailed in the Bluestone and Leonhardt articles?

8. According to Leonhardt, what are the costs of not "remaking" the U.S. economy and making public investment in areas that generate faster long-term growth?

9. What is an "investment gap"? According to Leonhardt, will simply filling an investment gap restore U.S. growth? Explain. What are some of the potential short-term effects of these public investment efforts?

10. Leonhardt quotes economist Paul Romer as saying "The choices that determine a country's growth rate 'dwarf all other economic policy concerns.'" Why are these choices so important? What can get in the way of growth and growth policies? Why do some kinds of economic activity promote more growth than others? Why is it necessary to have public rather than private investment for these efforts?

# Forget Bush and Gore; Our Economy Needs Another Khrushchev

*Barry Bluestone*

...the conventional wisdom holds that it took three initiatives to restart the American growth machine. The first was Reagan's effort to get government regulation and social spending under control beginning in the 1980s. The second was President Clinton's getting the deficit under control after 1993. And the third was the amazing prowess of Federal Reserve Chairman Alan Greenspan in keeping inflation under control despite strong consumer demand and extraordinarily low unemployment.

In the bad old days, according to this logic, regulations undercut corporate intentions to invest, while public borrowing forced up interest rates to the point that borrowing became too expensive. The threat of inflation dampened enthusiasm for new capital improvements. Consequently, productivity suffered and economic growth slowed.

The annual growth in the nation's real gross domestic product fell from 4.4 percent in the 1960s to 3.2 in the 1970s to 3.0 in the 1980s and finally to only 2.3 percent during the first half of the 1990s. Only *after* Clinton and Congress moved decisively to reduce the federal deficit, and only after Greenspan snuffed out any hint of inflation, could the economy grow again.

That story sounds plausible, and the timing seems exquisite. Yet it's mostly wrong.The best data tracking the U.S. economy reveal that corporations were already investing heavily before the 1990s even though deficits were soaring and we were still worrying about inflation. Moreover, the investments were paying off, the proof being that productivity completely rebounded in the United States' manufacturing sector by the mid-1980s. It was the service sector that was dragging down overall productivity growth, but even in that labor-intensive sector, productivity began to pick up by the early 1990s. So even before we reined in federal deficits and stopped inflation cold, the economy was perched to take off.

Our rapid growth today has its roots in a technological revolution that has been underway for nearly three decades. Since it takes so long for business to move up the "learning curves" of new technologies, and often longer still to diffuse those technologies throughout the economy, there has always been a long lag time between the introduction of innovations and their payoff in the marketplace.

After the introduction of the steam engine in the early nineteenth century, it took nearly two decades for the new technology to yield a growth premium. Only after years of tinkering with that revolutionary technology and teaching a generation of mechanics how to use it did the steam engine provide for a sustained period of economic growth. The same lag pattern occurred between the introduction of the electric motor at the end of the nineteenth century and the realization of long-term growth we witnessed at the beginning of the twentieth century.

The lag phenomenon has recurred with the revolution brought about by the integrated circuit, the computer, and sophisticated software. It took more than two decades for the information-age technology to become sufficiently user-friendly that it could revolutionize production in nearly every goods-producing industry and in the service sector. During the same period, we were educating a work force to operate these marvels. As a result, productivity is now rising at better than 3 percent a year—three times faster than during the early 1990s. Tied to a labor supply growing at 1 percent annually, we have seen better than 4 percent growth for the past five years, every bit as high as we enjoyed during the booming post–World War II era.

Whom do we have to thank for all this? Reagan? Clinton? Greenspan? A more likely candidate is Nikita Khrushchev. Behind the information-age revolution were investments the federal government made beginning decades ago in basic research, education, and training. Khrushchev, the podium-thumping leader of the Soviet empire, challenged the United States to a nuclear arms race and then a space race beginning at the end of the 1950s. We took that challenge.

Massive computing power stuffed into the cramped quarters of missile cones was needed to guide ICBMs and rockets. The government, therefore, paid for the development of the first integrated circuits and microprocessors. Software was needed for the instruction sets for those minicomputers, and the government paid for that as well. The personal computer and all that followed were the direct descendants of those federally sponsored Cold War research projects. Later, it was the Department of Defense's investment in the ARPANET that led to the modern-day Internet.

Without those investments, today's ubiquitous e-commerce would never have come about—or at least it would have been delayed by decades. Moreover, money the federal government poured into science and math education after the launch of Sputnik in 1957 was critical for preparing a generation of scientists and engineers who developed all the new technology.

Alas, Khrushchev is gone, the Cold War is over, and Americans refuse to lavish money on the civilian side to anywhere near the extent we once did on the military. As a result, the federal government has been unwittingly destroying vital elements of the public-private research partnership....

Constrained by the number-one goal of paying down the federal debt as fast as possible, the amount spent on federal research and education has been plummeting, and these new initiatives would do little to reverse that downward trajectory. Back in the mid-1960s, federal spending on research and development was equivalent to 2.15 percent of the gross domestic product. Today, it has fallen to only .8 percent. Over the same period, federal spending on education as a proportion of the GDP has declined by almost half, from 1.07 percent to .56 percent. If *all* of President Clinton's spending plans for education were implemented over the next five years, the share of discretionary spending by the federal government allocated to this vital area would increase from just 5.0 percent to 5.8 percent—and basic research would fare no better. As a percentage of GDP, both education and basic research would continue to decline.

It would be nice to think that the private sector could make up the difference. But increased cost pressures from global competition and the deregulation of such industries as telecommunications have made it more difficult for private firms to set aside funds for basic research. Such investment is highly speculative, the payoffs are distant, and it is often impossible to restrict the benefits to those who paid for the research in the first place. As a result, while private research support is growing, only a small fraction pays for the kind of basic research that powers technological revolutions. And, of course, the private sector finances only a small portion of basic education.

So where is Khrushchev when we need him? We need something like the civilian equivalent of the Cold War to assure us of a continuing stream of technological breakthroughs that can fuel sustained prosperity.

There are many candidates for such government-sponsored research investments. Mounting a fully financed "war on cancer" and other medical scourges is one. Adding to the research on nanotechnology and biotechnology are two more. Certainly we could use more research into alternative fuel supplies and other efforts aimed at the problem of global warming.

On the education front, the federal government could underwrite a program to assure every child in the United States a prekindergarten year of schooling to help them get off on the right foot. Further expansion of federal backing for science and math education could be important as well, especially given the fact that the proportion of college students majoring in science and engineering has not increased since the 1970s....Unfortunately, the tax-cut nostrums of the Republicans and the debt obsession of many Democrats divert our attention from the growing federal-investment deficit that could ultimately condemn the nation to slower growth.

Source: Barry Bluestone, "Forget Bush and Gore; Our Economy Needs Another Khrushchev," *The Chronicle Review*, Jan. 5, 2001, pp. 311–312. Copyright © Barry Bluestone. Used with permission.

## The Big Fix
*David Leonhardt*

### I. Whither Growth?

The economy will recover. It won't recover anytime soon. It is likely to get significantly worse over the course of 2009, no matter what President Obama and Congress do. And resolving the financial crisis will require both aggressiveness and creativity. In fact, the main lesson from other crises of the past century is that governments tend to err on the side of too much caution—of taking the punch bowl away before the party has truly started up again. "The mistake the United States made during the Depression and the Japanese made during the '90s was too much start–stop in their policies," said Timothy Geithner, Obama's choice for Treasury secretary, when I went to visit him in his transition office a few weeks ago. Japan announced stimulus measures even as it was cutting other government spending. Franklin Roosevelt flirted with fiscal discipline midway through the New Deal, and the country slipped back into decline....

Once governments finally decide to use the enormous resources at their disposal, they have typically been able to shock an economy back to life. They can put to work the people, money and equipment sitting idle, until the private sector is willing to begin using them again. The prescription developed almost a century ago by John Maynard Keynes does appear to work.

But while Washington has been preoccupied with stimulus and bailouts, another, equally important issue has received far less attention—and the resolution of it is far more uncertain. What will happen once the paddles have been applied and the economy's heart starts beating again? How should the new American economy be remade? Above all, how fast will it grow?

That last question may sound abstract, even technical, compared with the current crisis. Yet the consequences of a country's growth rate are not abstract at all. Slow growth makes almost all problems worse. Fast growth helps solve them. As Paul Romer, an economist at Stanford University, has said, the choices that determine a country's growth rate "dwarf all other economic-policy concerns."

Growth is the only way for a government to pay off its debts in a relatively quick and painless fashion, allowing tax revenues to increase without tax rates having to rise. That is essentially what happened in the years after World War II. When the war ended, the federal government's debt equaled 120 percent of the gross domestic product (more than twice as high as its likely level by the end of next year). The rapid economic growth of the 1950s and '60s—more than 4 percent a year, compared with 2.5 percent in this decade—quickly whittled that debt away. Over the coming 25 years, if growth could be lifted by just one-tenth of a percentage point a year, the extra tax revenue would completely pay for an $800 billion stimulus package.

Yet there are real concerns that the United States' economy won't grow enough to pay off its debts easily and ensure rising living standards, as happened in the postwar decades. The fraternity of growth experts in the economics profession predicts that the economy, on its current path, will grow more slowly in the next couple of decades than over the past couple. They are concerned in part because two of the economy's most powerful recent engines have been exposed as a mirage: the explosion in consumer debt and spending, which lifted short-term growth at the expense of future growth, and the great Wall Street boom, which depended partly on activities that had very little real value.

Richard Freeman, a Harvard economist, argues that our bubble economy had something in common with the old Soviet economy. The Soviet Union's growth was artificially raised by massive industrial output that ended up having little use. Ours was artificially raised by mortgage-backed securities, collateralized debt obligations and even the occasional Ponzi scheme.

Where will new, real sources of growth come from? Wall Street is not likely to cure the nation's economic problems. Neither, obviously, is Detroit. Nor is Silicon Valley, at least not by itself. Well before the housing bubble burst, the big productivity gains brought about by the 1990s technology boom seemed to be petering out, which suggests that the Internet may not be able to fuel decades of economic growth in the way that the industrial inventions of the early 20th century did. Annual economic growth in the current decade, even excluding the dismal contributions that 2008 and 2009 will make to the average, has been the slowest of any decade since the 1930s.

So for the first time in more than 70 years, the epicenter of the American economy can be placed outside of California or New York or the industrial Midwest. It can be placed in Washington. Washington won't merely be given the task of pulling the economy out of the immediate crisis. It will also have to figure out how to put the American economy on a more sustainable path—to help it achieve fast, broadly shared growth and do so without the benefit of a bubble. Obama said as much in his inauguration speech when he pledged to overhaul Washington's approach to education, health care, science and infrastructure, all in an effort to "lay a new foundation for growth."

For centuries, people have worried that economic growth had limits—that the only way for one group to prosper was at the expense of another. The pessimists, from Malthus and the Luddites and on, have been proved wrong again and again. Growth is not finite. But it is also not inevitable. It requires a strategy....

III. The Investment Gap

One good way to understand the current growth slowdown is to think of the debt-fueled consumer-spending spree of the past 20 years as a symbol of an even larger problem. As a country we have been spending too much on the present and not enough on the future. We have been consuming rather than investing. We're suffering from investment-deficit disorder.

You can find examples of this disorder in just about any realm of American life. Walk into a doctor's office and you will be asked to fill out a long form with the most basic kinds of information that you have provided dozens of times before. Walk into a doctor's office in many other rich countries and that information—as well as your medical history—will be stored in computers. These electronic records not only reduce hassle; they also reduce medical errors. Americans cannot avail themselves of this innovation despite the fact that the United States spends far more on health care, per person, than any other country. We are spending our money to consume medical treatments, many of which have only marginal health benefits, rather than to invest it in ways that would eventually have far broader benefits.

Along similar lines, Americans are indefatigable buyers of consumer electronics, yet a smaller share of households in the United States has broadband Internet service than in Canada, Japan, Britain, South Korea and about a dozen other countries. Then there's education: this country once led the world in educational attainment by a wide margin. It no longer does. And transportation: a trip from Boston to Washington, on the fastest train in this country, takes six-and-a-half hours. A trip from Paris to Marseilles, roughly the same distance, takes three hours—a result of the French government's commitment to infrastructure.

These are only a few examples. Tucked away in the many statistical tables at the Commerce Department are numbers on how much the government and the private sector spend on investment and research—on highways, software, medical research and other things likely to yield future benefits. Spending by the private sector hasn't changed much over time. It was equal to 17 percent of G.D.P. 50 years ago, and it is about 17 percent now. But spending by the government—federal, state and local—has changed. It has dropped from about 7 percent of G.D.P. in the 1950s to about 4 percent now.

Governments have a unique role to play in making investments for two main reasons. Some activities, like mass transportation and pollution reduction, have societal benefits but not necessarily financial ones, and the private sector simply won't undertake them. And while many other kinds of investments do bring big financial returns, only a fraction of those returns go to the original investor. This makes the private sector reluctant to jump in. As a result, economists say that the private sector tends to spend less on research and investment than is economically ideal....

Even so, the idea that the government would be playing a much larger role in promoting economic growth would have sounded radical, even among Democrats, until just a few months ago. After all, the European countries that have tried guiding huge swaths of their economies—that have kept their arms around the "commanding heights," in Lenin's enduring phrase—have grown even more slowly than this country in recent years. But the credit crunch and the deepening recession have changed the discussion here. The federal government seems as if it was doing too little to take advantage of the American economy's enormous assets: its size, its openness and its mobile, risk-taking work force. The government is also one of the few large entities today able to borrow at a low interest rate. It alone can raise the capital that could transform the economy in the kind of fundamental ways....

IV. Stimulus vs. Transformation

The Obama administration's first chance to build a new economy—an investment economy—is the stimulus package that has been dominating policy discussions in Washington. Obama has repeatedly said he wants it to be a down payment on solving bigger problems. The twin goals, he said recently, are to "immediately jump-start job creation and long-term growth." But it is not easy to balance those goals....

Sometimes a project can give an economy a lift and also lead to transformation, but sometimes the goals are at odds, at least in the short term. Nothing demonstrates this quandary quite so well as green jobs, which are often cited as the single best hope for driving the post-bubble economy. Obama himself makes this case. Consumer spending has been the economic engine of the past two decades, he has said. Alternative energy will supposedly be the engine of the future—a way to save the planet, reduce the amount of money flowing to hostile oil-producing countries and revive the American economy, all at once. Put in these terms, green jobs sounds like a free lunch.

Green jobs can certainly provide stimulus. Obama's proposal includes subsidies for companies that make wind turbines, solar power and other alternative energy sources, and these subsidies will create some jobs. But the subsidies will not be nearly enough to eliminate the gap between the cost of dirty, carbon-based energy and clean energy. Dirty-energy sources—oil, gas and coal—are cheap. That's why we have become so dependent on them.

The only way to create huge numbers of clean-energy jobs would be to raise the cost of dirty-energy sources, as Obama's proposed cap-and-trade carbon-reduction program would do, to make them more expensive than clean energy. This is where the green-jobs dream gets complicated.

For starters, of the $700 billion we spend each year on energy, more than half stays inside this country. It goes to coal companies or utilities here, not to Iran or Russia. If we begin to use less electricity, those utilities will cut jobs. Just as important, the current, relatively low price of energy allows other companies—manufacturers, retailers, even white-collar enterprises—to sell all sorts of things at a profit. Raising that cost would raise the cost of almost everything that businesses do. Some projects that would have been profitable to Boeing, Kroger or Microsoft in the current economy no longer will be. Jobs that would otherwise have been created won't be. As Rob Stavins, a leading environmental economist, says, "Green jobs will, to some degree, displace other jobs." Just think about what happened when gas prices began soaring last spring: sales of some hybrids increased, but vehicle sales fell overall.

None of this means that Obama's climate policy is a mistake. Raising the price of carbon makes urgent sense, for the well-being of the planet and of the human race. And the economic costs of a serious climate policy are unlikely to be nearly as big as the alarmists—lobbyists and members of Congress trying to protect old-line energy industries—suggest. Various analyses of Obama's cap-and-trade plan, including one by Stavins, suggest that after it is fully implemented, it would cost less than 1 percent of gross domestic product a year, or about $100 billion in today's terms. That cost is entirely manageable. But it's still a cost.

Or perhaps we should think of it as an investment. Like so much in the economy, our energy policy has been geared toward the short term. Inexpensive energy made daily life easier and less expensive for all of us. Building a green economy, on the other hand, will require some sacrifice. In the end, that sacrifice should pay a handsome return in the form of icecaps that don't melt and droughts that don't happen—events with costs of their own. Over time, the direct economic costs of a new energy policy may also fall. A cap-and-trade program will create incentives for the private sector to invest in alternative energy, which will lead to innovations and lower prices. Some of the new clean-energy spending, meanwhile, really will replace money now flowing overseas and create jobs here.

But all those benefits will come later. The costs will come sooner, which is a big reason we do not already have a green economy—or an investment economy.

## V. Curing Inefficiencies

Washington's challenge on energy policy is to rewrite the rules so that the private sector can start building one of tomorrow's big industries. On health care, the challenge is keeping one of tomorrow's industries from growing too large.

For almost two decades, spending on health care grew rapidly, no matter what the rest of the economy was doing. Some of this is only natural. As a society gets richer and the basic comforts of life become commonplace, people will choose to spend more of their money on health and longevity instead of a third car or a fourth television.

Much of the increases in health care spending, however, are a result of government rules that have made the sector a fabulously—some say uniquely—inefficient sector. These inefficiencies have left the United States spending far more than other countries on medicine and, by many measures, getting worse results. The costs of health care are now so large that it has become one problem that cannot be solved by growth alone. It's qualitatively different from the other budget problems facing the government, like the Wall Street bailout, the stimulus, the war in Iraq or Social Security.

You can see that by looking at various costs as a share of one year of economic output—that is, gross domestic product. Surprisingly, the debt that the federal government has already accumulated doesn't present much of a problem. It is equal to about $6 trillion, or 40 percent of G.D.P., a level that is slightly lower than the average of the past six decades. The bailout, the stimulus and the rest of the deficits over the next two years will probably add about 15 percent of G.D.P. to the debt. That will take debt to almost 60 percent, which is above its long-term average but well below the levels of the 1950s. But the unfinanced parts of Medicare, the spending that the government has promised over and above the taxes it will collect in the coming decades requires another decimal place. They are equal to more than 200 percent of current G.D.P.

During the campaign, Obama talked about the need to control medical costs and mentioned a few ideas for doing so, but he rarely lingered on the topic. He spent more time talking about expanding health-insurance coverage, which would raise the government's bill. After the election, however, when time came to name a budget director, Obama sent a different message. He appointed Peter Orszag, who over the last two years has become one of the country's leading experts on the looming budget mess that is health care....

"One of the blessings in the current environment is that we have significant capacity to expand and sell Treasury debt," he [Orszag] told me recently. "If we didn't have that, and if the financial markets didn't have confidence that we would repay that debt, we would be in even more dire straits than we are." Absent a health care overhaul, the federal government's lenders around the world may eventually grow nervous about its ability to repay its debts. That, in turn, will cause them to demand higher interest rates to cover their risk when lending to the United States. Facing higher interest rates, the government won't be able to afford the kind of loans needed to respond to a future crisis, be it financial or military. The higher rates will also depress economic growth, aggravating every other problem....

Orszag would begin his talks by explaining that the problem is not one of demographics but one of medicine. "It's not primarily that we're going to have more 85-year-olds," he said during a September speech in California. "It's primarily that each 85-year-old in the future will cost us a lot more than they cost us today." The medical system will keep coming up with expensive new treatments, and Medicare will keep reimbursing them, even if they bring little benefit....

## VI. Graduates Equal Growth

A great appeal of green jobs—or, for that matter, of a growing and efficient health care sector—is that they make it possible to imagine what tomorrow's economy might look like. They are concrete. When somebody wonders, What will replace Wall Street? What will replace housing? they can be given an answer.

As answers go, green jobs and health care are fine. But they probably aren't the best answers. The best one is less concrete. It also has a lot more historical evidence on its side.

Last year, two labor economists, Claudia Goldin and Lawrence Katz, published a book called "The Race Between Education and Technology." It is as much a work of history—the history of education—as it is a work of economics. Goldin and Katz set out to answer the question of how much an education really matters. They are themselves products of public schools, she of New York and he of Los Angeles, and they have been a couple for two decades. They are liberals (Katz served as the chief economist under Robert Reich in Bill Clinton's Labor Department), but their book has been praised by both the right and the left. "I read the Katz and Goldin book," Matthew Slaughter, an associate dean of Dartmouth's business school who was an economic adviser to George W. Bush, recently told me, "and there's part of me that can't fathom that half the presidential debates weren't about a couple of facts in that book." Summers wrote a blurb for the book, calling it "the definitive treatment" of income inequality.

The book's central fact is that the United States has lost its once-wide lead in educational attainment. South Korea and Denmark graduate a larger share of their population from college—and Australia, Japan and the United Kingdom are close on our heels.

Goldin and Katz explain that the original purpose of American education was political, to educate the citizens of a democracy. By the start of the 20th century, though, the purpose had become blatantly economic. As parents saw that high-school graduates were getting most of the good jobs, they started a grass-roots movement, known as the high-school movement, to demand free, public high schools in their communities. "Middletown," the classic 1929 sociological study of life in Indiana, reported that education "evokes the fervor of a religion, a means of salvation, among a large section of the population."

At the time, some European intellectuals dismissed the new American high schools as wasteful. Instead of offering narrowly tailored apprentice programs, the United States was accused of overeducating its masses (or at least its white masses). But Goldin and Katz, digging into old population surveys, show that the American system paid huge dividends. High-school graduates filled the ranks of companies like General Electric and John Deere and used their broad base of skills to help their employers become global powers. And these new white-collar workers weren't the only ones to benefit. A high-school education also paid off for blue-collar workers. Those with a diploma were far more likely to enter newer, better-paying, more technologically advanced industries. They became plumbers, jewelers, electricians, auto mechanics and railroad engineers.

Not only did mass education increase the size of the nation's economic pie; it also evened out the distribution. The spread of high schools—by 1940, half of teenagers were getting a diploma—meant that graduates were no longer an elite group. In economic terms, their supply had increased, which meant that the wage premium that came with a diploma was now spread among a larger group of workers. Sure enough, inequality fell rapidly in the middle decades of the 20th century.

But then the great education boom petered out, starting in the late 1960s. The country's worst high schools never got their graduation rates close to 100 percent, while many of the fast-growing community colleges and public colleges, which were educating middle-class and poorer students, had low graduation rates. Between the early 1950s and early '80s, the share of young adults receiving a bachelor's degree jumped to 24 percent, from 7 percent. In the 30 years since, the share has only risen to 32 percent. Nearly all of the recent gains have come among women. For the first time on record, young men in the last couple of decades haven't been much more educated than their fathers were.

Goldin and Katz are careful to say that economic growth is not simply a matter of investing in education. And we can all name exceptions to the general rule. Bill Gates dropped out of college (though, as Malcolm Gladwell explains in his recent book, "Outliers," Gates received a fabulously intense computer-programming education while in high school). Some college graduates struggle to make a good living, and many will lose their jobs in this recession. But these are exceptions. Goldin's and Katz's thesis is that the 20th century was the American century in large part because this country led the world in education. The last 30 years, when educational gains slowed markedly, have been years of slower growth and rising inequality.

Their argument happens to be supported by a rich body of economic literature that didn't even make it into the book. More-educated people are healthier, live longer and, of course, make more money. Countries that educate more of their citizens tend to grow faster than similar countries that do not. The same is true of states and regions within this country. Crucially, the income gains tend to come after the education gains. What distinguishes thriving Boston from the other struggling cities of New England? Part of the answer is the relative share of children who graduate from college. The two most affluent immigrant groups in modern America—Asian-Americans and Jews—are also the most educated. In recent decades, as the educational attainment of men has stagnated, so have their wages. The median male worker is roughly as educated as he was 30 years ago and makes roughly the same in hourly pay. The median female worker is far more educated than she was 30 years ago and makes 30 percent more than she did then.

There really is no mystery about why education would be the lifeblood of economic growth. On the most basic level, education helps people figure out how to make objects and accomplish tasks more efficiently. It allows companies to make complex products that the rest of the world wants to buy and thus creates high-wage jobs. Education may not be as tangible as green jobs. But it helps a society leverage every other investment it makes, be it in medicine, transportation or alternative energy. Education—educating more people and educating them better—appears to be the best single bet that a society can make....

The Obama administration has suggested that education reform is an important goal. The education secretary is Arne Duncan, the former school superintendent in Chicago, who pushed for education changes there based on empirical data. Obama advisers say that the administration plans to use the education money in the stimulus package as leverage. States that reward good teaching and use uniform testing standards—rather than the choose-your-own-yardstick approach of the No Child Left Behind law—may get more money.

But it is still unclear just how much of a push the administration will make. With the financial crisis looming so large, something as sprawling and perennially plagued as education can seem like a sideshow. Given everything else on its agenda, the Obama administration could end up financing a few promising pilot programs without actually changing much. States, for their part, will be cutting education spending to balance their budgets....

Economists don't talk much about cultural norms. They prefer to emphasize prices, taxes and other incentives. And the transformation of the American economy will depend very much on such incentives: financial aid, Medicare reimbursements, energy prices and marginal tax rates. But it will also depend on forces that aren't quite so easy to quantify.

Orszag, on his barnstorming tour to talk about the health care system, argued that his fellow economists were making a mistake by paying so little attention to norms. After all, doctors in Minnesota don't work under a different Medicare system than doctors in New Jersey. But they do act differently.

The norms of the last two decades or so—consume before invest; worry about the short term, not the long term—have been more than just a reflection of the economy. They have also *affected* the economy. Chief executives have fought for paychecks that their predecessors would have considered obscenely large. Technocrats inside Washington's regulatory agencies, after listening to their bosses talk endlessly about the dangers of overregulation, made quite sure that they weren't regulating too much. Financial engineering became a more appealing career track than actual engineering or science. In one of the small gems in their book, Goldin and Katz write that towns and cities with a large elderly population once devoted a higher-than-average share of their taxes to schools. Apparently, age made them see the benefits of education. In recent decades, though, the relationship switched. Older towns spent less than average on schools. You can imagine voters in these places asking themselves, "What's in it for me?"

By any standard, the Obama administration faces an imposing economic to-do list. It will try to end the financial crisis and recession as quickly as possible, even as it starts work on an agenda that will inspire opposition from a murderers' row of interest groups: Wall Street, Big Oil, Big Coal, the American Medical Association and teachers' unions. Some items on the agenda will fail.

But the same was true of the New Deal and the decades after World War II, the period that is obviously the model for the Obama years. Roosevelt and

Truman both failed to pass universal health insurance or even a program like Medicare. Yet the successes of those years—Social Security, the highway system, the G.I. Bill, the National Science Foundation, the National Labor Relations Board—had a huge effect on the culture.

The American economy didn't simply grow rapidly in the late 1940s, 1950s and 1960s. It grew rapidly and gave an increasing share of its bounty to the vast middle class. Middle-class incomes soared during those years, while income growth at the very top of the ladder, which had been so great in the 1920s, slowed down. The effects were too great to be explained by a neat package of policies, just as the last few decades can't be explained only by education, investment and the like.

When Washington sets out to rewrite the rules for the economy, it can pass new laws and shift money from one program to another. But the effects of those changes are not likely to be merely the obvious ones. The changes can also send signals. They can influence millions of individual decisions—about the schools people attend, the jobs they choose, the medical care they request—and, in the process, reshape the economy.

*Source:* David Leonhardt. "The Big Fix," February 1, 2008. *The New York Times.*

The Washington Post.

# International Trade and Interdependence

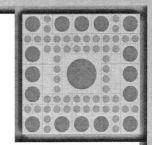

## Introduction

Interdependence among nations is a major feature of the modern world economy. To understand this concept properly and apply it to the problems we will be examining, we must be more specific. By the term economic interdependence, *we mean that all countries are affected by the events of an economic nature that occur in many other countries. For example, many industrialized nations rely on developing nations for raw materials and other resources. In turn, many developing nations import manufactured finished goods from industrialized nations. The degree of interdependence is, of course, different for every nation. For example, the Japanese economy is seriously affected by increased oil prices yet relatively unaffected by Costa Rica's decision to increase banana prices. On the other hand, the Costa Rican economy, also strongly affected by an oil price increase, has the flexibility to shift its imports of steel from the United States to Japan.*

*Economic interdependence describes the effect of the complex international flow of goods, services, and capital among nations. It helps us understand how individuals, businesses, and nations must first exchange their currencies before exchanging goods and services. To acquire Japanese Toyotas, a U.S. auto importer must first exchange dollars for yen in a currency market. Then, the automobile transaction can be completed.*

*Financial markets are interdependent as well. For example, if real interest rates fall in Germany and at the same time rise in the United States, investors are likely to sell their German bonds and invest the proceeds in U.S. bonds generating a better return. If Mexico experiences political instability or increasing inflation, domestic and foreign investors will likely transfer funds from Mexico to the United States or Europe. Information and communications technology has increased both the magnitude and speed of these transfers and facilitated international interdependence.*

*The nature of this contemporary interdependence involves not only the exchange of goods and services but technology transfers, financial capital movements, and factors affecting the*

From Chapter 19 of *Economics: A Tool for Critically Understanding Society*, 9/e. Tom Riddell. Jean Shackelford. Geoffrey Schneider. Steve Stamos. Copyright © 2011 by Pearson Education. Published by Addison-Wesley. All rights reserved.

*international division of labor. For the past four centuries, raw materials and resources as well as technology provided the impetus for trade. Indeed, much of the motivation for the geographical explorations of the fifteenth century was the search for trade routes and later for colonies from which raw materials could be exported cheaply. Later, with the Industrial Revolution, the ability to manufacture and export products cheaply became a motivation for trade. While capital has always been highly mobile, seeking the highest profits worldwide, today the transfer of technology has made it very easy to set up operations in places where wages and other production costs are low. Increasingly, industrialized nations are losing jobs and exports to developing countries, which offer an abundance of low-wage labor.*

## INTERNATIONAL TRADE AND INTERDEPENDENCE

The 1990s brought forward a decade of rapid globalization. This globalization was characterized by the increased volume of international trade in goods and services, financial flows and services, the migration of labor, and technological changes in the areas of communications, information, finance, and production. The global economic and financial system was fundamentally transformed in this decade. Combined with a prevailing economic philosophy that focused on the benefits of free markets, free trade, unrestricted capital flows, and deregulation, there were distinct uneven outcomes between nations and between citizens within nations. By the end of the 1990s, there was a worldwide anti-globalization movement calling into question the efficacy of the liberalization character of the new global system.

The first decade of the twenty-first century has seen the continuation of this debate as the rapid and impressive economic growth of both China and India benefited from markets open to them. In this decade China and Japan have used their large trade surplus to buy U.S. debt, thus financing both public and private U.S. expenditures financed by borrowing. The global financial crisis and great recession that began in late 2007 and continued through 2009 left the global financial and economic system facing many serious challenges and questions. In addition, the issues of global poverty, unemployment, public health, environmental degradation, energy sustainability, food supply and prices, and climate change present serious long-term challenges for the global community.

## WORLD TRADE

Figures 1 and 2 show the rapid process of globalization and trade liberalization that has resulted in a sustained increase in the growth of world real GDP growth. Figure 3 shows the slowing of the world trade volume, beginning in 2007. In Fig. 1, we can observe that the trend for world real GDP growth rose to around 4 percent by 2005, yet fell dramatically in 2009 to a negative 1.6 percent. It is expected to recover to its historic trend line after 2012. Figure 2 shows that between 2000 and 2007, emerging and developing economies grew at rates between 4 and 8 percent while advanced economies grew rates of 3.5 percent or less. The economic downturn in late 2007 slowed emerging and developing economies growth rates to 2 percent, while advanced economies saw growth fall by −4 percent. Nevertheless, the International Monetary Fund in its 2009 *Global Prospects and Policies Report* estimates a return to positive trends when the recession ends.

**FIGURE 1** The Rapid Growth of Globalization

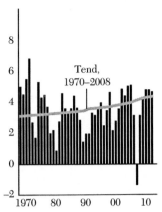

Note: *Annual percent change unless otherwise noted.*

The global economy is undergoing its most severe recession of the postwar period. World real GDP dropped in 2009, with advanced economies experiencing deep contractions and emerging and developing economies slowing abruptly. Trade volumes fell sharply, while inflation subsided quickly.

*Source: IMF Global Prospects: Policies, Chapter 1, 2009.*

## The Impact of International Trade on the United States

Since the early 1980s, international trade has continued to become a larger and larger share of the U.S. economy. By 2000, imports of goods represented 13 percent of the GDP and exports of goods represented 8 percent of the GDP, together representing more than 20 percent of the GDP. Since the early 1980s, the United States has experienced a trade deficit. By 1987, the trade deficit had increased to $40 billion. With a change in policies and a determined depreciation of

**FIGURE 2** Real GDP Growth—1970–2010

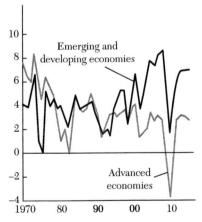

Note: Annual percent change unless otherwise noted.

*Source: IMF Global Prospects: Policies, Chapter 1, 2009.*

**FIGURE 3**   World Trade Volume (goods and services)

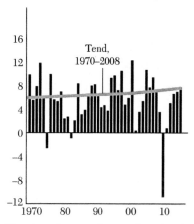

Note: Annual percent change unless otherwise noted.

*Source: IMF Global Prospects: Policies,* Chapter 1, 2009.

the U.S. dollar (to make exports more competitive and imports more expensive), the U.S. trade deficit narrowed in 1991 to less than $10 billion. Yet, in the 1990s, globalization and the global movement toward the liberalization of trade and markets along with a returning strong U.S. dollar produced a trend toward larger trade deficits. This process accelerated from the period 1997 to the present.

**Table 1**   GDP and Merchandise Trade by Region, 2006–2008 (Annual % change at constant prices)

|  | GDP | | | Exports | | | Imports | | |
|---|---|---|---|---|---|---|---|---|---|
|  | 2006 | 2007 | 2008 | 2006 | 2007 | 2008 | 2006 | 2007 | 2008 |
| World | 3.7 | 3.5 | 1.7 | 8.5 | 6.0 | 2.0 | 8.0 | 6.0 | 2.0 |
| North America | 2.9 | 2.1 | 1.1 | 8.5 | 5.0 | 1.5 | 6.0 | 2.0 | −2.5 |
|   United States | 2.8 | 2.0 | 1.1 | 10.5 | 7.0 | 5.5 | 5.5 | 1.0 | −4.0 |
| South and Central America[a] | 6.1 | 6.6 | 5.3 | 4.0 | 3.0 | 1.5 | 15.5 | 17.5 | 15.5 |
| Europe | 3.1 | 2.8 | 1.0 | 7.5 | 4.0 | 0.5 | 7.5 | 4.0 | −1.0 |
|   European Union (27) | 3.0 | 2.8 | 1.0 | 7.5 | 3.5 | 0.0 | 7.0 | 3.5 | −1.0 |
| Commonwealth of Independent States (CIS) | 7.5 | 8.4 | 5.5 | 6.0 | 7.5 | 6.0 | 20.5 | 20.0 | 15.0 |
| Africa | 5.7 | 5.8 | 5.0 | 1.5 | 4.5 | 3.0 | 10.0 | 14.0 | 13.0 |
| Middle East | 5.2 | 5.5 | 5.7 | 3.0 | 4.0 | 3.0 | 5.5 | 14.0 | 10.0 |
| Asia | 4.6 | 4.9 | 2.0 | 13.5 | 11.5 | 4.5 | 8.5 | 8.0 | 4.0 |
|   China | 11.6 | 11.9 | 9.0 | 22.0 | 19.5 | 8.5 | 16.5 | 13.5 | 4.0 |
|   Japan | 2.0 | 2.4 | −0.7 | 10.0 | 9.5 | 2.5 | 2.0 | 1.5 | −1.0 |
|   India | 9.8 | 9.3 | 7.9 | 11.0 | 13.0 | 7.0 | 8.0 | 16.0 | 12.5 |
|   Newly industrialized economies (4)[b] | 5.6 | 5.6 | 1.7 | 13.0 | 9.0 | 3.5 | 8.0 | 6.0 | 3.5 |

[a]Includes the Caribbean.
[b]Hong Kong, China; Republic of Korea; Singapore and Chinese Taipei.

Source: World Trade Secretariat 2009.

**Table 2**  World Merchandise Trade by Region and Selected Country, 2008 ($bn and %)

| | Exports | | Imports | |
|---|---|---|---|---|
| | **Value 2008** | **Annual % change 2000–2008** | **Value 2008** | **Annual % change 2000–2008** |
| World | 15,775 | 12 | 16,120 | 12 |
| North America | 2,049 | 7 | 2,909 | 7 |
| United States | 1,301 | 7 | 2,166 | 7 |
| Canada | 456 | 6 | 418 | 7 |
| Mexico | 292 | 7 | 323 | 7 |
| South and Central America[a] | 602 | 15 | 595 | 14 |
| Brazil | 198 | 17 | 183 | 15 |
| Other South and Central America[a] | 404 | 14 | 413 | 14 |
| Europe | 6,456 | 12 | 6,833 | 12 |
| European Union (27) | 5,913 | 12 | 6,268 | 12 |
| Germany | 1,465 | 13 | 1,206 | 12 |
| France | 609 | 8 | 708 | 10 |
| Netherlands | 634 | 13 | 574 | 13 |
| Italy | 540 | 11 | 556 | 11 |
| United Kingdom[b] | 458 | 6 | 632 | 8 |
| Commonwealth of Independent States (CIS) | 703 | 22 | 493 | 25 |
| Russian Federation[c] | 472 | 21 | 292 | 26 |
| Africa | 561 | 18 | 466 | 17 |
| South Africa | 81 | 13 | 99 | 16 |
| Africa less South Africa | 481 | 19 | 367 | 18 |
| Oil exporters[d] | 347 | 21 | 137 | 21 |
| Non-oil exporters | 133 | 15 | 229 | 16 |
| Middle East | 1,047 | 19 | 575 | 17 |
| Asia | 4,355 | 13 | 4,247 | 14 |
| China | 1,428 | 24 | 1,133 | 22 |
| Japan | 782 | 6 | 762 | 9 |
| India | 179 | 20 | 292 | 24 |
| Newly Industrialized economies (4)[e] | 1,033 | 10 | 1,093 | 10 |
| Memorandum Items | | | | |
| Developing economies | 6,025 | 15 | 5,494 | 15 |
| MERCOSUR[f] | 279 | 16 | 259 | 14 |
| ASEAN[g] | 990 | 11 | 936 | 12 |
| EU (27) extra-trade | 1,928 | 12 | 2,283 | 12 |
| Least Developed Countries (LDCs) | 176 | 22 | 157 | 17 |

[a]Includes the Caribbean. For composition of groups see the Technical Notes of WTO, International Trade Statistics, 2008.
[b]The 2007 annual change was affected by a reduction in trade associated with fraudulent VAT declaration. For further information, refer to the special notes of the monthly UK Trade First Release.
[c]Imports are valued f.o.b.
[d]Algeria, Angola, Cameroon, Chad, Congo, Equatorial Guinea, Gabon, Libya, Nigeria, Sudan.
[e]Hong Kong, China; Republic of Korea; Singapore and Chinese Taipei.
[f]Common Market of the Southern Cone: Argentina, Brazil, Paraguay, Uruguay
[g]Association of Southeast Asian Nations: Brunei, Cambodia, Indonesia, Laos, Malaysia, Myanmar, Philippines, Singapore, Thailand, Viet Nam.

Source: World Trade Secretariat 2009.

**Table 3**  World Exports of Commercial Services by Region and Selected Country, 2008 ($bn and %)

| | Exports | | Imports | |
|---|---|---|---|---|
| | Value 2008 | Annual % change 2000–2008 | Value 2008 | Annual % change 2000–2008 |
| World | 3,730 | 12 | 3,470 | 12 |
| North America | 603 | 8 | 473 | 7 |
| United States | 522 | 8 | 364 | 7 |
| South and Central America[b] | 109 | 11 | 117 | 10 |
| Brazil | 29 | 16 | 44 | 14 |
| Europe | 1,919 | 13 | 1,628 | 12 |
| European Union (27) | 1,738 | 13 | 1,516 | 12 |
| Germany | 235 | 15 | 285 | 10 |
| United Kingdom | 283 | 12 | 199 | 9 |
| France | 153 | 9 | 137 | 11 |
| Italy | 123 | 10 | 132 | 12 |
| Spain | 143 | 13 | 108 | 16 |
| Commonwealth of Independent States (CIS) | 83 | 22 | 114 | 22 |
| Russian Federation | 50 | 23 | 75 | 21 |
| Africa | 88 | 14 | 121 | 16 |
| Egypt | 25 | 12 | 16 | 11 |
| South Africa[a] | 13 | 13 | 17 | 15 |
| Middle East | 94 | 14 | 158 | 16 |
| Israel | 24 | 6 | 20 | 7 |
| Asia | 837 | 13 | 858 | 11 |
| Japan | 144 | 10 | 166 | 6 |
| China[a] | 137 | — | 152 | — |
| India[a] | 106 | — | 91 | — |
| Four East Asian traders[c] | 271 | 11 | 247 | 10 |

[a]Secretariat estimates.
[b]Includes the Caribbean. For composition of groups see Chapter IV Metadata of WTO International Trade Statistics, 2008.
[c]Chinese Taipei; Hong Kong, China; Republic of Korea and Singapore.

Note: While provisional full year data were available in early March for 50 countries accounting for more than two-thirds of world commercial services trade, estimates for most other countries are based on data for the first three quarters (the first six months in the case of China).

Source: World Trade Secretariat 2009.

**Table 4**  Merchandise Trade: Leading Exporters and Importers, 2008 ($bn and %)

| Rank Exporters | Value | Share | Annual % Change | Rank Importers | Value | Share | Annual % Change |
|---|---|---|---|---|---|---|---|
| 1. Germany | 1,465 | 9.1 | 11 | 1. United States | 2,166 | 13.2 | 7 |
| 2. China | 1,428 | 8.9 | 17 | 2. Germany | 1,206 | 7.3 | 14 |
| 3. United States | 1,301 | 8.1 | 12 | 3. China | 1,133 | 6.9 | 19 |
| 4. Japan | 782 | 4.9 | 10 | 4. Japan | 762 | 4.6 | 22 |
| 5. Netherlands | 634 | 3.9 | 15 | 5. France | 708 | 4.3 | 14 |
| 6. France | 609 | 3.8 | 10 | 6. United Kingdom | 632 | 3.8 | 1 |

**Table 4**  Continued

| Rank Exporters | Value | Share | Annual % Change | Rank Importers | Value | Share | Annual % Change |
|---|---|---|---|---|---|---|---|
| 7. Italy | 540 | 3.3 | 10 | 7. Netherlands | 574 | 3.5 | 16 |
| 8. Belgium | 477 | 3.0 | 10 | 8. Italy | 556 | 3.4 | 10 |
| 9. Russian Federation | 472 | 2.9 | 33 | 9. Belgium | 470 | 2.9 | 14 |
| 10. United Kingdom | 458 | 2.8 | 4 | 10. Korea, Republic of | 435 | 2.7 | 22 |
| 11. Canada | 456 | 2.8 | 8 | 11. Canada | 418 | 2.5 | 7 |
| 12. Korea, Republic of | 422 | 2.6 | 14 | 12. Spain | 402 | 2.5 | 3 |
| 13. Hong Kong, China | 370 | 2.3 | 6 | 13. Hong Kong, China | 393 | 2.4 | 6 |
| - domestic exports | 17 | 0.1 | — | - retained imports | 98 | 0.6 | — |
| - re-exports | 353 | 2.2 | — | | | | |
| 14. Singapore | 338 | 2.1 | 13 | 14. Mexico | 323 | 2.0 | 9 |
| - domestic exports | 176 | 1.1 | 13 | | | | |
| - re-exports | 162 | 1.0 | 13 | | | | |
| 15. Saudi Arabia[a] | 329 | 2.0 | 40 | 15. Singapore | 320 | 1.9 | 22 |
| | | | | - retained imports[b] | 157 | 1.0 | 31 |
| 16. Mexico | 292 | 1.8 | 7 | 16. Russian Federation[c] | 292 | 1.8 | 31 |
| 17. Spain | 268 | 1.7 | 6 | 17. India | 292 | 1.8 | 35 |
| 18. Taipei, Chinese | 256 | 1.6 | 4 | 18. Taipei, Chinese | 240 | 1.5 | 10 |
| 19. United Arab Emirates[a] | 232 | 1.4 | 28 | 19. Poland | 204 | 1.2 | 23 |
| 20. Switzerland | 200 | 1.2 | 16 | 20. Turkey | 202 | 1.2 | 19 |
| 21. Malaysia | 200 | 1.2 | 13 | 21. Australia | 200 | 1.2 | 21 |
| 22. Brazil | 198 | 1.2 | 23 | 22. Austria | 184 | 1.1 | 13 |
| 23. Australia | 187 | 1.2 | 33 | 23. Switzerland | 183 | 1.1 | 14 |
| 24. Sweden | 184 | 1.1 | 9 | 24. Brazil | 183 | 1.1 | 44 |
| 25. Austria | 182 | 1.1 | 11 | 25. Thailand | 179 | 1.1 | 28 |
| 26. India | 179 | 1.1 | 22 | 26. Sweden | 167 | 1.0 | 10 |
| 27. Thailand | 178 | 1.1 | 17 | 27. United Arab Emirates[a] | 159 | 1.0 | 20 |
| 28. Poland | 168 | 1.0 | 20 | 28. Malaysia | 157 | 1.0 | 7 |
| 29. Norway | 168 | 1.0 | 23 | 29. Czech Republic | 142 | 0.9 | 20 |
| 30. Czech Republic | 147 | 0.9 | 20 | 30. Indonesia · | 126 | 0.8 | 36 |
| Total of above[d] | 13,120 | 81.4 | — | Total of above[d] | 13,409 | 81.7 | — |
| World[d] | 16,127 | 100.0 | 15 | World[d] | 16,415 | 100.0 | 15 |

[a]Secretariat estimates.
[b]Singapore's retained imports are defined as imports less re-exports.
[c]Imports are valued f.o.b.
[d]Includes significant re-exports or imports for re-export.

Source: WTO Secretariat 2009.

**Table 5** Leading Exporters and Importers in World Trade in Commercial Services, 2008 ($bn and %)

| Rank | Exporters | Value | Share | Annual % change | Rank | Importers | Value | Share | Annual % change |
|---|---|---|---|---|---|---|---|---|---|
| 1 | United States | 522 | 14.0 | 10 | 1 | United States | 364 | 10.5 | 7 |
| 2 | United Kingdom | 283 | 7.6 | 2 | 2 | Germany | 285 | 8.2 | 11 |
| 3 | Germany | 235 | 6.3 | 11 | 3 | United Kingdom | 199 | 5.7 | 1 |
| 4 | France | 153 | 4.1 | 6 | 4 | Japan | 166 | 4.8 | 11 |
| 5 | Japan | 144 | 3.9 | 13 | 5 | China[a] | 152 | 4.4 | — |
| 6 | Spain | 143 | 3.8 | 11 | 6 | France | 137 | 3.9 | 6 |
| 7 | China[a] | 137 | 3.7 | — | 7 | Italy | 132 | 3.8 | 12 |
| 8 | Italy | 123 | 3.3 | 12 | 8 | Spain | 108 | 3.1 | 10 |
| 9 | India[a] | 106 | 2.8 | — | 9 | Ireland[a] | 103 | 3.0 | 9 |
| 10 | Netherlands[a] | 102 | 2.7 | 8 | 10 | Korea, Republic of | 93 | 2.7 | 12 |
| 11 | Ireland[a] | 96 | 2.6 | 8 | 11 | Netherlands[a] | 92 | 2.6 | 10 |
| 12 | Hong Kong, China | 91 | 2.4 | 9 | 12 | India[a] | 91 | 2.6 | — |
| 13 | Belgium[a] | 89 | 2.4 | 16 | 13 | Canada | 84 | 2.4 | 5 |
| 14 | Switzerland | 74 | 2.0 | 15 | 14 | Belgium[a] | 84 | 2.4 | 16 |
| 15 | Korea, Republic of | 74 | 2.0 | 20 | 15 | Singapore | 76 | 2.2 | 6 |
| 16 | Denmark | 72 | 1.9 | 17 | 16 | Russian Federation | 75 | 2.2 | 29 |
| 17 | Singapore | 72 | 1.9 | 3 | 17 | Denmark | 62 | 1.8 | 16 |
| 18 | Sweden | 71 | 1.9 | 13 | 18 | Sweden | 54 | 1.6 | 13 |
| 19 | Luxembourg[a] | 68 | 1.8 | 5 | 19 | Thailand | 46 | 1.3 | 22 |
| 20 | Canada | 62 | 1.7 | 2 | 20 | Australia | 45 | 1.3 | 18 |

**Table 5** Continued

| Rank | Exporters | Value | Share | Annual % change | Rank | Importers | Value | Share | Annual % change |
|---|---|---|---|---|---|---|---|---|---|
| 21 | Austria | 62 | 1.7 | 12 | 21 | Brazil | 44 | 1.3 | 28 |
| 22 | Russian Federation | 50 | 1.3 | 29 | 22 | Hong Kong, China | 44 | 1.3 | 7 |
| 23 | Greece | 50 | 1.3 | 16 | 23 | Norway | 44 | 1.3 | 12 |
| 24 | Norway | 46 | 1.2 | 13 | 24 | Austria | 42 | 1.2 | 8 |
| 25 | Australia | 46 | 1.2 | 15 | 25 | Luxembourg[a] | 40 | 1.2 | 8 |
| 26 | Poland | 35 | 0.9 | 20 | 26 | Switzerland | 37 | 1.1 | 10 |
| 27 | Turkey | 34 | 0.9 | 22 | 27 | United Arab Emirates[a] | 35 | 1.0 | — |
| 28 | Taipei, Chinese | 34 | 0.9 | 8 | 28 | Saudi Arabia[a] | 34 | 1.0 | — |
| 29 | Thailand | 33 | 0.9 | 11 | 29 | Taipei, Chinese | 34 | 1.0 | -2 |
| 30 | Malaysia | 30 | 0.8 | 5 | 30 | Poland | 30 | 0.9 | 25 |
| | Total of above | 3,135 | 84.1 | — | | Total of above | 2,835 | 81.7 | — |
| | World | 3,730 | 100.0 | 11 | | World | 3,470 | 100.0 | 11 |

[a]Secretariat estimates.

Note: While provisional full year data were available in early March for 50 countries accounting for more than two-thirds of world commercial services trade, estimates for most other countries are based on data for the first three quarters (the first six months in the case of China).

Source: World Trade Secretariat 2009.

**FIGURE 4**   International Trade–Goods and Services, Percent of GDP

*Source:* Federal Reserve Bank, St. Louis, 2009.

Figure 4 shows the share of exports and share of imports as a percentage of the U.S. GDP. Together, exports and imports were 29 percent by 2008 (18 percent for exports and 13 percent for imports). As a consequence of accelerated demand for imports over exports, Figure 5 shows that the U.S. trade deficit reached record levels before plummeting in 2009 as a

**FIGURE 5**   Trade Deficit in Goods and Services, Billions of Dollars, Monthly Rate

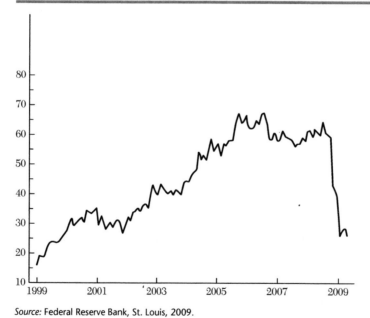

*Source:* Federal Reserve Bank, St. Louis, 2009.

**FIGURE 6** U.S. Goods Export & Import Shares, 2008

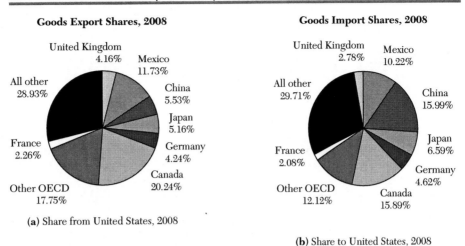

**Goods Export Shares, 2008**

United Kingdom 4.16%
Mexico 11.73%
All other 28.93%
China 5.53%
Japan 5.16%
France 2.26%
Germany 4.24%
Other OECD 17.75%
Canada 20.24%

**(a)** Share from United States, 2008

**Goods Import Shares, 2008**

United Kingdom 2.78%
Mexico 10.22%
All other 29.71%
China 15.99%
Japan 6.59%
France 2.08%
Germany 4.62%
Other OECD 12.12%
Canada 15.89%

**(b)** Share to United States, 2008

*Source:* Research Division, Federal Reserve Bank of St. Louis, 2009.

result of the global recession. By 2006, the U.S. trade deficit was more than $600 billion and was at a level that represented more than 6 percent of the GDP. More than two-thirds ($400 billion) of this trade deficit is with China and Japan.

The United States trades with many countries, and Figure 6, shows that Canada is the major trading partner with the United States. In 2008 the United States exported over 20 percent of its goods to Canada and imported nearly 16 percent of its goods from Canada, while 16 percent of the goods entering the United States came from China, China received only 5.5 percent of U.S. exports.

## THE MODERN THEORY OF INTERNATIONAL TRADE

Modern economic interdependence and the influence of multinational corporations led to more complex national trade questions in the 1990s. Before examining those questions, however, we need to understand why trade takes place. The simple answer to this question relies on the **theory of comparative advantage,** which suggests that free trade is most beneficial to world economies. We shall examine the theory behind international trade, a few of the more convincing arguments for protection, and current trends toward free trade as well as the critics of such attempts.

# THE **BIG** PICTURE

## Comparative Advantage

The theory of comparative advantage explains why nations gain from specialization in production and trade. Two countries will benefit if they both specialize in producing goods in which they have a relative advantage and trade those goods freely. One way to think about this is by comparing the resources or inputs it takes to produce two goods, textiles and computers, in two countries, the United States and Mexico, and examine how each might benefit from specialization and trade.

Suppose that the United States is more efficient in producing both textiles and computers than Mexico. (Using the same amount of inputs, the United States can produce more computers and textiles). Suppose furthermore that the United States is twice as productive in textile production and four times as productive in computer production. We can say that the United States has an *absolute* advantage in both goods, that is, it can produce both textiles and computers more efficiently). However, if we look at the relative advantage of each nation, we find that the United States has a relative (and absolute advantage) in producing computers, while Mexico has a relative (but not an absolute) advantage in producing textiles.

Production with same resource inputs:

| United States | Mexico |
|---------------|--------|
| 200 Textiles | 100 textiles |
| 400 Computers | 100 computers |

The United States can produce computers relatively more efficiently than it can produce textiles and Mexico can produce textiles relatively more efficiently than it can produce computers—given the same input or resource requirements. Thus, the United States has a *comparative* advantage in computers and Mexico has a *comparative* advantage in textiles. Given that the United States has limited resources, the United States will benefit from specializing in computer production, and importing textiles from Mexico, which should specialize in textile production, and Mexico will benefit from trading textiles for computers. When each country specializes in the good that it is relatively best at producing and trades that good freely, total production or output of both goods increases. After trade occurs, the standard of living in both countries increases.

This is illustrated in Figure BP.1 below. Before trade occurs, both countries produce both goods. Given that the United States can produce either 200 Textiles or 400 Computers with its resources, suppose it decides to devote 1/4 of its resources to producing 50 Textiles and 3/4 of its resources to producing 300

**FIGURE BP.1**

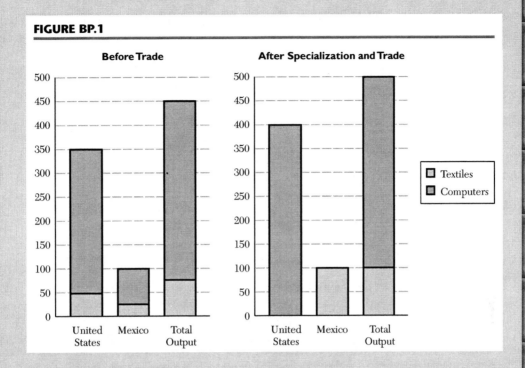

Computers. Similarly, Mexico can produce either 100 Textiles or 100 Computers, and chooses to produce 25 Textiles and 75 Computers. Total output of both countries is then 75 Textiles and 375 Computers before trade. After trade, the United States specializes entirely in computer production, producing 400 Computers, and Mexico specializes entirely in textile production, producing 100 Textiles. Production of both goods has increased, and both countries can now consume more of both goods due to specialization and trade based on comparative advantage.

If this process is extended to more countries, then specialization and trade based on the theory of comparative advantage should increase global efficiency and enhance the standard of living of all trading countries. The section below outlines the theory of comparative advantage in more detail, and then lays out some of the problems with this theory when applied to the modern global economy.

## Who Trades What, and Why?

How does an individual nation assume its place in the world economy? Why does one nation specialize in production of groundnuts; a second, textiles; a third, aircraft; and a fourth, financial services? One of the first economists to deal with this question was Adam Smith, and in 1817 David Ricardo refined Smith's ideas to develop the general approach that we still use today. This approach to understanding trade is based on two basic concepts, absolute and comparative advantage.

Some assumptions will greatly facilitate matters by allowing us to deal with the essentials. In our hypothetical world, we have two nations, producing two goods. Perfect competition exists everywhere, there are no transportation costs, and labor and capital cannot move between the two nations. The costs of production in terms of labor hours are assumed to be as follows:

| | Cost to Produce 1 Unit (Hours of Labor) | |
| --- | --- | --- |
| | Wheat | Cloth |
| United Kingdom | 10 | 20 |
| France | 15 | 45 |

Under these assumptions, the United Kingdom can produce both goods with less labor cost than can France. The United Kingdom, therefore, has an absolute advantage in producing both wheat and cloth, and France has an absolute disadvantage in each. Having an **absolute advantage** simply means that a nation can produce goods (in this case, both wheat and cloth) more efficiently than another.

This does not mean, however, that the United Kingdom produces and exports both goods and that France produces neither of them. To find out what production and exchange will take place, we must examine the production trade-off ratios between products within each nation; that is, we must see how much cloth must be given up to produce more wheat. In our example, one unit of wheat is produced in the United Kingdom with half the amount of labor time that it takes to produce a unit of cloth; with other factors constant, one unit of cloth will exchange for two units of wheat. In France—again, because of the relative costs of production—one unit of cloth can be exchanged for three units of wheat. This gives us the following internal rates of exchange of cloth for wheat:

United Kingdom 1 cloth = 2 wheat

France 1 cloth = 3 wheat

or

United Kingdom 1/2 cloth = 1 wheat

France 1/3 cloth = 1 wheat

By comparing the internal rates of exchange in each of the two countries, a trader might reason, "If I could buy one unit of wheat in Paris, ship it to London, and exchange it there for cloth, I could get one-half of a unit of cloth; if I exchanged it in France, I would get only one-third of a unit of cloth. My gain from this trade is one-sixth of a unit of cloth. On the other hand, taking one unit of cloth from Paris to London and exchanging it for wheat would bring me only two units of wheat, whereas I could have gotten three units of wheat at home in France. I lose one unit of wheat in the process." Note that taking one unit of cloth from London to Paris results in a gain of one unit of wheat (two units of wheat in the United Kingdom but three units in France).

Our trader would quickly conclude that France has a comparative advantage in the production and export of wheat, even though France has an absolute disadvantage in both goods. By similar reasoning, we conclude that the United Kingdom has a comparative advantage in the production of cloth. A **comparative advantage** means that one nation can produce a product relatively, not absolutely, more efficiently than another nation. (A nation with an absolute advantage can produce a variety of products more efficiently than another.) Trade is expanded when nations produce products where they possess a comparative advantage.

Although the assumptions underlying this theory are "unreal" in today's world, economists since David Ricardo's time have shown that his comparative advantage model is valid for a world of many nations producing many different goods. Other economists have demonstrated that dropping the assumptions of perfect competition and zero transportation costs reduces the gain from specialization and trade but does not invalidate the theory. The only assumption crucial to these results is labor immobility. If workers migrated freely from country to country, we could have exchanges of labor rather than exchanges of products.

## Comparative Advantage and Output

In the following example, we can see what happens to total output of two goods (here, units of wheat and cloth) when trade occurs. We can also use a production possibilities curve to help us understand the effect of trade on total output. Unlike our previous example, we don't know the amount of labor involved in the production of each of these outputs, nor do we know the size of the labor forces. While we cannot calculate total output precisely, the production levels shown in Table 6 are consistent with our hypothetical costs and rates of exchange.

For the production levels given, France has the absolute advantage in the production of both products. If neither country is involved in international trade, each must use part of its resources to produce some of each product to meet domestic demand. If France uses half of its resources to produce wheat and half to produce cloth, cloth production will be 400 units and wheat production 1,200 units. If Brazil divides its labor resources so that six-sevenths produce wheat and one-seventh produces cloth, 600 units of wheat and 100 units of cloth will be produced. Total world output will be that shown in Table 7. Figure 7 shows the production possibilities curves for this example.

1. In what product does Brazil have the comparative advantage? Why would France want to trade with Brazil at all?

**Table 6** Total Country Production

| | Units per Year | | |
|---|---|---|---|
| | **Wheat** | | **Cloth** |
| Brazil | 700 | or | 700 |
| France | 2,400 | or | 800 |

**Table 7** Total World Output Without Trade

| | Units per Year | |
| --- | --- | --- |
| | **Wheat** | **Cloth** |
| Brazil | 600 | 100 |
| France | 1,200 | 400 |
| Total | 1,800 | 500 |

The two countries can expand total output by specializing. France has a comparative advantage in wheat production, and Brazil has a comparative advantage in cloth. If each country produces only its specialty, world output expands as shown in Table 8.

**FIGURE 7** Production Possibilities without Trade

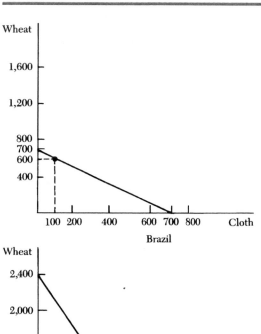

Brazil

France

**Table 8**  Total World Output with Specialization

| | Units per Year | |
| --- | --- | --- |
| | **Wheat** | **Cloth** |
| Brazil | 0 | 700 |
| France | 2,400 | 0 |
| Total | 2,400 | 700 |

With trade, the countries can exchange some of their expanded output so that both countries have both products. Of the wheat France produces, it uses some for domestic consumption and exports the rest. Of the cloth Brazil produces, it uses some for domestic consumption and exports the rest. After trading, many results are possible, but we might get a result similar to that shown in Table 9. In this case, the countries exchange 1,000 units of wheat from France for 500 units of cloth from Brazil. Figure 8 shows the production possibilities curves of Brazil and France with trade.

2. Who has gained what through specialization and trade?

3. In the example just given, what are some other possible combinations of exchange?

Thus, if each nation specializes in the product in which it has a comparative advantage, world output of both commodities is increased—in this case by 600 units of wheat and 200 units of cloth. If specialization and trade result in some reasonable distribution of this gain, both countries are better off than they would be in the absence of trade. This is the essence, then, of the argument for free trade.

## Terms of Trade

In the example from the previous section, not only can we determine whether Brazil and France can benefit from specialization and trade, we can also examine exchange ratios or **terms of trade** in which both will gain. By looking at the internal or domestic production ratios within each nation—the production possibilities in Table 6—we can determine how much wheat must be given up in order to produce an additional unit of cloth. Brazil can produce 700 units of

**Table 9**  Total World Output with Specialization and Trade

| | Units per Year | |
| --- | --- | --- |
| | **Wheat** | **Cloth** |
| Brazil | 1,000 | 200 |
| France | 1,400 | 500 |
| Total | 2,400 | 700 |

**FIGURE 8** Production Possibilities with Trade

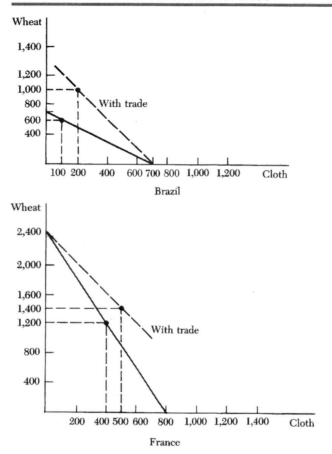

Brazil

France

wheat or 700 units of cloth during a year, so producing an additional unit of wheat necessarily means reducing cloth production by 1 unit. France can produce 2,400 units of wheat or 800 units of cloth, so the internal production trade-off is 3 units of wheat for each additional unit of cloth produced. To produce an additional unit of cloth, French wheat production must be reduced by 3 units.

With the internal production trade-off at 1 unit of wheat for 1 unit of cloth in Brazil (1W:1C) and 3 units of wheat for 1 unit of cloth in France (3W:1C), we can look for a terms of trade somewhere between those two ratios and show that each nation will gain from trade. The simplest trading ratio within that range is 2W:1C. Both nations gain with a 2:1 terms of trade. Brazil is able to exchange 1 unit of cloth for 2 units of wheat (twice as much as domestic production would allow), and France is able to exchange 2 units of its wheat for 1 unit of cloth, rather than sacrificing a full 3 units for an additional unit.

Several other trading ratios are possible in this example. In practice, the final terms of trade will depend on the bargaining strength of each nation as well as other economic and political factors. Each nation will want to negotiate the best possible terms of trade for itself.

To measure the terms of trade, we compare import and export price ratios—that is, we measure the price a country pays for imports and the price it receives for exports. We can express this as an index number:

$$\text{terms of trade} = \frac{\text{index of export prices}}{\text{index of import prices}} \times 100$$

For example, suppose the U.S. export price index was 113 in 1997 and the import price index was 95, both beginning from a base year of 1992 (at 100). In this case, the terms of trade would be $113/95 \times 100 = 119$. The terms of trade over the 1992–1997 period increased from 100 to 119, a 19 percent improvement. This improvement in terms of trade allowed the United States to give up 19 percent less in exports to obtain the same amount of imports.

For developing countries, the terms of trade is a very important influence on their capability to carry out their development plans and strategies. If their terms of trade decline, they have to pay relatively more for imports than they receive for their exports (that is, they must pay greater amounts of exports in return for imports).

## Problems with the Theoretical Assumptions of Free Trade

This theoretical model of comparative advantage clearly shows that international trade benefits the trading nations. Since the 1800s, this theory has become the rationale for most economists' belief that free trade is good and anything that interferes with it—such as tariffs, quotas, and other protectionist measures—is, by definition, bad. But the theory itself has serious problems. As is often the case in economic analysis, these problems involve the assumptions of the model.

When Ricardo first developed the theory of comparative advantage, he assumed that costs remain constant no matter what the level of production. Therefore, a nation could increase its production to satisfy the needs of other nations without increasing its own costs. But modern economics has documented, to the satisfaction of most, that since production is subject to diminishing returns, it is also subject to increasing costs—sooner or later, depending on what is being produced. In such a case, the increased costs may cancel out much, if not all, of the benefits of comparative advantage.

Ricardo also did not consider the large transportation costs that may be involved in international trade. These often raise the costs of imported goods considerably over those produced domestically and cancel out some of the benefits of international trade.

Finally, Ricardo assumed that the factors of production that are mobile within a country may be immobile internationally. These days labor still is fairly immobile, but capital funds move freely internationally. It is not so easy, as the modern era has shown, for a country to abandon production of one product and move resources into the production of another without serious reallocation problems. Further, moving resources from one industry to another can cause serious political difficulties beyond the practical economic realities.

Despite these limitations, the theory of comparative advantage does provide a useful perspective for viewing the trading process. However, it cannot alone explain the much more complicated process of the internationalization of world production.

## Restrictions to Free Trade: Protectionism

Free trade exists if there are no barriers to the export and import of goods and services. But, historically, when unemployment, job loss, reduced profits, and recession threaten a nation, domestic industry, or region, the predictable response is a call for increased protection of domestic goods and thus domestic jobs.

Nations use several types of trade restrictions, but the most common have been tariffs and quotas. **Tariffs** are simply taxes on goods imported or exported, while **quotas** are limits on the quantities of goods imported or exported. More recently, orderly marketing agreements (OMAs) have been popular. OMAs are nonmonetary barriers that absolutely or quantitatively limit imports and thus limit the choice between imported and domestic goods. Importers reap the profits from the higher prices commanded by the limited supply (assuming that there is a relatively inelastic demand for the product).

In general, tariffs and quotas succeed in their objective—they protect a special interest at the expense of the whole population. In other words, a few people are helped a lot, while all citizens are hurt a little because they pay higher prices for the goods and services on which tariff duties are imposed.

**Arguments for Protectionism.**   Nations establish trade barriers for many reasons. Most often protectionist measures are designed to protect some interest in the home country. Special interest groups in the United States often appeal to Congress for protection. Industries also seek protection from "unfair trade practices." For example, some governments subsidize particular industries, giving those products a price advantage over other viable producers. Representatives of new industries also use the "infant industries" argument that they need help to gain a foothold in world markets already flush with producers that might "overpower" the infant industry in a competitive marketplace. This argument is common in developing nations hoping to diversify their primarily agricultural base with a new industry. With time, however, particularly in the industrialized countries, the infant industry might grow to be a major competitor in the market, offering a better product at a better price.

Included in the protectionists' argument is another reason for tariff levies—retaliation. Governments have often increased tariffs in response to increases by trading partners. The 1930 Smoot-Hawley tariff, for example, set off a worldwide round of tariff increases. This "do unto others as they have done unto you" philosophy has also been used simply for the sake of self-esteem. As a result, consumers in both nations pay the higher price. At worst, such retaliation can compound recession into worldwide depression. During the 1930s, international trade almost disappeared—one important factor in the length and depth of the Great Depression. In the 1990s, the United States threatened retaliatory action against French wine.

At times Congress has considered proposals that it levy tariffs for the purpose of raising revenue, since the proceeds from the tax are collected by the government. This is well and good, but there are many more effective ways of raising revenue. Besides, if the tariff prices the imported good above that of the domestic product, the government will not collect any revenue, since the consumer will be priced out of the import market and will purchase only the domestic product.

Another protectionist argument centers on the need to reduce the competition of cheap foreign labor to protect domestic labor and domestic wage rates.

Protection is also very sensitive to political cycles. For example, during presidential elections, some candidates propose protectionism to win political support from some areas of the United States hurt by exports.

Other arguments on trade policy have run from the rather dry and abstract to the invective. The "national defense" argument falls into both categories. The merchant marine and the oil industry have argued for protection, since they are essential in times of national emergency.

4. Congress adopted import quotas to protect the oil industry for "defense" reasons from 1954 to 1973. How did these protective quotas, designed to encourage U.S. oil production, work during the OPEC oil embargo of 1973? As a consequence, what happened to domestic reserves of oil?

**Costs of Protectionism.**   Despite the many arguments in support of protectionist policies, an analysis of the consequences for consumers in each nation and the overall international trading system shows that one group may gain while another loses, and the entire trading system often suffers. The practice of protectionism results in all consumers paying higher prices for goods and services. The higher cost of imported goods may contribute to inflationary pressures. Protected jobs and firms may be sheltered from the competitive dynamics of the market, which would normally force them to allocate their scarce resources more efficiently and more productively.

The costs of protectionism can be high. Australia's Center for International Economics in 1990 concluded that if all regions in the global trading system reduced their tariff and nontariff barriers by 50 percent, the total gains from freer trade, measured in terms of increases in worldwide output, would be around $740 billion (more than $130 per person). A 1988 report issued by the Organization for Economic Cooperation and Development (the OECD, which includes the twenty-two advanced Western countries) concluded that agricultural protectionism cost the OECD countries about $72 billion a year. With free trade in agriculture, the study argues, personal incomes would increase by 1 percent, and less than 1 percent of the workforce would be displaced. The cost per farm job saved was estimated at $20,000 per year. In addition, free trade in agriculture would potentially increase Third World nations' agricultural exports by $30 billion a year.

In the 1997 *Economic Report of the President*, the Clinton administration noted the costs and benefits of free trade:

> Defenders of free trade can do it a disservice by promoting it as a way to create more jobs or to reduce bilateral trade deficits. Jobs, the unemployment rate, and the overall balance of payments [see Chapter 20] are ultimately a consequence of macroeconomic policies, not trade barriers. The real objective of free trade is to raise living standards by ensuring that more Americans are working in areas where the United States is comparatively more productive than its trading partners. In a full-employment economy, trade has more impact on the distribution of jobs than on the quantity of jobs.

—*Economic Report of the President*, 1997, p. 21.

## U.S. Steelmakers Accuse China of Dumping

Since late 2007 and throughout 2008, there has been a discernable rise in U.S. imports of steel from China and Canada. As a consequence, U.S. steelmakers have asserted that China is flooding the United States markets with steel subsidized by the Chinese government, thus enabling exporters to sell steel in the United States at prices below the cost of production. This practice, if true, is called **dumping**, which is illegal in international trade law.

As a consequence, U.S. steelmakers want the U.S. government to impose higher import tariffs (taxes) so that domestic producers can hold on to market share that they are losing and at the same time recover from the recession and the crisis in the U.S. automobile market.

The World Trade Organization allows countries to raise their import tariffs on goods that have suffered from dumping. But, the case most be proved and won for this to be given approval. This is an example of what generally takes place in the context of a global slowdown in trade. China no doubt needs to keep its steel plants operating to maintain employment for thousands of its citizens. The United States has the same motivation.

*Source:* Ellen Zhu and Robert Guy Matthews, "U.S. Steelmakers to Seek Higher Tariffs," the *Wall Street Journal*, February 20, 2009.

**FIGURE 9** Monthly U.S. Steel-Product Imports from China

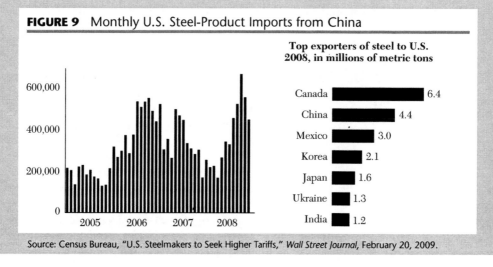

Top exporters of steel to U.S. 2008, in millions of metric tons

| Country | Millions of metric tons |
|---|---|
| Canada | 6.4 |
| China | 4.4 |
| Mexico | 3.0 |
| Korea | 2.1 |
| Japan | 1.6 |
| Ukraine | 1.3 |
| India | 1.2 |

Source: Census Bureau, "U.S. Steelmakers to Seek Higher Tariffs," *Wall Street Journal*, February 20, 2009.

One major issue in recent trade negotiations has been the large agricultural subsidies of developed countries, including the United States, Canada, Japan and the European Union. These subsidies benefit developed-country farmers at the expense of poor farmers in developing countries. And, the subsidies encourage production in locations that have a higher opportunity cost, thereby reducing economies efficiency.

## INTERNATIONAL TRADE ISSUES

As the volume of world trade has grown, nations have joined together in agreements to reduce trade barriers between them and to move toward freer trade. These agreements have included establishing trading blocs among a group of specific countries to reduce barriers among themselves (increasing both trade and the size of the market), as well as multinational agreements to reduce barriers throughout the world. Among the trade agreements important to the United States (as well as to the other countries involved) are the North American Free Trade Agreement (NAFTA) signed in 1992, and the Asia-Pacific Economic Cooperation (APEC) agreements joining twelve Asia-Pacific countries. Meanwhile, the integration of Europe continued with the Maastricht Treaty officially establishing the European Union in 1993. The decade of the 1990s brought much progress on the trade front. The WTO advanced the liberalization and globalization dynamics and established an economic and political framework for advancing free markets and along with them the goal of free trade. By the beginning of the twenty-first century, the .com bubble had burst and the results of the 1990s experience with globalization, trade, and financial liberalization policies documented the winners and losers, with results unevenly distributed. A strong antiglobalization movement emerged at the WTO meetings in Seattle in 1999 with protesters in the streets. Following the terror attacks on September 11, 2001, and subsequent wars in Afghanistan and Iraq (2003), the WTO-led push for enhanced trade liberalization began to crumble. Following the Seattle experience, the Doha Round in 2001 again focused on the importance of linking trade liberalization with the development goals and objectives of developing nations, which argued that trade liberalization was not contributing to their development agenda. The Doha Round encountered nothing but difficulty. The followup meetings in Cancun, Mexico, in 2003 collapsed after the fourth day, with the majority of members from the developing countries walking away in anger. The more recent meetings in Hong Kong in 2005 were no more successful. In 2006 there was a faint-hearted effort to breathe life back into the Doha agenda at the meeting of the World Economic Forum in Davos, Switzerland, but there were no expectations that anything would come of it. In the opinion of many experts, by 2006 it appeared that the era of multilateral trade liberalization was over. However, many critics and experts, like Joseph Stiglitz (author of *Making Globalization Work*, 2006), argue that there is a comprehensive set of proposals for reform that would make it possible for trade liberalization to work. This would effectively mean creating a fair trade environment in which all subsidies and trade restraints are eliminated. His point is that this is not the case today, especially for the advanced countries, even though they claimed to advocate free trade.

Much criticism has been leveled at China over the past few years as it has moved to protect several of its domestic markets, including books, songs, and movies. The following article, "W.T.O. Rules against China's Limits on Imports," examines the arguments and the ruling of the World Trade Organization after multiple complaints of protectionism.

## W.T.O. Rules Against China's Limits on Imports

HONG KONG — The World Trade Organization gave the United States a victory on Wednesday in its trade battle with China, ruling that Beijing had violated international rules by limiting imports of books, songs and movies.

The W.T.O. panel decision in Geneva buttresses growing complaints from the United States and Europe that China is becoming increasingly nationalistic in its trade policies. It also offers some hope that China will remove its restrictions on media and reduce rampant piracy of intellectual property, though the country can appeal.

But even if China changes its policy in light of the decision, Western companies could struggle to increase their sales anytime soon. The ruling does not affect a quota that caps at 20 the number of foreign films that can be released in Chinese movie theaters each year.

Also, because of piracy, Chinese consumers are so accustomed to paying very little for DVDs, or downloading movies or songs free on the Internet, that American movie companies already sell authorized DVDs of their movies for much less in China than in the United States—and still struggle to find buyers.

Still, Ron Kirk, the United States trade representative, praised the panel's legal finding. "This decision promises to level the playing field for American companies working to distribute high-quality entertainment products in China," Mr. Kirk said, "so that legitimate American products can get to market and beat out the pirates."

For the American media industry, the ruling essentially means that the W.T.O. supports demands by United States movie studios, book and newspaper publishers, and record labels that they be allowed to sell more directly to the Chinese consumer, rather than first going through a middleman, often a state-owned enterprise, as China has required. It does not necessarily mean the Chinese consumer will have access to a broader array of American films, books and music — although those industries hope that may eventually occur.

"American companies now have the right to trade without going through a Chinese intermediary at the border," said James Bacchus, a lawyer at Greenberg Traurig in Washington who represented the China Copyright Alliance, a consortium of media companies, in the case. ...

Either side may appeal the panel's ruling. It is difficult, although not impossible, for a panel decision like this one to clear the way for the petitioning country to impose trade sanctions on the country that broke the rules.

The ruling goes to the heart of one of the biggest trade issues pending between China and the West: whether intellectual property, like copyrighted songs, books and movies, should be granted the same kind of protection from discriminatory trade practices as manufactured goods.

China has enjoyed double-digit economic growth through most of the last three decades in part because of rapid expansion of exports, virtually all of which have been manufactured goods. But Chinese imports have grown much more slowly, particularly if imports of goods for export are excluded, like computer chips from Japan that are assembled in China into consumer electronics for shipment to the United States.

One reason for the slow growth in imports has been China's restrictions on imported books, movies and other content. Demand is met by pirated copies made in China; the latest Hollywood movies are on DVDs on street corners across China within days of their release, at a cost of $1 or less—much less in inland cities and for the buyer who bargains aggressively.

The Chinese government had no immediate reaction to the decision, which was released late at night Beijing time. Chinese state media also initially ignored the decision. Officials sometimes wait a day or two to respond to adverse trade developments. ...

The panel stopped short of endorsing an American request for a ruling on whether Chinese censorship had unfairly restricted imports. The panel said that this question was outside its purview; for the same reason, the panel also declined to rule on whether China's approval processes were too onerous for would-be distributors of imported entertainment.

Like the United Nations, the W.T.O. has limited power to enforce decisions. But criticism from the W.T.O. can shame countries, and panel rulings against other countries have frequently become the basis for bilateral or multilateral negotiations that result in policy changes.

The Bush administration filed the original complaint in 2007, partly to head off possible legislation requiring a more confrontational trade policy toward China. The Obama administration now faces pressure from the Democratic majority in Congress to take more assertive action in response to China's trade surplus during the current recession, and could use the ruling as evidence that the issue is already being addressed. It may also use the victory as a precedent to take more cases against China to the trade organization, said Gary Clyde Hufbauer, a trade expert at the Peterson Institute for International Economics.

But while China has lost two other W.T.O. panel rulings in the last 13 months, regarding high taxes on imported auto parts and lax enforcement of counterfeiting laws, China has not changed its policies in either case.

"They've got a poor record of compliance. They keep filing appeals," said Lyle Vander Schaaf, a partner in Washington at the law firm Bryan Cave who specializes in W.T.O. dispute panels and has not advised either side in any of the three panel decisions against China.

—*Tim Arango and Gerry Shih contributed reporting from New York and Helene Cooper from Washington.*

1. What exactly are intellectual property rights? What is the issue of piracy with regard to intellectual property rights? Why is it so difficult to resolve this kind of issue?

2. Why would China want to cap the official inflow of foreign films at 20 per year?

3. What are the likely impacts and consequences of the World Trade Organization decision?

Source: Keith Bradsher, "W.T.O. Rules against China's Limits on Imports," *The New York Times*, August 13, 2009.

Next, we will briefly examine the experience of the North American Free Trade Agreement between the United States, Canada, and Mexico.

## North American Free Trade Agreement (NAFTA)

In 1992, the North American Free Trade Agreement joined Canada, the United States, and Mexico into a multilateral trading bloc. NAFTA provides guiding principles for the reduction of tariffs on goods traded among these countries over fifteen years, until trade barriers no longer exist among the three. The NAFTA agreement was signed by President Bush in 1992 and ratified by Congress in late 1993, despite considerable debate in the 1992 presidential campaign (with Ross Perot opposing NAFTA and Bill Clinton supporting a modified NAFTA agreement). Some changes were negotiated in the areas of the environment and job loss.

NAFTA was hotly debated. Opponents argued that job losses would offset increased profits to manufacturers and lower consumer prices. Supporters argued that more jobs and increased wealth would result for all three nations. Since implementation in 1994, critics point to data validating their predictions. In the first two years of the agreement, Mexico imported fewer U.S. goods than in previous years; at the same time the level of Mexican exports to the United States rose dramatically. Even supporters of the agreement adjusted their earlier prediction of U.S. job growth. A currency crisis in the Mexican peso complicated interpretation of early results of the treaty. While some argue that the jury is still out on NAFTA, others—politicians and economists alike—look ahead to more free trade agreements in South America and the establishment of a Free Trade Area of the Americas (FTAA).

Since NAFTA began, proponents and critics have been studying the experience in order to be able to argue that it has indeed been successful or that it has been a disappointment or, even, a failure. By 2007, there had been several major and highly reputable studies on the performance of NAFTA (the World Bank, Institute for International Economics, AFL-CIO, etc.). Obviously, everyone can make a case for his or her position. Nevertheless, this is a very controversial and important debate as it sheds light not just on the experience of NAFTA but the recent passage of the Central American Free Trade Agreement (CAFTA).

The following article by James Parks, "NAFTA, CAFTA Not Working" (AFL-CIO, September 12, 2006), is an example of the case that critics make of NAFTA and CAFTA.

## NAFTA, CAFTA Not Working

James Parks

They are the twin pillars of recent U.S. trade policy—NAFTA and DR-CAFTA. And neither of them is working.

After 12 years, NAFTA (North American Free Trade Agreement) has not brought prosperity to working people in Mexico, Canada and United States, as promised.

And like NAFTA and other bad U.S. trade agreements, DR-CAFTA (Dominican Republic–Central American Free Trade Agreement) does not contain enforceable workers' rights or environmental protections. The agreement, which went into effect in January, is already failing after just eight months, according to a report released Tuesday.

In testimony submitted Sept. 11 to the Senate Finance Subcommittee on International Trade for NAFTA hearings, AFL-CIO Policy Director Thea Lee noted that "rather than encouraging sustainable and equitable growth, NAFTA has contributed to the loss of jobs and incomes of workers, while enriching the very few."

NAFTA's main outcome has been to strengthen the clout and bargaining power of multinational corporations, to limit the scope of governments to regulate in the public interest and to force workers into more direct competition with each other, while assuring them fewer rights and protections. The increased capital mobility afforded by NAFTA has hurt workers, the environment and communities in all three NAFTA countries.

Since 1994, the U.S. combined trade deficit with Mexico and Canada has ballooned from $9 billion to $127 billion, Lee says. The Department of Labor has certified that well over half a million U.S. workers lost their jobs due to NAFTA, and the nonprofit Economic Policy Institute (EPI) estimates the skyrocketing NAFTA trade deficit contributed to the loss of more than 1 million jobs and job opportunities.

Mexican workers haven't fared any better. Real wages in Mexico are actually lower today than before NAFTA went into effect in 1994, and the number of people in poverty grew from 62 million to 69 million through 2003, Lee says.

The NAFTA model was the starting point for CAFTA. In *Monitoring Report: DR-CAFTA in Year One*, prepared by the Stop CAFTA Coalition, Katherine Hoyt of the Nicaragua Network, one of the members of the coalition, says CAFTA has fueled the deterioration of workers' rights. For example, according to the report:

* Few collective bargaining agreements exist with noncompany unions in the free-trade zones of Central America, and corporations continue to fire union leadership in order to quash organizing efforts.
* Despite promises from the El Salvadoran government and the Bush administration, the cost of living is increasing, including the price of food. The White House had assured Salvadoran farmers that increased food exports from the United States would lead to lower food prices.
* In Nicaragua, funds from a program to support farmers are going to rich, powerful large producers, not to small farmers who desperately need them.
* Using a section of CAFTA, El Salvador's government is preparing a new law to privatize the nation's water system, an action that traditionally leads to huge cost increases and the loss of water by poor farmers and workers.

With Congress poised to consider new NAFTA-type trade agreements with Peru and Colombia, lawmakers need to take a look at what has happened in Central America and Mexico, Lee says:

Trade agreements must include enforceable protections for workers' core rights and must preserve our ability to use our domestic trade laws effectively. They must protect our government's ability to regulate in the public interest, to use procurement dollars to promote economic development and other legitimate social goals, and to provide high-quality public services. Finally, it is essential that workers, their unions and other civil society organizations be able to participate meaningfully in our government's trade policy process, on an equal footing with corporate interests.

The success or failure of any future trade and investment agreements will hinge on government's willingness and ability to negotiate agreements that appropriately address all of the social, economic and political dimensions of trade and investment, not just those of concern to corporations. Unfortunately, NAFTA is precisely the wrong starting point.  ·

1. What is the case against NAFTA?

2. Can you find information (data) that would support or contradict this argument? What is it?

3. What are the lessons of NAFTA for CAFTA?

4. What would make for a more "fair" agreement?

## The WTO and GATT

Despite debates over protectionism, much of the post–World War II period has seen an overall reduction in the excessive protection of the Great Depression years. Nations have, of course, disagreed as to which goods should be exempt from tariff reductions and where tariff levels should be set. Protectionist tendencies are particularly prevalent during periods of severe recession as countries compete for shrinking markets. Still, primarily through international negotiations in organizations such as the **General Agreement on Tariffs and Trade (GATT),** treaties increase trade through agreed-on reductions in tariffs.

Ninety-nine nations participated in the General Agreement on Tariffs and Trade, Multilateral Trade Negotiations, or the Tokyo Rounds, which concluded in 1979 after five years of negotiation over tariff reductions and the elimination of nontariff impediments and distortions to trade. In 1986, GATT attempted to reduce barriers in Punta del Este, Uruguay, and continued through 1993. Delegates negotiated reductions in both tariff and nontariff barriers, on everything from intellectual property, including patents and copyrights, to services such as telecommunications.

The most controversial part of the Uruguay Round was the agreement to establish the World Trade Organization (WTO) as the institution responsible for governing international trade. The WTO represents more than 120 countries. The WTO has the duty of implementing the agreements in the Uruguay Round by administering the agreements and providing a forum for settling disputes. The WTO replaced GATT as the central institution working to eliminate trade barriers. In its early years of existence, the WTO had its share of critics and supporters. Critics argued that the WTO oversteps its bounds in issues of national sovereignty. As the WTO makes more decisions, the organization has come under increased scrutiny from its supporters, who want increased powers and enforcement of those powers, and critics, who want to reduce WTO's importance.

## European Integration

Twelve European nations with a total population of 320 million and a GDP rivaling that of the United States formally merged into the European Union in 1993. There are currently 27 member states with a population nearing 500 million. The latest in a series of European organizational efforts beginning in 1952 with the European Coal and Steel Community, the EU trading bloc was designed to liberalize trade between member nations, encourage cooperation in intergovernmental and security affairs, and facilitate the movement toward a single currency. The economic goal of the EU is to synchronize economic policies promoting European economic growth and stabilization. Gains from integration are predicted at around 6.2 percent of combined GDP, or $230 billion.

Continued integration efforts are not easy. Strikes by French farmers and German miners emphasize the discord within member nations, as the EU places regional economic decisions above national ones. The EU is opening its doors to trade with the rest of the world, and thus opening a growing European market to U.S. products, even though trade among member nations receives greater emphasis. For U.S. trade, the future direction of EU economic policy is an important one. The majority of EU members moved to a common currency (the euro) in January 2000.

12. If a nation encourages free trade, what happens to the laborer whose job is threatened by increased domestic demand for imported substitutes?

## Japan as a Neomercantilist Trading Partner

While NAFTA, APEC, FTAA, the WTO, and the European Union aim at reducing the potential for trade wars, fears of such disputes have not vanished.

In particular, some concern persists regarding Japan's remaining neomercantilist trade policies. Some policy makers working on Japan trade issues have concluded that prior to the mid-1990s, Japan's trade policies were mercantilist in nature and that free trade interrupted their organized markets.

Japanese exports to U.S. markets account for more than half of Japan's total trade surplus. Needless to say, there is concern over Japanese trade policies, which are generally exclusionary and sometimes violate international trade law. The strategies with which the Japanese encourage strategic industries often puts U.S. domestic competitors at a disadvantage.

U.S. government and trade officials and businesspeople have long been frustrated with the Japanese. Intensive rounds of bilateral trade negotiations have increased the frustration on both sides. Tariff barriers *have* fallen over the past few years, but other restrictive practices have made entry into some Japanese markets difficult.

# Conclusion

*With protectionist measures, there is always an undercurrent of possible retaliation and trade wars similar to those of the 1930s, during which time international trade almost disappeared. In the past decade, however, the fear of retaliation seems not to have been an issue. Increasingly more economists are calling for the introduction of trade strategies as an improvement on free trade.*

*Developing countries are especially concerned about protectionist tendencies. They need to increase their exports in order to earn much-needed dollars and foreign currencies with which to repay the enormous debt that they have accrued in the past. A quota on imported steel would greatly affect a nation such as Brazil, which relies heavily on steel exports to earn foreign exchange. These nations have learned to play the game of protection as well. Several of the developing countries are using import controls as well as export subsidies to improve their trade positions. This trend has been caused by a minimal weakening of inflationary activity and the persistence of high unemployment levels.*

*Protection or free trade? Retaliation? Negotiated trade agreements? More than 30 years ago, in his 1977 presidential address to the twelfth biannual convention of the AFL-CIO, George Meany declared, "Free trade is a joke and a myth, and a government policy dedicated to 'free trade' is more than a joke—it is a prescription for disaster. The answer is fair trade—do unto others as they do unto you—barrier for barrier, closed door for closed door."*

*The 2001 U.S. economic recession that followed the collapse of the technology bubble and boom of the late 1990s resulted in a worldwide economic slowdown. The critics of globalization, free trade, and economic liberalization gathered more and more influence. This put enormous pressure on the World Trade Organization and other regional economic integration initiatives. By 2003 and into the early months of 2004, WTO trade discussions broke down in Cancun, Mexico, and Miami, Florida. Rising protectionist sentiment was visible throughout the global economy especially as the global economic downturn caused by the financial crisis threatened jobs and slowed economic growth.*

*From 2005 to 2009, the Doha Round talks continued to produce little if any progress. The Bush administration continued to be preoccupied with the Iraq War and the ongoing war in Afghanistan. The twin deficits (budget and trade) persisted in the face of sluggish economic growth. Oil prices continued to rise as the increased demand for petroleum from China and India and speculation by oil traders pushed prices to the highest nominal and real levels ever—over $145 per barrel. As growth remained robust in emerging nations and with China's appetite for natural resources to fuel its 10 percent growth rate, a commodity boom emerged, causing prices for raw materials to soar. This generated a strong trade dynamic and allowed many emerging nations to generate a favorable trade surplus. Yet, by late 2007, signs of the emerging global financial crisis were self-evident and the global recession was underway. The global recession continued through early to mid-2009. With the economic downturn, the slowdown in international trade, and soaring unemployment rates, protectionist policies emerged.*

*There can be no doubt that arguments over free trade will continue in the future, and the effects will be felt on currencies and domestic policies.*

## Review Questions

1. What factors have brought about the dynamic process of globalization and international economic interdependence?

2. What are some of the more dominant trends with respect to international trade? What can be said of the role and position of the United States with regard to international trade?

3. What is the basic theory of free trade? What are the pros and cons of free trade in theory? In practice?

4. What are the arguments for protectionism?

5. What is the reality of farm subsidies in the United States? Should they be maintained, reduced, or eliminated? Explain.

6. What has been the overall experience of NAFTA given its goals and objectives?

7. What since 2000 has been the trade relationship between the United States and China? What are the apparent benefits and costs of this relationship to each country?

8. What has the global financial crisis and economic recession done to global economic growth and international trade since 2008?

9. How would you categorize President Obama's trade policy and strategy? Do you agree or disagree with it? Explain.

# International Finance

From Chapter 20 of *Economics: A Tool for Critically Understanding Society*, 9/e. Tom Riddell. Jean Shackelford. Geoffrey Schneider. Steve Stamos. Copyright © 2011 by Pearson Education. Published by Addison-Wesley. All rights reserved.

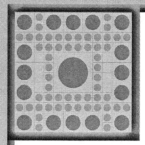

# International Finance

## ◆Introduction

**H**aving considered the theory and the recent history of international trade, we shall now turn our attention to issues of international finance and to accounting for the international exchange of goods, services, investment, and other capital flows. Monies flow from one nation to another when citizens or institutions of a given nation decide to lend to or borrow from foreigners and to import or export goods and services.

We begin our examination with a discussion of the **balance of payments,** which is the accounting scheme that governments and international organizations use for measuring trade and capital flows between nations. We shall then move to a discussion of exchange rates and review how they respond to trade and financial transactions. Our discussion of exchange rates includes how international trade flows alter these rates, and how systems of exchange have changed over time.

## THE BALANCE OF PAYMENTS

All nations must eventually adjust their national economic policies to meet the demands of the international trading and financial system. Nations commonly keep track of these demands with a mechanism called the balance-of-payments accounting system. A balance-of-payments account is a statement of a nation's aggregate international financial transactions over a period of time, usually one year. The balance of payments is a statement that shows the exchange of a country's currency for foreign currencies for all of the international transactions of a country's citizens, businesses, and government during a year. It helps nations keep track of the flow of goods and services into and out of the country. In this accounting statement, all international economic and financial transactions must have either a positive or a negative effect on a nation's balance-of-payments accounts. Table 1 shows the effects of possible transactions.

**Table 1**  Credits and Debits in a Nation's Balance of Payments

| Credits (+) | Debits (−) |
|---|---|
| 1. Any *receipt* of foreign money | 1. Any *payment* to a foreign country |
| 2. Any *earnings* of an investment in a foreign country | 2. Any *earnings* on domestic investments by a foreign country |
| 3. Any sale of goods or services abroad (*export*) | 3. Any purchase of goods and services from abroad (*import*) |
| 4. Any gift or aid *from* a foreign country | 4. Any gift or aid *given* abroad |
| 5. Any *sale* of stocks or bonds abroad | 5. Any *purchase* of foreign stocks or bonds |
| 6. Any foreign investment in this country | 6. Any investment in a foreign country |

The balance-of-payments accounting statement is divided into three major classifications: the current account, the capital account, and the financial account. (In June 1999, the Bureau of Economic Analysis changed the way that it accounts for financial transactions in its international account. The BEA had previously used only a current account and capital account; by adding the financial account, the BEA conforms more closely to the international guidelines of the International Monetary Fund.) For each of these accounts, subtracting payments from receipts results in an account balance.

## The Current Account

The **current account** includes the import and export of all goods and services, investment income, and most unilateral transfers during a year. Exports of goods and services create a receipt of income, while imports of goods command payments abroad, resulting in an outflow of income. Table 2 shows the magnitude of these components of the current account for 2005, 2007 and 2008.

By far the largest category under the current account is the export and import of goods—cars, steel, raw materials, machines, and so forth. In 2007 U.S. goods exported totaled $1.148 trillion, and goods imported totaled an outflow $1.98 trillion. The balance referred to as the **balance of trade** represents the value of exports of goods and services minus the value of imports. For 2007, the balance of trade was −$700.4 billion. The balance is negative because payments were larger than receipts in 2007.

Besides merchandise trade, the current account records investment income and services of various types. When we total all of the transactions in the current account, we get the current account balance. For 2007, this balance was −$706 billion.

Just as we examined the budget deficit within the framework of our leakages and injections model of National Income Accounting, we can look at trade deficits within the same context. In equilibrium, leakages equal injections:

$$\text{leakages } = \text{injections}$$

$$S + Tx + M = I + G + X$$

**Table 2**  U.S. International Transactions, 2005, 2007, and 2008

| Transaction | Amount (in millions) | | |
|---|---|---|---|
| | 2005 | 2007 | 2008 |
| **Current Account** | | | |
| (1)  Exports of goods and services and income receipts | $1,749.9 | $2,463.5 | $2,591.3 |
| (2)      Goods, balance-of-payment basis | 894.6 | 1,148.4 | 1,277.0 |
| (3)      Services | 380.6 | 497.2 | 549.6 |
| (4)      Income Receipts | 474.6 | 817.8 | 764.6 |
| (5)  Imports of goods and services and income payments | −2,455.3 | −3,082.0 | −3,168.9 |
| (6)      Goods, balance-of-payment basis | −1,677.4 | −1,967.8 | −2,117.2 |
| (7)      Services | −314.6 | −378.1 | −405.3 |
| (8)      Income Payments | −463.4 | −736.0 | −646.4 |
| (9)  Unilateral current transfers, net | −86.1 | −112.7 | −128.1 |
| (10) Balance on current account = (1) + (5) + (9) | −791.5 | −731.2 | −706.0 |
| **Capital Account** | | | |
| (11) Capital Account transactions, net | −4.4 | −1.8 | 1.0 |
| **Financial Account** | | | |
| (12) U.S.-owned assets abroad, net (increase/financial outflow excluding financial derivatives (−)) | −426.8 | −1,289.9 | −0.1 |
| (13)      U.S. official reserve assets, net | 14.1 | −0.1 | −4.8 |
| (14)      U.S. government assets, other than official reserves assets, net | 5.5 | −22.2 | −529.5 |
| (15)      U.S. private assets, net | −446.4 | −1,267.5 | 481.9 |
| (16) Foreign-owned assets in the United States, net excluding financial derivatives (increase/financial inflow (+)) | 1,212.3 | 2,057.7 | 534.1 |
| (17)      Foreign official assets in the United States, net | 199.4 | 411.1 | 477.7 |
| (18)      Other foreign assets in the United States, net | 1,012.7 | 1,646.6 | 177.7 |
| (19) Financial Derivatives, net | N/A | 6.5 | N/A |
| (20) Balance of capital financial flows = (16) − (12) | 785.4 | 767.8 | 537.0 |
| (21) Statistical discrepancy (sum of above items with sign reversed) | 10.4 | −41.3 | −129.3 |
| Balance of payments = (1) + (5) + (9) + (11) + (12) + (16) + (20) + (21) | 0 | 0 | 0 |
| Balance of trade = (2) + (3) + (6) + (7) | −716.7 | −700.4 | −695.9 |

Source: Bureau of Economic Analysis, *Survey of Current Business*, June 2006, July 2009.

Next, we can rewrite the equation in terms of the current account balance, which is in deficit in this case:

$$X - M = S - I - G + Tx,$$

where $I$ is domestic investment, $G$ is government expenditures, $X - M$ is net exports (and here serves as a measure of the current account deficit or surplus), $S$ is private domestic saving, and $Tx$ is domestic tax receipts.

$$(X - M) = S - I - (G - Tx),$$

where $X - M$ is the current account balance and $G - Tx$ is the government deficit. This balance is linked to fiscal and/or saving imbalances.

## The Capital Account

The amount in the nation's **capital account** is small. The only transactions included are a few unilateral transfers that had been included in the current account until the Bureau of Economic Analysis changed its accounting for financial transactions in 1999. The BEA provides the following definition:

> The newly defined capital account consists of capital transfers and the acquisition or disposal of nonproduced nonfinancial assets. They are major types of capital transfers and are debt forgiveness and migrant's transfers (goods and financial assets accompanying migrants as they leave or enter the country). "Other" capital transfers include the transfer of title to fixed assets and the transfer of funds linked to the sale or acquisition of fixed assets, gift and inheritance taxes, death duties, uninsured damage to fixed assets, and legacies. The acquisition and disposal of nonproduced nonfinancial assets includes the sales and purchases of nonproduced assets, such as the rights to natural resources, and the sales and purchases of intangible assets, such as patents, copyrights, trademarks, franchises, and leases.

Although these capital account transactions are relatively small in the U.S. accounts, they are more important to other countries and may become more important to U.S. accounts. In 2007, these transactions amounted to −$1 billion.

## The Financial Account

The financial account includes all financial flows in and out of the United States. U.S. financial outflow represents the purchase of capital assets outside of the United States by the government, citizens, or corporations. The dollars used to purchase these assets flow out of the country. In return, the government, citizen, or business now owns an asset abroad. U.S. citizens or businesses might make bank deposits in other countries, purchase foreign stocks and bonds, or even buy foreign productive facilities (a plant, office, McDonald's franchise, etc.). All of these activities produce an increase in U.S. assets abroad, or an outflow of dollars—a payment in the balance of payments. On the other hand, if U.S. residents were to sell their foreign assets and bring the proceeds back home, this would be recorded as a receipt. In 2007, the net outflow of U.S. private assets amounted to −$1.23 trillion, which represented payments in the financial account. Financial inflow into the United States, which occurs when foreign governments, institutions, corporations, or individuals increase their assets in the United States, amounted to $2.1 trillion in 2007. In Table 2, entries in the financial account in 2008 are significantly different from other years because of the global financial crisis. Note the vast change in row 12 for U.S.-owned assets abroad. These dropped by $1 trillion between 2007 and 2008. This was due to dramatic changes in row 15 because of U.S. claims reported by banks. Looking at foreign-owned assets in the United States, U.S. liabilities reported by banks is reflected in changes in row 18. The world credit market crisis is reflected in the financial account of the balance of payments in 2008.

1. What do we lose by foreign direct investment in the United States? What do we gain when it occurs?

## Balancing the Accounts

The balance of payments always "balances." Whatever surplus (net inflow) or deficit (net outflow) these transactions generate is offset by the use of official reserve assets of the U.S. government and the statistical discrepancy.

The *statistical discrepancy* category is in one sense an accounting mechanism for balancing the accounts. It is simply the total of the items in the current, capital, and financial account measurements with the sign reversed. One reason this account is necessary is that the measurement of all international transactions is extremely complex. The government cannot accurately measure all of these transactions, particularly illegal ones; some transactions, both legal and illegal, will escape measurement. For 2007, the deficit in the U.S. current, capital, and financial account items indicates an outflow of dollars. This number could represent any one or a combination of possible activities. The deficit would put downward pressure on the dollar, reducing its value and "balancing" the deficit. Alternatively, other nations could hold on to the dollars that they had received because of U.S. imports from their countries or U.S. capital flows to their countries. They might want to hold these dollars for future use. Whatever the specifics, to compensate for the imprecision involved in attempting to measure all international economic activities, the statistical discrepancy category mechanically balances the international accounts.

2. If investment by Canada in the United States results in a "receipt" or positive effect on the U.S. balance of payments in the financial account, is this investment necessarily good for the United States? Why or why not?

3. What would be an example of a merchandise export? A government transfer payment? If you took $1,000 out of your bank account in the United States and put it in a bank in London, what effect would it have on the balance of payments accounts?

## Trade Deficits

When reporters, economists, and politicians speak of balance-of-payments deficits (outflows of dollars) and surpluses (inflows of dollars), they may be referring only to the transactions in the current account or the current and financial accounts—and not in the balancing cash, gold, or bond transactions. The *basic balance* includes the balance on the current account added to the long-term capital movements. This basic balance normally shows a payments deficit (payments < receipts) or surplus (receipts > payments).

If we look only at the merchandise balance in the current account (the balance of trade), we find that the U.S. "balance" has historically been a surplus.

In every year from 1893 until 1971, merchandise exports exceeded merchandise imports. Beginning in the 1970s, however, the balance of trade has shown deficits—large ones in the late 1970s and even larger in the 1980s and late 1990s, after simply large deficits in the early 1990s. The trade deficits of the early to mid-1970s resulted primarily from the large increase in the price of imported oil. During the first half of the 1980s, the trade deficits were caused by a very strong dollar, which made U.S. goods much more expensive than imported goods. This price shift decreased U.S. exports and increased foreign imports. In the latter half of the decade, the value of the dollar fell, and the trade deficit began to decrease in 1988, having reached a record $152.9 billion in 1987. Deficits in the trade balance continued to narrow until 1992. Since 1992 trade deficits climbed to record levels. Figure 1 shows the pattern for international transactions balances between 1983 and 2008.

Trade deficits in the current account have been offset by larger financial inflows into the United States, which have reduced the deficit in the basic balance. Until recently the financial account has historically run deficits, since it records U.S. corporate investment in foreign nations.

> During the period when imports by Americans do exceed our exports to the rest of the world, foreigners must accept additional dollar securities in exchange for our excess imports. In different words, we finance the excess imports by borrowing from the rest of the world or by selling U.S. assets to foreigners. This accommodating flow of credit or capital to the United States is an inevitable corollary of the trade deficit.
>
> —Martin Feldstein, "Why the Dollar Is Strong," *Challenge*, January/February 1984

**FIGURE 1**   Current Account, Trade, and Investment Income Balances

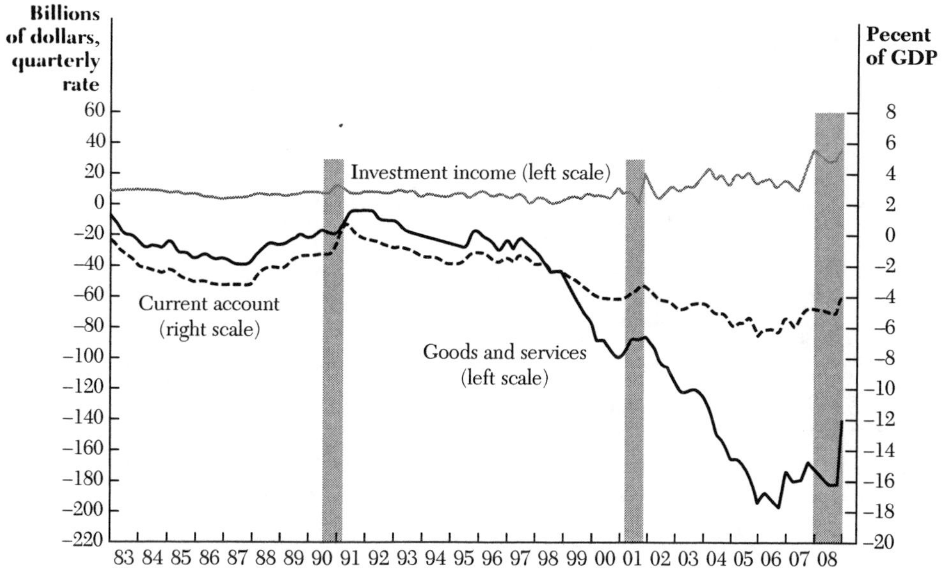

*Source:* Federal Reserve Bank, St. Louis, 2009.

One of the problems a nation encounters in trade, just as in life, is that it must pay for the goods and services received. An individual can use either cash or an IOU to offset a debt. In the international sphere, several alternatives are available. Payments are accepted in cash (dollars), gold, or special drawing rights (a bookkeeping form of international money).

If a nation's exports exceed its imports, it will have attained a balance-of-trade surplus. The reward for this is increased employment and income at home. The penalty is higher prices. Why? As exports of goods and services rise, income ($Y$) and hence GDP increase. As income increases, consumption increases. As consumption increases, more dollars are competing for fewer domestic goods, and prices will tend to rise.

A trade deficit (imports greater than exports) earns a nation's economic and political leaders criticism and economic disadvantages. Strains are placed on the value of a nation's currency with respect to other currencies. If these strains become too severe, the country's currency will **depreciate** (be worth less) with respect to other, stronger currencies, so imported goods will cost more. On the other hand, exports should become cheaper and thus more attractive to foreign nations. In following sections of this chapter, we will see how this happens.

A country cannot do away with a trade deficit simply by removing or reducing a "big" item on the balance-of-payments statement. For example, it is not true that, as opponents of foreign aid have argued, this expenditure caused deficits in the basic trade balance for many years. Much foreign aid is "tied"; that is, it must be spent on goods produced in the United States. So if the United States cut foreign aid by $1 billion, U.S. exports might be reduced by as much as $800 million. The gain would be very small indeed. Many of the items in the balance of payments are related to other items in this way.

It is, however, legitimate to note that when a particular item is in surplus, the country has the freedom to run up a deficit in some other item without creating pressure against its currency. This sort of situation can be created in either of two ways: There may be items that in the working out of "basic economic forces" generate a surplus, or other countries in the world economy may "allow" deficits to exist without exerting pressure for policy measures that would reduce them. An example of the former is the flow of investment income into the United States. In the past, the net income on U.S. investments abroad allowed the United States to, among other things, increase its ownership of factories and mines in other countries and finance military expenditures abroad. An example of the second situation would be the willingness of countries to hold onto dollars accumulated from U.S. deficits because dollars are valuable to them.

# EXCHANGE RATES AND THE BALANCE OF PAYMENTS

As we mentioned earlier, trade imbalances can create pressures on a nation's currency. Let's examine how the value (exchange rate) of the dollar is determined and how it influences the balance of payments.

The value of a nation's currency, the exchange rate, is determined by the supply of and demand for that currency. The supply of a nation's currency

# THE BIG PICTURE

## Exchange Rates

The supply and demand model is used to determine exchange rates. There are a number of determinants that affect exchange rates, and this can make fluctuations in exchange rates difficult to understand. But the logic behind the supply and demand model for exchange rates, and thus behind fluctuations in exchange rates, is straightforward. When international actors (including consumers, investors, businesses, speculators, and governments) want more of a particular country's goods, services, or assets, they will demand more of that country's currency to pay for those goods, services, or assets. As shown in Figure BP.1, any increase in the demand for a nation's currency will cause that currency to increase (or appreciate) in value relative to the currency of its trading partner (whose currency will in turn decrease, or depreciate, in value). When international actors want less of a particular nation's goods, services, or assets, they will demand less of that nation's currency. Any decrease in the demand for a nation's currency will cause that currency to decrease (or depreciate) in value relative to the currency of its trading partner(s). There are, of course, a number of variations to this story, and we explore the nuances of changes in exchange rates in the rest of the chapter.

**FIGURE BP.1** The Market for Dollars Responds to an Increase in Demand

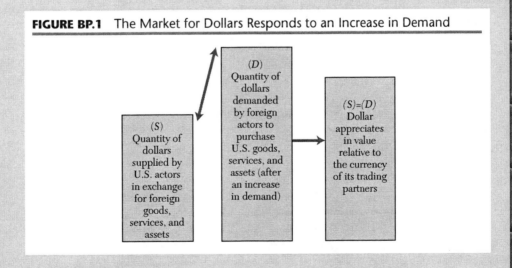

**FIGURE 2** An Increase in the Supply of Dollars

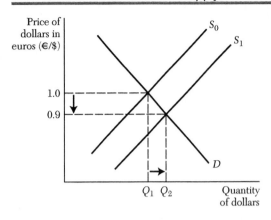

comes from the country's central bank as well as its citizens who desire to purchase foreign goods, services, securities, and other assets. For example, the supply of U.S. dollars would increase if the Fed supplied more dollars in order to purchase foreign currencies, if U.S. citizens wanted to purchase more imported goods, or if U.S. investors wanted to invest in foreign asset markets. Figure 2 shows that an increase in the supply of dollars in exchange for euros causes the value of the dollar in terms of foreign currency to depreciate (decrease in price relative to the euro). A depreciation of the dollar means that each U.S. dollar buys less foreign currency than it used to, making foreign goods more expensive to purchase.

The demand for a nation's currency comes from foreign citizens who want to purchase the home country's goods and assets. For example, the demand for dollars would increase if the prices of U.S. goods fell relative to foreign goods (causing foreign citizens to desire more U.S. goods), if foreign citizens wanted to invest more in U.S. bonds, or if foreign citizens wanted to hold more dollars as assets. As Figure 3 shows, an increase in

**FIGURE 3** An Increase in the Demand for Dollars

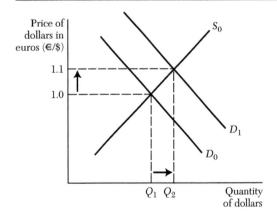

the demand for dollars by European citizens would shift the demand curve for the dollar to the right, causing the dollar to appreciate (increase in price relative to the euro). An appreciation of the dollar means that each dollar can purchase more foreign currency than it used to, making foreign goods cheaper to U.S. citizens.

**The Dollar and the Euro**   In fact, the dollar was strong relative to the euro from 1999 to 2001 and weak from 2001 to 2009. As the U.S. economy slowed in 2001, the stock market plummeted, and the Fed slashed interest rates to try to stave off a recession. Normally, economists would expect declining stock prices and low interest rates on bonds to scare off foreign investors, causing a decrease in the demand for dollars and a depreciation of the dollar.

While the dollar fell with respect to the euro and other European currencies, including the pound and kroner, Asian currencies held up the sagging dollar—at least for a while. During much of the period from 2003–2008 the United States was very dependent on Asian central banks to finance the current account deficit.

**Determinants of Exchange Rates**   To understand shifts in the supply and demand curves for a currency, we must understand the determinants of exchange rates. Table 3 lists some of the factors that cause shifts in the supply of and demand for a currency. The supply of a currency is affected by the central bank's decisions to supply more or less of the currency, as well as domestic consumer and producer decisions regarding foreign goods, services, and assets. The demand for a nation's currency is affected by the demand for a nation's products and the prices of those products. The lower the price of the products, the greater the demand, and thus the greater the demand for the nation's currency, since currency is needed to purchase the products. Other factors that often influence exchange rates include tastes and preferences for the country's products, productivity increases, the inflation rate, and the domestic interest rate relative to other countries' rates. In Figure 4, an increased demand in the United States for Japanese-produced Toyotas increases the demand for yen and thus increases the exchange rate of the yen in terms of dollars. Each dollar will purchase fewer yen as the price of yen in dollars rises. From the opposite perspective, the price of dollars in terms of yen has decreased.

Given the current U.S. trade deficits, we might expect the value of the dollar to be falling with respect to many other currencies, since the demand for U.S. exports is low (contributing to a low demand for dollars) and the demand for imported goods is high (contributing to a large supply of dollars). But other factors affect the demand for a nation's currency. Nontrade pressures, which are not influenced by the demand for a nation's products, might dramatically influence the value, or the exchange rate, of the dollar. Currencies are used not only to purchase goods and services, but also to make money—that is, to earn a rate of return, or interest. The Fed's tightening of monetary policy in the fall of 1979, in late 1989, and from 1997 to 2000 did curb the growth rate of the money supply, but the resulting higher interest rate and a growing confidence that the United States was a "safe haven" for assets created a demand for dollars

**Table 3** Shifts in the Supply and Demand for a Currency (Dollars)

| Determinant Change | Supply of Dollars | Demand for Dollars | Value of the Dollars |
|---|---|---|---|
| U.S. prices increase. | U.S. citizens want cheaper foreign goods; supply of dollars increases. | Foreign citizens want fewer U.S. goods; demand for dollars decreases. | Depreciates |
| U.S. demand for foreign goods, services, and assets increases. | U.S. citizens want more foreign items; supply of dollars increases. | Foreign citizens do not change the amount of U.S. goods they purchase; demand for dollars does not shift. | Depreciates |
| Foreign demand for U.S. goods, services, and assets increases. | U.S. citizens do not change the amount of foreign goods they purchase; supply of dollars does not change. | Foreign citizens want more U.S. items; demand for dollars increases. | Appreciates |
| U.S. productivity increases, lowering the prices of U.S. goods. | U.S. citizens prefer cheaper U.S. goods to many foreign goods; supply of dollars decreases. | Foreign citizens want more U.S. goods now that the price has fallen; demand for dollars increases. | Appreciates |
| U.S. interest rates increase. | U.S. investors move their money from foreign banks back to U.S. banks to get a higher return; supply of dollars decreases. | Foreign investors put more money in U.S. banks to get a higher return; demand for dollars increases. | Appreciates |

**FIGURE 4** Supply and Demand for Toyotas and Yen

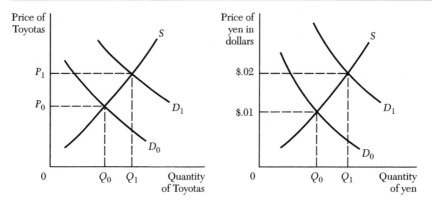

**FIGURE 5** Supply and Demand for Dollars When U.S. Interest Rates Increase

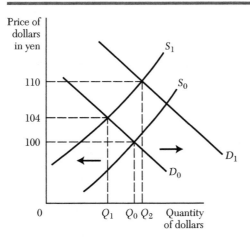

among foreign corporations and investors. In early 2009, foreign investors were again attracted to the U.S. safe haven.

To illustrate this, we will assume that before the Fed initiative, $1 would purchase 100 yen. In Figure 5, a Fed reduction in the growth rate of the money supply is shown by the shift in the supply curve of dollars from $S_0$ to $S_1$. A higher interest rate created by the reduced money supply will attract foreign investment and thus increase the demand for dollars. This is shown by a shift in the demand curve from $D_0$ to $D_1$.

In this example, the dollar has become very strong. Therefore, it commands or purchases a larger quantity of other foreign currencies and thus more foreign goods and services. Before the Fed's contractionary monetary policy, $1 would purchase 100 yen, but with less supply and greater demand, $1 purchases 110 yen. Japanese products have become relatively cheaper for U.S. consumers. That will tend to increase Japanese (foreign) imports, which increases the tendency for the U.S. balance of trade to run a deficit. At the same time, 1 yen commands fewer dollars, its buying power having fallen from $.010 worth of U.S. products to only $.009 worth. Therefore, each U.S. product costs Japanese consumers more. Even though the prices of U.S. products have not changed in absolute terms, for a Japanese consumer they are relatively higher, since the yen's dollar-purchasing power has declined. As a result, fewer U.S. goods are exported to Japan, leading to further deterioration in the balance of trade. In this example, the dollar has appreciated, or gained in value with respect to the yen, while the yen has depreciated, or lost value with respect to the dollar.

## The Value of the Dollar Since the 1970s

During the 1970s, the U.S. dollar experienced a spectacular decline in value relative to other major trading currencies. Beginning in the fall of 1979, the dollar began an upward roll, eventually reaching new highs against most

Discount store, Tokyo, Japan.
(Eddie Stanger/SuperStock, Inc.)

major currencies (major currency index) in early 1985 (see Figure 6). The decline in the 1970s reflected major weaknesses in the U.S. economy: slow growth, an impressive economic challenge by Germany and Japan, and relatively high and continuing inflation in the United States. Factors responsible for sustaining the high dollar value in the 1980s included the high U.S. budget deficits, high real interest rates, and low levels of inflation with respect to those in other industrial nations. The dollar peaked against the yen in 1985 at $1 = 260$ yen.

Between 1985 and 1993, the dollar began to drop, particularly in relation to the German mark and the Japanese yen. In September of 1985, the Group of Five (the United States, United Kingdom, France, West Germany, and Japan—also known as G-5), agreed in the Plaza Accord* to intervene in foreign exchange markets to lower the value of the soaring dollar in order to promote more even-handed economic growth.[†] After 1993, the dollar had fallen to its post–World War II low against the yen at $1 = 100.9$ yen. The dollar had depreciated more than 50 percent from its peak in 1985, as interest rates in the

---

*The Plaza Accord was so named after the location of the September 1985 meeting at New York City's Plaza Hotel.

[†]Currency intervention occurs when a nation (or nations) purchase (or sell) the currency of a particular nation to establish a higher (or lower) rate of exchange. In this case, the G-5 nations agreed to sell dollars so as to lower the dollar's value with respect to other trading currencies. This is truly a managed float!

## FIGURE 6   EXCHANGE RATES

Source: Federal Reserve Bank of St. Louis, 2009.

*ECU–the precursor to the Euro.

United States and oil prices continued to fall. Since 1993, the dollar strengthened against the yen and many other major currencies and by early 1997 had moved to 125 yen per dollar.

The period between 1971 and 1997 shows a complete cycle of exchange rate movements that respond to domestic inflation, interest rates, and intervention in currency markets. Some economists argue that the U.S. merchandise trade balance was not reduced by a greater magnitude during the period of dollar decline because many foreign producers cut their profit margins in order to keep export prices low and thus maintain their share of the market. These economists also point out that the dollar depreciation was much greater with respect to the yen and German mark than to other currencies. Thus, prices of goods imported from those areas remained attractive to U.S. consumers.

4. What kind of sale on U.S.-produced goods were Japanese consumers and businesses treated to with the fall in the value of the dollar between 1985 and 1993? How would U.S. retailers advertise such a deal?

In 1997 the value of the dollar was again turning upward. The threat of increased inflation caused the Fed to institute a somewhat more restrictive monetary policy and thus an increase in interest rates in the United States. Japanese investors, still concerned with domestic banking and stock market crises, moved some of their funds to the United States and Europe to seek higher yields and perhaps greater stability. As the movement continued, the U.S. trade balance felt increased pressure as imports became more attractive to U.S. consumers and exports lost their exchange advantage in international markets.

The U.S. dollar continued to grow stronger from 1997 to the early months of 2001. As Figure 6 illustrates, the weak dollar of the late 1970s gave way to the strong dollar of the early 1980s, only to weaken from 1985 to 1990. From 1990 to 1995, the dollar maintained its general strength but was weaker to the yen and stronger to the euro. From 1995, the dollar began its rise for the remainder of the decade, growing stronger against the yen and the euro. Much of the strength of the dollar was related to the increased demand for dollars generated by the strong foreign demand for U.S. financial instruments and for direct investment in the United States. In addition, the demand for U.S. exports began to increase in the late 1990s.

The U.S. dollar, as measured by the major currency index in Figure 6, strengthened from 1999 to the beginning of 2002. After 2002, the dollar declined through 2006 into early 2008, with the U.S. economic downturn. Continued concerns about the U.S. economic recovery, contributed to the dollar's fall. By mid-2008 the dollar had strengthened against many major currencies as investors perceived the U.S. dollar as a safe haven. By mid-2009 the dollar again began to lose value, particularly against the euro. The growing U.S. trade and current account deficit and the domestic budget deficit were also major factors contributing to this decline.

## THE FUTURE OF THE INTERNATIONAL FINANCIAL SYSTEM

As the twenty-first century began, global capital markets became more integrated. Economic policy makers and central bankers from all countries realized that their ability to control their respective domestic economies, in the context of rapid global change, was increasingly more difficult and less effective. Capital was highly mobile. It could move quickly. Currency values were increasingly volatile.

The countries with the eight largest industrial economies (the United States, Canada, United Kingdom, France, Germany, Italy, Russia, and Japan), together known as the G-8 countries, responded by voluntarily coordinating some of their economic policies. Their ongoing effort to cooperate has been mildly successful. Still, without the discipline of an enforcement mechanism, countries tend to do only what is self-serving and politically expedient. Annual economic summits have served largely to bring together the members of the G-8 for public relations, ritual identification of the problems they face collectively, and only moderate cooperation.

By 2006, the global economy was marked by rapid and dramatic forces of change. Developing countries in Asia, Latin America, and Africa were moving toward market economies and democratic governments. Other nations in transition in Eastern Europe, Central Europe, and the Commonwealth of Independent States were also following the path toward establishing market economies, drawing enormous attention to the potential opportunities afforded by these emerging market economies. In these countries there was a new interest in stock and bond markets, along with investment scandals, such as the one in Albania in 1997, which produced riots and a governmental crisis. Increased capital flows in the form of direct private foreign investment in these countries led many international commercial banks and investment banks to aggressively establish themselves there.

From the 1990s to the early years of the twenty-first century, China and India emerged as powerful new players in the global economy. Western Europe continued to adapt to the changes and challenges of European economic integration and monetary union for most of the EU members. West Germany's integration with East Germany slowed the locomotive for European economic growth a bit. And while all this had been taking place, the competitive pressures of the marketplace were pushing even more rapid change.

The mid-1990s found Japan coming out of three years of recession, only to have its economy collapse again in 1998 as fears of a currency crisis gripped Asia and spread to Latin America. In 2001, Japan continued to try to solve many internal financial and political problems as well as confront new competitive pressures in its own backyard. By 2004, the United States and the global economy were entering a period of synchronized growth and economic recovery. But the U.S. occupation of Iraq, the terrorist train bombing in Madrid, and the continued instability in the Middle East provided a context for an underlying concern about the prospects for continued growth and stability.

Economic growth continued until 2008 when the effects of the financial and economic crisis began to spread. The effects of the housing market bubble bursting lasting through 2009. The low interest rates that provided for easy access to credit and financing generated housing price increases, near zero savings, and rising household debt in the United States. Regulators were late to recognize the potential consequences of this situation while it was brewing. When the crisis hit, both the U.S. and global economy went into a tailspin. Global growth and international trade slowed dramatically, or ceased, as frozen credit markets prevented even the most basic economic activities, such as borrowing and lending, from taking place.

At the end of 2009, the United States was left with twin deficits including a budget deficit due to the growing public debt and a considerable current account deficit. Major issues and challenges for the United States remained, including restoring economic growth, fiscal integrity, and re-regulating the financial sector to prevent another crisis. There was also the need for international coordination and cooperation to address the structural and regulatory aspects of the current crisis. Indeed, European leaders called for a new international conference similar to that held in Bretton Woods after World War II (see box below) to focus on institutions and policies and regulations to provide sound footing for future world trade and finance. Another issue for such a conference would be the future role of the U.S. dollar in the global economy. The United States has depended on borrowing from other countries to finance both public and private spending. In the following article, "China's Leader Says He Is 'Worried' Over U.S. Treasuries," Michael Wines, Keith Bradsher, and Mark Landler report on China's growing concern about U.S. policies and its ability to repay debt in the future.

# Exchange Rate Systems: An Historical Perspective

Some type of international financial system is required to deal with the "imbalances" in the balance-of-payments positions among nations. If the United States, for example, has an overall balance-of-trade deficit with the rest of the world, some mechanism must exist for "balancing" that deficit. Throughout the history of modern world capitalism, several different systems have existed for accomplishing this task, including fixed and fluctuating exchange standards.

## The Gold Standard

Gold served as the external form of payment in the international system from the Middle Ages until the twentieth century. Under a gold standard, a country's currency is convertible into gold at a fixed price. The price of the currency expressed in terms of gold is known as its *parity value*. The United States and the United Kingdom once defined their currencies in terms of gold. As a result, surpluses and deficits in the balance of payments were equivalent to a certain amount of gold.

This mechanism was relatively simple and had some attractive results. The flow of gold from the United Kingdom would reduce the money supply in the United Kingdom and increase it in the United States. As an automatic reaction, prices would fall in the United Kingdom and rise in the United States, since less (more) money would tend to force prices downward (upward) and since gold was a part of the money supply. Consumers in each country would then respond to the price changes. Exports of U.S. goods would tend to fall, and those of the United Kingdom would tend to increase. Consequently, the balance-of-payments surplus of the United States would tend to decline, all without any government intervention.

The concept of liquidity is vital to trade in that transactions require some standard of "moneyness" that is universally accepted, and the trading parties must have this liquidity. Under the gold standard, if countries do not have enough gold reserves (or gold mines) to facilitate trade or if output of goods and services outstrips the output of gold, a liquidity crisis results. The health of domestic economies is therefore at the mercy of the world's ability to produce gold. In practice, the gold standard limited the amount of international trade that could be financed and tended to restrict some domestic economies. As nations and trade grew, the limited gold resources could not satisfy the needs of world trade.

## The International Monetary Fund and the Bretton Woods System

Two world wars separated by the Great Depression dealt fatal blows to the gold standard. The framework for the system that forms the official organizational structure of today's international financial negotiations was formulated in 1944 at a conference in Bretton Woods, New Hampshire, and became known as the **Bretton Woods system.** The institutional arrangements settled on were to be overseen by a new organization, the **International Monetary Fund (IMF).** The IMF was established to provide an institutional framework for monetary cooperation and consultation when problems arose. It was charged with facilitating expansion and balanced growth of trade with high levels of domestic income and employment.

To accomplish this goal, the participants established a system of fixed exchange rates. Under the fixed exchange system, currencies were defined in terms of one another. The IMF was to provide for stable exchange rates between currencies. Consistency was assured, with each nation defining its currency in terms of both gold and the U.S. dollar. The U.S. dollar maintained a passive role in the Bretton Woods system because it was chosen to serve as the key or reserve currency, making it as acceptable as gold in international transactions. The Bretton Woods system functioned with this fixed exchange system until 1973.

## International Monetary Crisis

The IMF was created and designed to guarantee the working of the Bretton Woods system, but problems sent the fixed exchange system into periods of confusion and disarray, never quite fulfilling the dreams of its creators. According to the design of the Bretton Woods system, exchange rate adjustments should occur in cases of persistent balance-of-payments difficulties. However, because the dollar was the reserve currency and essential for international liquidity, necessary dollar adjustments were avoided. In addition, more serious trouble lay deeper than this. Currency realignments were rare under the Bretton Woods system. Many believed depreciation was a sign of national weakness, while appreciation was viewed not as a sign of strength but as a compromise to a weaker economic position. Many nations' exchange rates were out of kilter, since they remained at essentially the same parity rates that existed at the end of World War II.

With ever-increasing deficits in the balance of payments, U.S. policy remained much the same during the 1960s. During this period, the IMF virtually conceded its operations to the Group of Ten, consisting of the ten most economically powerful countries in the world. At their meetings they discussed and acted at any indication of weakness in currency operations—but prompt realignment of parity rates did not occur. A system of emergency capital flows developed, with funds being shuttled from one weak currency to the next. This led only to greater instability within the Bretton Woods system.

In August 1971, President Nixon introduced the New Economic Policy (NEP), which, along with domestic wage and price controls, called for a temporary 10 percent surcharge on all imports as well as a "temporary" halt in the convertibility of dollars into gold. (This temporary condition still exists, and it is now understood that August 15, 1971, marked the complete end of the gold exchange standard. Although U.S. citizens have not been able to exchange their dollar holdings for gold from the U.S. Treasury since 1934, foreign dollar holders continued to exchange dollars for gold until this suspension.) Under the burden of inflation and the high costs of the war in Vietnam, the U.S. balance-of-payments deficit was larger and more pressing than it had been at any time in the nation's history.

## Floating Exchange Rates

On December 18, 1971, President Nixon committed what a few years earlier would have been political suicide and devalued the dollar. The "historic" Smithsonian agreement called for an 8 percent devaluation of the dollar and a realignment of other currencies to reflect the lower value of the dollar. As pressures continued, nations began to let their currencies float (adjust to daily changes in the supply of and demand for each currency).

Since 1973, *de facto* currency depreciations or appreciations occur without official IMF sanction. The overvalued dollar was allowed to seek its own worth in the somewhat free international currency markets. The IMF was given the power to "oversee the exchange rate regime, adopt principles to guide national policies, and encourage international cooperation."

In the years since the introduction of floating exchange rates, the international monetary system has adjusted surprisingly well, even though the central banks of most major industrial countries have intervened at one time or another to "manage" or intervene in their exchange rates. Floating exchange rates have presented special problems for developing economies, however. Because few of these nations had well-developed currency markets, they tied or pegged their currency to that of their major industrial trading partner. A developing nation whose currency was pegged to the British pound found that its currency, like the pound, depreciated by almost 25 percent between mid-1975 and the end of 1976. These kinds of exchange rate movements can cause severe inflationary pressures in developing countries where inflation is often a persistent problem.

## China's Leader Says He Is "Worried" Over U.S. Treasuries

BEIJING — The Chinese prime minister, Wen Jiabao, spoke in unusually blunt terms on Friday about the "safety" of China's $1 trillion investment in American government debt, the world's largest such holding, and urged the Obama administration to offer assurances that the securities would maintain their value.

Speaking ahead of a meeting of finance ministers and bankers this weekend near London to lay the groundwork for next month's Group of 20 summit meeting of the nations with the 20 largest economies, Mr. Wen said that he was "worried" about China's holdings of United States Treasury bonds and other debt, and that China was watching economic developments in the United States closely.

As the financial crisis has unfolded, China has become increasingly vocal about what it perceives as Washington's mismanagement of the global economy and financial system, joining a chorus of foreign critics of unbridled American capitalism. On Thursday, for example, France and Germany rebuffed American calls to coordinate a global stimulus package at the G-20 meeting, saying financial regulation should come first.

In January, Mr. Wen gave a speech criticizing what he called an "unsustainable model of development characterized by prolonged low savings and high consumption." There was little doubt that he was referring to the United States....

With budget deficits mounting rapidly, the United States needs China if it is to finance all that new debt at low interest rates.

"President Obama and his new government have adopted a series of measures to deal with the financial crisis. We have expectations as to the effects of these measures," Mr. Wen said. "We have lent a huge amount of money to the U.S. Of course we are concerned about the safety of our assets. To be honest, I am definitely a little worried."

He called on the United States to "maintain its good credit, to honor its promises and to guarantee the safety of China's assets." What he did not mention was that Chinese investments in the United States helped drive the debt-fueled boom of the last decade, during which China grew increasingly dependent on the American market—a point that was driven home earlier this week when China reported a record 26 percent drop in exports in February.

He stopped short of any threat to reduce purchases of American bonds, much less sell any of them, underscoring the two countries' mutual dependency.

Some specialists say that China's investment in American debt is now so vast that it would be impossible for Beijing to unload its Treasury securities without flooding the market and driving down their price....

While economists dismiss the possibility of the United States defaulting on its obligations, they say China could face steep losses in the event of a sharp rise in United States interest rates or a plunge in the value of the dollar.

Mr. Wen praised China's comparatively healthy economy and said his government would take whatever steps were needed to end the country's slump. He also predicted that the world economy would improve in 2010....

Mr. Wen's confident performance also underscored the growing financial and geopolitical importance of China, one of the few countries to retain enormous spending power despite slowing growth. It has the world's largest reserves of foreign exchange, estimated at $2 trillion, the product of years of double-digit growth.

Economists say at least half of that money has been invested in United States Treasury notes and other government-backed debt, mostly bonds issued by the Treasury and government-sponsored enterprises, Fannie Mae and Freddie Mac.

Much of the Treasury debt China purchased in recent years carries a low interest rate and would plunge in value if interest rates were to rise sharply in the United States. Some financial experts have warned that measures taken to combat the financial crisis — running large budget deficits and expanding the money supply — may eventually lead to higher interest rates.

"The United States government is going to have to sell a huge amount of paper, and the market may react by demanding a higher interest rate," said Nicholas R. Lardy, an expert in the Chinese economy at the Peterson Institute for International Economics. "This will force down the price of outstanding treasuries, imposing large paper losses on the Chinese."

The conflicting financial currents pose a dilemma for Beijing. The smaller the United States stimulus, the less its borrowing, which could help prevent interest rates from rising. But less government spending in the United States could also mean a slower recovery for the American economy and reduced American demand for Chinese goods.

The sharp narrowing of China's trade surplus with the United States may result in reduced Chinese purchases of American bonds in any case. By some accounts, China's trade surplus could fall by as much as half this year, to around $155 billion. That would leave China with fewer dollars to buy foreign bonds, particularly as the pace of investment flows into China has also slowed sharply.

During her visit here last month, Secretary of State Hillary Rodham Clinton publicly assured China that its American holdings remained a reliable investment. But the sheer size of China's holdings of American debt ensure that the countries' partnership will endure, some analysts say. "The only possibility, really, is that China will have to hold these bonds until maturity," said Shen Minggao, the chief economist at Caijing, a Beijing-based business magazine. "If you start to sell those bonds, the market may collapse."

*Michael Wines reported from Beijing, Keith Bradsher from Hong Kong, and Mark Landler from Washington.*

*Source:* Michael Wines, Keith Bradsher, and Mark Landler, "China's Leader says He Is 'Worried' Over U.S. Tressuries." *The New York Times,* March 14, 2009.

# Conclusion

*With all of these changes taking place, what will become of the international financial system? A number of factors currently drive this system with interactive effects. The context of these changes is a competitive system characterized by deregulation, free markets, and innovation. Deregulation and innovation have generated exchange rate volatility as financial entities have applied new computer and information system technologies to their operations and the development of new products and services.*

*Clearly, these issues confound simple Keynesian solutions to macroeconomic problems. As we move further into this millennium, global policy makers will continue to be challenged to find workable solutions that promote worldwide economic stability.*

## Review Questions

**1.** What is the international balance of payments? What does it mean to have a balance-of-payments surplus or deficit?

**2.** What kinds of activities contribute positive credits (+) to a nation's balance of payments?

**3.** How can you use the National Income Accounting framework to illustrate a trade deficit?

**4.** What has been the experience of the United States with trade deficits and current account deficits since 1990?

**5.** What has been the experience of the U.S. dollar since 2000? What is the situation for the U.S. dollar today?

**6.** What are the primary determinants of the value of a nation's currency (exchange rate)?

**7.** What can explain the appreciation of the dollar? The depreciation of the dollar?

**8.** What have been the yen/dollar and euro/dollar relationship since 2006? What is your analysis of these relationships?

# Glossary

**Absolute advantage** In international trade, a condition in which one nation can produce more of a particular commodity with the same amount of resources as another nation uses for producing that commodity.

**Aggregate demand** The total quantity of goods and services demanded by households, businesses, government, and the international sector at various prices.

**Aggregate supply** The total quantity of goods and services producers are willing to supply at varying price levels.

**Alienation** The condition resulting from the separation of the worker from the means of production. Alienation from the worker's point of view results from no control over the product, no control of the means of producing it, and an antagonistic relationship of workers and owners.

**Antitrust policy** Laws that attempt to limit the degree of monopoly in the economy and to promote competition. In the United States, the passage, interpretation, and enforcement of antitrust laws have involved varying degrees of emphasis on market performance, market conduct, and market structure. See *Sherman Antitrust Act*.

**Appreciation of currency** The relative strengthening of a currency in a flexible exchange rate system. The appreciated currency rises in cost and value relative to the depreciated currency.

**Assumption** A proposition that is accepted as true. Economists use simplifying assumptions in building economic models.

**Average cost** Total cost divided by the number of production units.

**Average fixed cost** Total fixed cost divided by total units of output.

**Average propensity to consume (APC)** Total consumption divided by total disposable income. This is the average consumption income ratio.

**Average propensity to save (APS)** Total saving divided by total disposable income.

**Average revenue** Total revenue divided by total output.

**Average variable cost (AVC)** Total variable cost divided by total output.

**Balance of payments** A summary record of a country's transactions that typically involves payments and receipt of foreign exchange. Credit items and debit items must balance, since each good that a country buys or sells must be paid for in one way or another.

**Balance of trade** The difference between the value of exports and the value of imports of visible items (goods and services).

**Barriers to entry** Obstacles to a firm's entry into new industries or markets. These obstacles may be political (such as tariffs or trade restrictions), economic (economies of scale or limited resources, especially in oligopolies), or legal (patents, copyrights, or monopoly).

**Board of Governors** A seven-member group members are appointed by the U.S. president and approved by the Congress to head the Federal Reserve. The board coordinates and regulates the nation's money supply. See *Federal Reserve System*.

**Breakeven point** (1) In national income accounting, the amount of income corresponding to consumption of the entire income. There is no saving or dissaving. (2) For an individual business, the amount of revenue corresponding to a production level at which revenues exactly equal costs. There are no profits or losses.

**Bretton Woods Agreement (1944)** The international agreement that formed the basis for today's international financial organizations. After World War II, the Allied nations agreed that international financial affairs would be overseen by the International Monetary Fund. GATT and the World Bank were also outcomes of Bretton Woods.

**Budget deficit**   The amount by which government expenditures exceed government revenues during the accounting period.

**Built-in stabilizers**   Automatic, nondiscretionary forms of fiscal policy that compensate for particular trends of aggregate changes in national income.

**Business cycle**   Recurrent ups and downs of business activity, shown in a host of business indicators. Expansion and contraction phases are both thought to have certain cumulative features. They may also contain the seeds of the turning points at the cycle's peak and trough.

**Capital**   A factor of production, along with labor and land; the stock of a society's produced means of production, including factories, buildings, machines, tools, and inventories of goods in stock.

**Capital account**   Unilateral and capital transfers in balance-of-payments, accounting; capital transfers of nonproduced, nonfinancial assets.

**Capitalism**   An economic system in which the basic resources and capital goods of the society are privately owned. Decisions are usually made by individual units, which may be relatively small (pure competition) or quite large (monopoly/oligopoly). Decisions tend to be based on profitability in the case of businesses, or, in the case of individuals, on economic self-interest.

**Cartel**   An organization of producers designed to limit or eliminate competition among its members, usually by agreeing to restrict output in an effort to achieve noncompetitive prices. An example is OPEC.

**Central Bank**   A Federal Reserve Board operation that serves the nation's banks. Besides its major responsibility—control of the money supply—it conducts some restriction, regulation, and investigation of the banking industry.

*Ceteris paribus*   Literally, "other things being equal"; a term used in economics to indicate that all variables except the ones specified are assumed not to change.

**Change in demand**   A shift in the demand curve due to a change in one of the determinants of demand.

**Change in supply**   A shift in the supply curve due to a change in one of the determinants of supply.

**Class**   In an economic sense, a group of people defined in terms of their relationship to production. For example, under capitalism, one class of people (proletariat) works the means of production, and another class (capitalists, bourgeoisie) owns the means of production. This concept was used largely by Karl Marx.

**Classical economics**   A school of economics that usually refers to the doctrines of the British Classical School of the late eighteenth and early nineteenth centuries, especially those of Adam Smith and followers. They emphasized competition, free trade, and minimal state intervention in the economy.

**Classical liberalism**   A doctrine stressing the importance of rationality, property rights, individual freedom, and laissez-faire.

**Collusion**   Agreements to avoid competition or to set prices.

**Commodity**   Marketable item produced to satisfy wants. Commodities may be either tangible goods or intangible services. Marx considered labor under the wage contract a commodity because it orders wage contracts and responds to supply-and-demand conditions.

**Communism**   An economic system characterized by socialization of labor, centralization of the ownership of the means of production, centralized coordination of production, centralization of credit policy through a central bank, and reduction of alienation and exploitation of the worker.

**Comparative advantage**   In international trade, a country's productive advantage with respect to a particular commodity, based on its ability to give up fewer other commodities to produce a unit of the commodity than another country would have to give up.

This relative cost of production is most significant in determining mutually beneficial patterns of trade among nations.

**Competition**   Theoretically, competition exists in a perfect and an imperfect form; the former is known as perfect competition, the latter as monopoly, oligopoly, and monopolistic competition.

**Concentration ratio**   The percentage of total sales in an industry that is accounted for by a specific number of firms.

**Conglomerate merger**   Companies in unrelated industries merge.

**Conservative economist**   An economist who advocates classical theory, classical liberalism, and classical economics (i.e., that government should intervene only when necessary, and then only minimally).

**Consumer Price Index (CPI)**   A government statistic that measures inflation in terms of the weighted average composite of goods and services commonly consumed by average families.

**Consumer sovereignty**   The doctrine that the market follows the dictates of consumers, and is driven solely by consumer tastes and preferences. Producers respond to consumer demand.

**Consumption**   Expenditures by households and individuals on consumer goods.

**Coordinated market economies**   Economies in which the government is involved in most major economic decisions, either directing, coordinating, or consulting with economic actors. Private firms still make many economic decisions, but labor unions and government officials also get input into most major economic decisions, and these groups have long-established relationships that facilitate cooperation and coordination.

**Corporation**   A form of business organization with a legal existence separate from that of the owners, in which ownership and financial responsibility are divided, limited, and shared among any number of individual and institutional shareholders.

**Cost-push inflation**   A general increase in prices associated with increases in the cost of production. Categorized as supply inflation.

**Creative destruction**   The process of the transformation of industries due to extraordinary innovations in which the most innovative actors tend to succeed while non-innovating establishments are destroyed.

**Crowding out**   Loss of funding as a result of the competition between economic units for the use of limited funds. The term usually refers to the federal budget deficit and the continued borrowing of the U.S. Treasury. Funds used to finance government spending deprive businesses of necessary capital, thus crowding out investment.

**Currency**   Any recognized material accepted as national money; almost always paper or coin.

**Current accounts**   In balance-of-payments accounting, the accounts that summarize the flow of goods and services between one nation and the rest of the world.

**Cyclical (budget) deficit**   The part of the federal deficit that fluctuates with the state of the economy. It increases when there is a downturn of the business cycle.

**Cyclical unemployment**   Measure of unemployment due to decreased demand during the troughs of business cycles, when output is curtailed. Workers who are cyclically unemployed are expected to be reinstated as the cycle moves upward.

**Deficit spending**   Government spending when net government revenues are less than net government expenditures.

**Demand**   (1) Quantity demanded. (2) The whole relationship of the quantity demanded to variables that determine it, such as tastes, income, population, and price. (3) The demand curve.

**Demand curve**   A hypothetical construction depicting how many units of a particular commodity consumers would be willing to buy over a period of time at all possible prices, assuming that the prices of other commodities, money incomes of consumers, and other factors are unchanged.

**Demand deposits**  Checking accounts in commercial banks. These deposits can be turned into currency "on demand," i.e., by writing a check. Demand deposits are a main form of money in the United States.

**Demand, law of**  A principle concerning the relationship between price and quantity demanded: All other things constant, the lower the price, the higher the quantity demanded. In other words, price and quantity demanded are inversely related.

**Demand-pull inflation**  A general increase in prices arising from increasing excess demand for a given level of output.

**Dependency model**  A model that assumes that underdevelopment is a consequence of the historical evolution of capitalism and the integration of developing countries into the expanding sphere of capitalist production globally.

**Depreciation**  (1) Loss of value in capital equipment due to use or obsolescence. (2) The loss of value in any valuable good or commodity due to use or market forces (such as currency exchange rates).

**Depression**  A prolonged downswing of economic activity exemplified by mass unemployment, a level of national income well below the potential level, and great excess capacity. A depression is more severe and longer lasting than a recession. The economic breakdown of the industrialized world in the 1930s was called the Great Depression. See *Recession*.

**Derived demand**  Demand of a good for use in the production of goods and services.

**Devaluation**  A downward revision in the value at which a country's currency is pegged in terms of a foreign currency.

**Dialectics**  The study of the contradictions within the essence of things; an exchange of a thesis and anti-thesis that results in a synthesis; the struggle of opposing forces in the economy that, according to Karl Marx, drives economic change.

**Discount rate**  Interest rate charged on loans from the Federal Reserve Bank to its member banks. The rate is pegged to the fed funds rate.

**Discretionary fiscal policy**  A fiscal policy designed to respond to a particular situation in the macroeconomy. These policies are implemented to achieve specific goals, usually high output, high employment, and stable prices.

**Diseconomies of scale**  The phenomenon of disproportional increasing costs as a firm's long-run productive capacity grows. Simply put, the growth of production costs in an expanding firm outstrips the growth in production.

**Disintermediation**  Resource allocation, particularly investment, by a firm that excludes intermediary institutions such as savings and loan institutions, banks, or brokerage firms.

**Disposable personal income**  Amount of personal income remaining after payment of various federal, state, and local taxes and other nontax payments.

**Dissaving**  Deficit or negative spending; that is, borrowing or drawing down other financial assets in order to consume.

**Distribution (of income)**  The division of the total product of a society among its members. The distribution is sometimes described by a classification according to income size or by a classification including factor payments.

**Division of labor**  Subdivision of a productive process into its component parts, which are then handled by specially skilled or trained laborers. Adam Smith believed it was a major source of increased productivity over time.

**Dumping**  Sale by an exporting nation of its product at a lower price in an importing country than in its own country. Dumping tends to ruin the importer's domestic industry while strengthening the exporter's market share.

**Economic dependence**  The relationship of unequal interdependence, endured by the less advanced countries with the developed countries. Theoretically, a country is in a state of economic dependence if the expansion of its economy depends on that of another country. See *Imperialism*.

**Economic development** Progressive changes in a society's ability to meet its economic tasks of production and distribution. Development is characterized by increasing output and the growth of economic institutions, relationships, and methods that facilitate society's ability to generate economic growth.

**Economic growth** Increase in productive capabilities beyond the necessary elements of survival. Expansion creates more jobs, goods, and income.

**Economic planning** The planning of investment, consumption, and similar decisions by one or more bodies. Several variants (among which are corporate planning, command planning, and indicative planning) demonstrate variety in what is to be planned and who does the planning.

**Economic profits** A return to capital above "normal profit"; profit remaining after opportunity costs have been taken into account.

**Economic system** The "mode of life" of a society; the manner in which people organize themselves for production and distribution.

**Economic theory** A theory of economics or resource allocation. Examples are Marxist, classical, and Keynesian theory. See *Theory*.

**Economics** The study of the allocation of resources, the production of goods and services, and their distribution in societies.

**Economies of scale** The phenomenon of decreasing average costs in large-scale production (usually oligopolistic production). The growth of production in an expanding firm outstrips the growth in costs.

**Efficiency** In economics, allocation of scarce resources to best meet the needs and wants of society.

**Elasticity** A function that describes the sensitivity of demand or supply of a product to changes in its price. Elasticity equals the percentage change in quantity demanded (supplied) divided by the percentage change in price.

**Employment Act of 1946** U.S. federal law that created a Council of Economic Advisers to advise the president on the state of the economy and on how best to achieve the goal of full employment.

**Enclosure movement** In England during the Middle Ages, a series of parliamentary acts by which the feudal nobility fenced off or enclosed lands formerly used for communal grazing, destroying feudal ties and creating a large, new "landless" labor force.

**Entrepreneur** In the classical liberal sense, an innovator and owner of the means of production. In the modern corporate world, an entrepreneur is often considered a businessperson.

**Equation of exchange** The quantity theory of money, expressed as $MV = PQ$, where $M$ is the money stock, $V$ is velocity of money, $P$ is price level, and $Q$ is real national income. It is a tautology, because $V$ is defined as $PQ/M$.

**Equilibrium** A state of balance in which there are no endogenous pressures for change. A market equilibrium is said to exist at the price where the quantity demanded equals the quantity supplied.

**Exchange rate** The price of a nation's currency in terms of another nation's currency.

**Exhaustive spending** Governmental purchases of goods and services.

**Exports** Any unit of production that leaves the country where it was produced for sale in another country.

**Externalities** Costs of productive activity that the firm is not obliged to bear. The costs are borne by the public as social costs of production. Also known as third-party effect. Externalities may be detrimental (external costs) or beneficial (external benefits).

**Factor of production** Any implement or agent whose services are used in the production of economic goods and services. Three basic factors are land, labor, and capital.

**Fed funds rate** The interest rate that banks charge when they lend reserves to other banks for short periods of time; the Federal Reserve currently targets the fed funds rate and uses policy tools to achieve the stated target.

**Federal Reserve System (Fed)** An independent agency of the federal government and instrumental in determining monetary policy. Its main tools are altering reserve requirements and conducting open-market purchases and sales of governmental securities. See *Discount rate; Monetary policy; Reserve requirements; Open Market Operations.*

**Feudalism** The economic system that preceded capitalism. Relations of class were between lord and serf. Feudalism existed in a society in which tradition and ceremony played the major roles.

**Financial account** In balance-of-payments accounting, all financial flows in and out of a country.

**Financial intermediaries** Institutions such as banks, savings and loans, insurance companies, mutual funds, pension funds, and finance companies that borrow funds from people with savings and then make loans to others (borrowers).

**Financial intermediation** Use of financial institutions to deposit or acquire funds from the public. Such institutions pool numerous funds and then provide them to businesses, governments, or individuals.

**Firm** Unit that makes decisions regarding the employment of factors of production and production of goods and services.

**Fiscal policy** Governmental policy concerned with the tax and expenditure activities of the federal government, including the size of public spending and the balancing or unbalancing of the federal budget. This policy is designed to promote certain macroeconomic objectives—usually full employment, stable prices, economic growth, and balance-of-payments equilibrium.

**Fixed exchange rate** A rate at which a currency is fixed (set) to establish its price relative either to a universal exchange (gold) or to another currency.

**Floating exchange rate** A currency exchange rate that rises or falls in response to the forces of international supply and demand. See *Exchange rate.*

**Forces of production** All of the necessary elements—tools, machines, factories, means of transportation, labor, science, technology, skills, knowledge, etc.—required to produce goods and services.

**Fractional reserve system** A banking system under which commercial banks are required to maintain reserves equal to a prescribed percentage of their demand or other deposits. See *Reserve requirement.*

**Free trade** A situation in which all commodities can be freely imported and exported without special taxes or restrictions being levied because of their status as imports or exports.

**Frictional unemployment** Loss of jobs caused by temporary mismatching of laborers with jobs due to differences between the needs of business and skills of labor.

**Full employment** A condition under which those who wish to work at the prevailing wage are able to find work. In the United States, full employment is defined as 4 percent unemployment.

**General Agreement on Tariffs and Trade (GATT)** An association of countries that "sets and regulates the code of international trade conduct and promotes free trade as part of the Bretton Woods System."

**Gini coefficient** A measure of inequality in income distribution derived from the Lorenz curve. To calculate it for a population, find the difference in area between a 45° line and the population's Lorenz curve, and divide the difference by the entire area below the 45° line.

**Glut** An excess of production over the amount purchased. This usually leads to a decline in production and possibly a recession.

**Gross domestic product (GDP)** The market value of all final goods and services produced in an accounting period by factors of production located within a country.

**Gross national product (GNP)** The market value of all final goods and services produced in an accounting period by factors of production owned by citizens of that country.

**Hidden unemployment** Workers who are unemployed or underemployed but are not counted in official unemployment statistics. Includes discouraged workers who are unemployed but have given up looking for a job, and workers who are working part-time but would like more hours of work.

**Historical materialism** Developed by Karl Marx, an in-depth historical study of material relations of people. The basis of social and economic change resides in class relations of people. The base of a society is its mode of production, and all class struggle emanates out of the relations of people to the mode of production. The superstructure, which is determined by the base, includes the philosophy, religion, ideology, etc., of the specific epoch.

**Horizontal merger** The combination of two companies in the same industry.

**Imperialism** One country's economic, social, political, and cultural dominance over another country. Imperialism, as developed by Lenin, Sweezy, Baran, Magdoff, and many others, is a historical problem and directly related to the growth and development of capitalism.

**Imports** Goods brought into a country for sale, having been produced elsewhere.

**Income elasticity of demand** The percentage change in quantity demanded divided by the percentage change in income. It measures how much the demand for a product changes when income changes.

**Income flow** The path that income follows in the economy. Businesses pay rents, wages, interest, and profits to households, which in turn spend their incomes to continue the flow.

**Income velocity of money** The rate of turnover of money in the economy. From the equation of exchange, velocity is GDP divided by the money supply. See *Equation of exchange.*

**Incomes policy** A governmental policy designed to limit inflation by instituting direct and indirect controls over prices, wages, profits, and other types of income.

**Index number** A weighted average of a given variable with a specified base number, usually 100.

**Indirect business taxes** Taxes imposed on the production and sale of goods. Examples include sales tax, excise tax, custom duties, and property taxes.

**Industry** The collective group of producers of a single good or service or closely related goods or services.

**Inefficiency in production** A condition in a noncompetitive market in which output is not at minimum average cost.

**Inefficiency in resource allocation** A condition in a noncompetitive market in which the good's price does not equal marginal cost.

**Infant industry** An industry that has recently been established in a country and has not yet had time to exploit possible economies of scale and other efficiencies. Such industries provide one of the traditional arguments for tariff protection.

**Inflation** A general rise in the average level of all prices in an economy as defined by some index (Consumer Price Index, wholesale price index, or GDP price deflator).

**Infrastructure** Necessary supports for development, such as transportation routes and social services.

**Innovation** A change for the better in technology or production. A change is considered "better" if it involves higher efficiency and/or lower production costs.

**Institutional economics** An approach to studying the economy that focuses on understanding the role and evolution of human-made institutions in shaping the economy and economic behavior.

**Institutionalist** Economists practicing institutional economics.

**Interest** (1) The price of borrowing money. (2) The rate of return to owners of financial capital.

**Interest rate** The amount of interest expressed as a percentage of the initial sum.

**International Monetary Fund (IMF)** International organization founded with the goal of encouraging trade by establishing an orderly procedure for stabilizing foreign exchange rates and for altering those rates in the case of fundamental balance-of-payments disequilibrium.

**International trade** Buying and selling of goods and services across national borders. The country that sells is the exporter, and the country that buys is the importer.

**Inventories** Stocks of goods kept on hand to meet orders from other producers and customers.

**Investment** An addition to a firm's or society's stock of capital (machines, buildings, inventories, etc.) in a certain period of time.

**"Invisible hand"** Term coined by Adam Smith to suggest that individuals who are motivated only by private (not social) interest will nevertheless be guided invisibly by the market to actions and decisions beneficial to the welfare of society.

**Kanban** The "just-in-time" system in which services and supplies are produced and delivered only when needed.

**Keiretsu** A production relation between a large core firm and its subsidiaries that allows for a stable, mutually beneficial long-term relationship.

**Keynesian economics** Theory characterized by its emphasis on macroeconomic problems, the special role of aggregate expenditure in determining national income, and the possibility of unemployment equilibrium; its attempt to synthesize real and monetary analysis; and its argument for a greater government involvement in the economy.

**Keynesian multiplier ($k$)** The number of dollars by which a $1 increase in spending ($C$, $I$, $G$) will raise the equilibrium level of national income. Represented as $k$, it can be expressed mathematically in relation to the marginal propensity to consume (MPC) or the marginal propensity to save (MPS):

$$k = \frac{1}{1 - \text{MPC}} \quad k = \frac{1}{\text{MPS}}$$

**Labor** The physical and mental contributions of humans to the production process. Collectively, labor refers to all workers.

**Labor force participation rate** Percentage of actual civilians participating in the labor force compared with the total number of civilians of working age.

**Labor theory of value** Theory held by Marx (and Smith in differing form) that the value of a commodity is proportional to the labor embodied in its production.

**Laissez-faire** A doctrine that the state should largely leave the economy to its own devices. Associated with Adam Smith.

**Land** A means of production that includes raw materials and the land upon which productive activity takes place (i.e., factory, farm).

**Law of diminishing returns** Principle that in the production of any commodity, as more units of a variable factor of production are added to a fixed quantity of other factors of production, the amount that each additional unit of the variable factor adds to the total product will eventually begin to diminish.

**Law of specialization** The tendency for productivity to increase when laborers specialize in one particular task.

**Liberal economist** An economist who accepts capitalism and advocates government intervention when market failures occur.

**Liberal market economies** Economies in which privately owned firms make the majority of economic decisions in competitive markets based on the forces of supply and demand. Economic relations tend to be legally based, and the government works to establish the appropriate legal environment for markets and to correct market failures, but does not direct economic activity most of the time.

**Liquidity** The ease with which an asset can be converted into cash. Considerations in measuring liquidity include the time necessary to acquire cash, the cost of conversion, and the predictability of the asset's value.

**Liquidity preference** Demand for money as a function of the interest rate; the willingness to hold money on hand.

**Liquidity trap** In Keynesian theory, the point in the economy when all economic agents desire to keep each additional dollar on hand. To them, the existing interest rate does not warrant the acquisition of bonds. The demand for money is thus perfectly elastic or horizontal, and monetary policy is completely ineffective in stimulating aggregate expenditures.

**Long run** Any extended period, usually longer than three to five years. For a firm, the time necessary to effect changes in "fixed" resources. Economists view the long run as the period in which equilibrium is reached.

**Lorenz curve** Graphs the extent of income inequality by charting the cumulative percentage of income against the cumulative percentage of families.

**Macroeconomics** The branch of economics concerned with large economic aggregates such as GDP, total employment, overall price level, and how these aggregates are determined.

**Malthus, Thomas** Economist who developed a theory that population tends to grow at a geometric rate while food supplies can, at best, grow at an arithmetic rate. Thus, in Malthus's eyes, extreme poverty, famine, plague, and war would continually beset humanity.

**Marginal cost (MC)** The change in total cost resulting from raising the rate of production by one unit.

**Marginal factor cost** The cost of an additional resource or factor of production (which in competition equals the price of the resource).

**Marginal physical product (of labor)** The additional output realized when one more unit of a variable input is used, assuming all other input levels are held constant.

**Marginal propensity to consume (MPC)** The change in consumption divided by the change in income ($MPC = \Delta C/\Delta Y$).

**Marginal propensity to save (MPS)** The change in saving divided by the change in income that brought it about ($MPS = \Delta S/\Delta Y$).

**Marginal revenue (MR)** The change in a firm's total revenue arising from the sale of one additional unit.

**Marginal revenue = marginal cost** In microeconomics, the point at which profits are maximized for a firm.

**Marginal revenue product** The additional revenue realized when one more unit of a variable input is used, assuming all other input levels are held constant.

**Market** (1) An area over which buyers and sellers negotiate the exchange of a well-defined commodity. (2) From the point of view of a household, the firms from which it can buy a well-defined product. (3) From the point of view of the firm, the buyers to whom it can sell a well-defined product.

**Market economy** An economy functioning largely through market forces (supply, demand, etc.).

**Market failure** The inability of the market to produce an efficient (or acceptable) result.

**Market power** A condition in which the firm can exercise control over the price of a good or service because the firm supplies the total quantity.

**Marxian economics** School of economics aimed at understanding the class system (or private property system); the methods of production and commodity exchange under capitalism.

**Materialism** In Marxian economics, the notion that production of goods and services for survival is the essential human activity in all societies. This activity colors and structures all other aspects of life.

**Medium of exchange** The function of money as intermediary. Since money is accepted in payment for goods and services and is valued for the goods and services it buys, money is a medium of exchange.

**Mercantilism** A characteristic European economic doctrine in the sixteenth to seventeenth centuries, emphasizing the role of money and trade in economic life and the desirability of active state intervention in the economy.

**Microeconomics** Branch of economics that deals with the interrelationships of individual businesses, firms, industries, consumers, laborers, and other factors of production that make up the economy. Focuses on markets.

**Mixed economy** An economy in which there are substantial public and private sectors, in which private enterprise and the market are significant determining factors, but in which the state also takes on certain basic economic responsibilities (e.g., full employment and business regulation). See *Capitalism.*

**Mode of production** In Marxian economics, the major economic structure, or base, of society, composed of the forces of production and the relations of production.

**Monetary aggregates** Various measures of the money supply used by the Federal Reserve System and include $M_1$ and $M_2$.

**Monetary policy** Governmental policy concerned with the supply of money and credit in the economy and the rate of interest. This policy is designed to promote certain macroeconomic objectives, usually full employment, stable prices, economic growth, stable exchange rates, or balance-of-payments equilibrium.

**Money** Anything that is generally accepted in payment for goods and services and in the repayment of debts.

**Monopolistic competition** A market structure in which each firm is relatively small, but each has a monopoly on its particular version of the product in question. Competition in such a framework includes advertising, easy entry product differentiation, limited price control, and other forms of non-price competition.

**Monopoly** A market structure in which there is a single seller of a commodity or service that has no close substitutes.

**Monopoly capitalism** An economy that marks the dominance of imperfect competition; productive forces or factors are extremely concentrated, and markets are imperfect. See *Capitalism.*

**Multinational corporation** A corporation that operates within more than one country.

**Multiplier** See *Keynesian multiplier; Transfer multiplier.*

**National debt** The net accumulation of federal budget deficits; the total indebtedness of the federal government.

**National income** The total income of factors of production in the current productive period.

**Neoliberal model** A model that assumes that developing nations must adopt modern capital and technology to have strong economic growth.

**Net national product (NNP)** Total output of final goods and services produced in an economy in a given period of time, including net rather than gross investment. NNP = GDP − depreciation or capital consumption allowances.

**Newly Industrializing Countries (NIC)** A group of countries (Hong Kong, Taiwan, Singapore, Malaysia, the Philippines, South Korea, Brazil, Mexico, and Argentina) that have allowed foreign firms to set up operations favorably and have generated sizable export capabilities.

**Oligopoly** A market structure in which a few large firms dominate the industry. Some of these industries produce an undifferentiated product, others a differentiated product. In either case, a special feature of oligopoly is that the firms recognize their interdependence.

**Open-market operations** Federal Reserve purchases and sales of government securities on the open market. These activities are an important instrument of monetary policy because sales of government securities reduce the money supply, while purchases increase it. See *Federal Reserve System.*

**Opportunity cost** The cost of an economic good as measured in terms of the alternative goods one must forgo to secure it.

**Organization of Petroleum Exporting Countries (OPEC)** Organization of oil-producing nations, largely in the Middle East, that have joined together for the purpose of controlling the production, export, and price of petroleum.

**Orthodox economics** The mainstream approach to economic theory, which emphasizes the rational, calculating nature of human behavior and seeks to model that behavior quantitatively and scientifically.

**Paradigms** A set of assumptions, concepts, values, practices, and so forth that inform a specific discipline (e.g. orthodox economics, Marxian economics, or institutional economics) during a particular period of time.

**Paradox of thrift** Economic principle, identified by Keynes, that an increase in the desire to save decreases output, even though investment may also increase.

**Peak (of business cycle)** The height of the business cycle; characterized by greatest economic activity and followed by contracting economic activity.

**Per capita income** Total national income divided by total population.

**Perfect competition** The market structure characterized by large numbers of small firms producing and selling a homogeneous product in a competitive market with easy entry and exit.

**Petrodollars** Dollars and currency in the form of monetary reserves controlled by the oil-exporting (largely OPEC) nations, accumulated by selling petroleum.

**Phillips curve** Graph showing the relationship between inflation and unemployment.

**Political business cycle** Distortion of the basic business cycle caused by the actions and policies of politicians bidding for reelection. Usually a four-year cycle in sequence with presidential elections.

**Political economy** Social science dealing with political policies and economic processes, their interrelationships, and their mutual influence on social institutions.

**Possessions** Personal items people own and use, including home, farm, or tools. Private property, in contrast, reflects ownership of impersonal property used by the owner only to collect rent on land, interest, and profits on capital; it is used (worked) by others.

**Postindustrial society** A society that has encountered the processes of industrialization and has gone beyond industrialization in terms of benefits accruing to the people. Some people consider the United States a postindustrial society.

**Praxis** Practical activity with an added twist, i.e., the dialectical interrelation of thought and practice. The term was used by the young Hegelians and especially Marx.

**Precautionary demand for money** Holding money in order to cover unexpected or temporary expenses or losses of income.

**Present value** The value today of a sum to be received or paid in the future, adjusted by a prevailing or assumed interest rate.

**Price** An amount of money that guides resource allocation and reflects the value of a good or service. Prices are transmitted by markets through which producers make decisions about what factors of production to use, and consumers decide what to consume.

**Price ceiling** A legally set, maximum price (price control), designed to keep prices in a particular market below the equilibrium price.

**Price elasticity of demand** The sensitivity of demand for a product to changes in its price.

**Price elasticity of supply** The sensitivity of supply of a product to changes in its price.

**Price index** See *Consumer Price Index; Index number.*

**Price leadership** The practice of a single firm in an industry announcing a price change and other firms following suit.

**Price stability** Price policy that aims to counter wide fluctuations in aggregate price levels. During a period of high inflation, for example, governments seeking price stability adopt anti-inflationary measures such as credit withdrawal, higher interest rates, and decreased government spending (or increased taxes).

**Price wars**   Progressive price cutting to increase sales.

**Primitive accumulation**   A way of accumulating wealth that fuels class conflict. In particular, the early formation of capital that accompanied the development of capitalism, often characterized by piracy and plunder.

**Product differentiation**   Business strategy in which substitute products retain some distinctive difference. Means of differentiating products include brand names, coloring, packaging, or advertising.

**Production possibilities curve**   Graph that illustrates scarcity and opportunity cost by showing that whenever society chooses to have more of one type of good, it must sacrifice some of another type of good.

**Productivity (of labor)**   The output produced per unit of input (output per hour of work).

**Profits**   Excess of revenues over costs. Normal profits are equal to the opportunity costs of management. Economic profits are the profits above the normal profit. Theoretically, in pure competition, economic profits equal zero in the long run. However, in imperfect market structures, they do not.

**Progressive income tax**   Tax that claims an ever-increasing percentage of income as the income level rises.

**Property**   Tangible or intangible possession that may be used to produce some product or aid in the selling of the product. Certain legal rights are attached to this "private property."

**Property rights**   In capitalism, where productive property is privately owned, owners' rights to control the use of these productive resources. See *Possessions*.

**Protectionism**   Policy that institutes high tariffs on incoming goods, so as to preserve domestic industry. Protectionism was prevalent during mercantilism. See *Infant industry*; *Tariff*.

**Public debt**   The amount of outstanding federal debt held by individuals, corporations, and nonfederal government agencies.

**Public goods**   Goods or resources that benefit the general public and are not necessarily directly paid for by all those who use them. Examples are street signs and public schools.

**Public sector**   Local, state, and federal governmental offices, organizations, and institutions.

**Putting-out system**   Labor system in which an owner would give workers the necessary materials and pay the worker to make a finished product. Replaced the handicraft type of industry and marked the emergence of private capital.

**Quantity demanded**   The specific number of units of a product in the economy that is desired by economic agents at a given price level.

**Quantity supplied**   The specific number of units of a product in the economy that is provided by producers at a given price level.

**Quantity theory of money**   Theory that the quantity of money in the economy largely determines the level of prices. Stated as $MV = PQ$, where $M$ is the quantity of money, $V$ is the income velocity of money, $P$ is the price level, and $Q$ is real national income. The theory postulates that $V$ is largely determined by institutional factors and $Q$ is determined by factor supplies and technology; hence changes in $M$ will be reflected in proportionate changes in $P$.

**Quotas**   Limits on the quantities of goods imported or exported.

**Radical economists**   Economists who are critical of classical and neoclassical theory and view economic problems as resulting directly from the capitalist system itself. Thus, the only serious relief to these problems is a change of economic system.

**Rational expectations**   An economics-based theory about the nature of economic agents, stating that all agents are rational, logical, and aware of what is best for them and what the consequences of decisions and developments in the economy will mean for their well-being. Agents will act logically to take advantage of changes in the economy and enhance their position.

**Real wages** Wages measured from a specific point; wages that reflect the rate of inflation. If a worker's wage level increases 10 percent and inflation increases 10 percent in the same period of time, then we say that the real wage remains the same. Usually contrasted with money wages, which in the example would reflect only the 10 percent increase in the worker's wage.

**Recession** A slowing down of economic activity, resulting in an increase in unemployment and in excess industrial capacity. Less severe than a depression. Sometimes defined in the United States in terms of a decline in GDP for two or more successive quarters of a year.

**Regulation Q** Federal regulation placing a ceiling on interest rates payable by banks on deposits. This regulation has been phased out.

**Relations of production** The relationships among people in the production process, especially the class structure (for example, slave/slaveowner, serf/lord, laborer/capitalist).

**Rent** (1) Payment for the services of a factor of production. (2) Payment for the use of land.

**Reserve army (industrial)** A term developed by Marx to describe the functioning of capitalism in which worker strength was greatly decreased, in proportion to the amount of unemployment.

**Reserve currency** A currency that is accepted in settlement of international exchanges.

**Reserve requirement** In banking, the fraction of public deposits that a bank holds in reserves.

**Ricardo, David** One of the reformers of classical liberalism, developed by Adam Smith. Ricardo's analysis was based on an economy composed of many small enterprises.

**Savings** All income received by households and not spent on the consumption of goods and services.

**Say's law** The doctrine (named after J. B. Say) that "supply creates its own demand."

The production of one good adds to both aggregate supply and aggregate demand. In this nonmonetary world, depression and mass unemployment are not possible.

**Scarcity** Inability of a society to produce or secure enough goods to satisfy all the wants, needs, and desires people have for these goods.

**Seasonal unemployment** Joblessness created by changing seasonal conditions or demand.

**Services** Duties (or work) for others that do not necessarily render a good but are nevertheless worth payment.

**Sherman Antitrust Act** A major U.S. antitrust law passed in 1890 prohibiting "every contract, combination in the form of trust or otherwise or conspiracy, in restraint of trade or commerce," and prescribing penalties for monopoly.

**Shortage** Disequilibrium situation wherein quantity demanded exceeds quantity supplied. In such a situation, price will tend to rise until it reaches an equilibrium level (where quantity supplied equals quantity demanded).

**Short-run** For a firm, the period in which some inputs are fixed.

**Smith, Adam** Economist who in 1776 published *The Wealth of Nations*, noting the foundation of a new individualist philosophy, classical liberalism.

**Socialism** An economic system in which property and the distribution of wealth are subject to control by the community.

**Special Drawing Rights (SDRs)** A bookkeeping device created by the International Monetary Fund to increase international liquidity. SDRs may be drawn by each country in proportion to its original fund contribution.

**Special Enterprise Zones (SEZs)** Areas in China, mostly in Southern China in coastal cities, where foreign companies are able to invest and operate freely as if they were in a capitalist market economy.

**Specialization (of labor)** Methods of production in which individual workers specialize in particular tasks rather than making everything for themselves.

**Speculative demand for money** Function that describes the amount of assets held by households and firms in the form of money, relative to the interest rate.

**Stagflation** Term coined in the 1970s to describe the coexistence of unemployment (stagnation) and inflation afflicting the United States and other countries.

**Standard of deferred payment** Acceptability as future payment; a characteristic of money.

**Stock** Shares of ownership in a corporation. May be common stock and/or preferred stock.

**Store of value** An asset that holds value into the future. Money has this characteristic.

**Structural (budget) deficit** The federal budget deficit which remains if the economy is at full employment.

**Structural unemployment** Type of permanent unemployment that stems from shifting demand and/or technological changes requiring new skills for workers. Disparities in geographic locations of workers and jobs also contribute to this phenomenon.

**Structuralist model** A model that assumes that domestic political and economic factors affect development.

**Superstructure** Society's ideals, institutions, and ideologies, including laws, politics, culture, ethics, religions, morals, and philosophy that, according to Marx, support the economic base of society and the existing mode of production.

**Supply** The amount of goods or services produced and available for purchase.

**Supply curve** The set of all points representing the amount of goods or services that will be offered at different price levels.

**Supply shock** Events that are unexpected and that limit the aggregate supply of goods and services.

**Supply, law of** Economic principle that says the lower the price, the lower the quantity supplied, all other things being constant. Price and quantity supplied are positively related.

**Surplus** A state of disequilibrium wherein quantity supplied exceeds quantity demanded. Price will tend to fall until it reaches an equilibrium (where quantity supplied equals quantity demanded).

**Surplus value** In Marxian terms, the amount by which the value of a worker's output exceeds his or her wage. Hence, a source of profit for the capitalist.

**Tariff** A tax applied to imports.

**Terms of trade** The prices of a country's exports in relation to its imports. Any improvement in a country's terms of trade means a relative increase in its export prices, while a deterioration in its terms of trade indicates a relative increase in its import prices.

**Theory** A cogently expressed group of related propositions declared as principles for explanation of a set of phenomena.

**Total cost** The cost of all factors of production involved in producing one good.

**Total fixed costs** The sum of all costs that do not change with varying output (in the short run). A firm incurs these costs regardless of production levels.

**Total revenue** The amount of funds credited to the firm for sales of its output; price multiplied by units sold.

**Total variable costs** The sum of all costs that fluctuate in relation to the activity of the firm and the productive process. The two major variable costs are labor and resources.

**Transactions demand for money** Function that indicates the amount of money balances that individuals desire for purchasing purposes. Considered relatively constant, given a level of income and consumption pattern.

**Transfer multiplier** The ratio that relates the change in the equilibrium level of income to a change in government transfer payments.

**Transfer payments** Government payments to individuals that are not compensation for currently productive activity.

**Trough (of business cycle)** The low point of the business cycle, representing the slowest level of business activity. Following this low point, the cycle begins an upward swing.

**Unemployed** A person sixteen years of age or older who is not working and is available for work and has made an effort to find work during the previous four weeks.

**Unemployment** A condition wherein workers who are ordinarily part of the labor force are unable to find work at prevailing wages. May take any of five specific forms: (1) Frictional unemployment arises from workers changing jobs, etc.; all labor markets have this kind. (2) Seasonal unemployment results from changing seasonal demand and supply for labor. (3) Structural unemployment results from changing or shifting product demand; i.e., it is a function of geographic and job skill mobility. (4) Cyclical unemployment arises from changes in demand of labor during the business cycle. (5) Hidden unemployment consists of frustrated potential workers who have given up looking for a job.

**Unemployment rate** The number of people unemployed expressed as a percentage of the total number of people in the labor force.

**Unit of account** A measure of value or the standard way of quoting prices and keeping accounts in an economy.

**Value added** Strictly, the value of a final product less the cost of production.

**Variable costs** Costs that fluctuate due to the activity of the firm and the productive process. The two major variable costs are labor and resources.

**Vertical merger** Companies in different stages of an industry merge.

**Wage and price controls** Mandatory regulation of wages and prices by the government in order to contain inflation. The U.S. government applied such controls to certain segments of the economy with varying force from 1971 to 1974.

**Wages** The price paid for units of labor or service supplied in the market per unit of time.

**World Bank** A bank that assists poor countries by lending or by insuring private loans to finance development projects. Officially the International Bank for Reconstruction and Development (IBRD) established after World War II to promote postwar reconstruction and development of underdeveloped countries.

# Index